Lectionary Texts
Year B

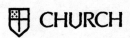 CHURCH

Church Publishing, New York

Introduction

Lectionary Texts is published in three separate volumes for Years A, B, and C. The selection of the readings is in strict accordance with The Lectionary of *The Book of Common Prayer (Proposed)*, pages 889-925, and pages 288-291 for the Great Vigil of Easter. The texts of the readings have been drawn from *The Common Bible* (Revised Standard Version, an Ecumenical Edition), whose accuracy and wide ecumenical acceptance are generally recognized. The texts in this book may, of course, be replaced by corresponding passages from any of the other versions of the Bible authorized for public worship in this Church.

The readings have been edited for liturgical use in accordance with the suggestions in *The Proposed Book of Common Prayer*, page 888. All alternatives cited have been included. In only a very few cases where exactly the same passages are to be read, rather than reprinting an entire passage, page references to a preceding or following page are given.

All optional passages have also been included. Those which may be omitted (cited in parentheses in the Lectionary), have been set off in separate indented paragraphs, and marked with a vertical bar line at the margin. In some of the passages, an opening phrase needed to clarify the context is printed in italics and set off in brackets. These italicized words should be omitted when the preceding section is read and the continuity of the entire reading is clear. An example will be found on pages 35-37, the reading from 2 Kings 4: (8-17) 18-21 (22-31) 32-37. Unless otherwise indicated, all page numbers refer to *The Book of Common Prayer*

In this book, citations from the Psalter are placed at the point where psalmody is normally used in the celebration of the Holy Eucharist, i.e., following the Old Testament Lesson. When the readings are used at a principal service of Morning or Evening Prayer, the Psalm is read at the place appointed in the service, i.e., before the Lessons. When used at the Office, the longer version of the Psalm is to be preferred. The shorter form is intended to be sung at the Eucharist.

The Church Hymnal Corporation wishes to record its deep appreciation to all who welcomed the publication of *Lectionary Texts: Year A*, especially to those who made valuable suggestions for improving subsequent volumes in this series. To the extent possible, these suggestions have been incorporated in the present volume.

The publishers hope that this book will enrich participation in worship by all the people, and will assist the clergy and other ministers in worthily proclaiming the Word of God at the principal service of Sundays and major Holy Days.

Lectionary Texts: Year B

First Sunday of Advent

A Reading (Lesson) from the Book of Isaiah [64:1-9a]

O that thou wouldst rend the heavens and come down, that the mountains might quake at thy presence — as when fire kindles brushwood and the fire causes water to boil — to make thy name known to thy adversaries, and that the nations might tremble at thy presence! When thou didst terrible things which we looked not for, thou camest down, the mountains quaked at thy presence. From of old no one has heard or perceived by the ear, no eye has seen a God besides thee, who works for those who wait for him. Thou meetest him that joyfully works righteousness, those that remember thee in thy ways. Behold, thou wast angry, and we sinned; in our sins we have been a long time, and shall we be saved? We have all become like one who is unclean, and all our righteous deeds are like a polluted garment. We all fade like a leaf, and our iniquities, like the wind, take us away. There is no one that calls upon thy name, that bestirs himself to take hold of thee; for thou hast hid thy face from us, and hast delivered us into the hand of our iniquities. Yet, O Lord, thou art our Father; we are the clay, and thou art our potter; we are all the work of thy hand. Be not exceedingly angry, O Lord, and remember not iniquity for ever.

Psalm 80 [page 702] or *Psalm 80:1-7* [page 702]

*A Reading (Lesson) from the First Letter of Paul
to the Corinthians* [1:1-9]

Paul, called by the will of God to be an apostle of Christ
Jesus, and our brother Sos'the-nes, to the church of God
which is at Corinth, to those sanctified in Christ Jesus, called
to be saints together with all those who in every place call on
the name of our Lord Jesus Christ, both their Lord and ours:
Grace to you and peace from God our Father and the Lord
Jesus Christ. I give thanks to God always for you because of
the grace of God which was given you in Christ Jesus, that in
every way you were enriched in him with all speech and all
knowledge — even as the testimony to Christ was confirmed
among you — so that you are not lacking in any spiritual
gift, as you wait for the revealing of our Lord Jesus Christ;
who will sustain you to the end, guiltless in the day of our
Lord Jesus Christ. God is faithful, by whom you were called
into the fellowship of his Son Jesus Christ our Lord.

✝ *The Holy Gospel of Our Lord Jesus Christ
According to Mark* [13:(24-32)33-37]

Jesus said, "In those days, after that tribulation, the sun
will be darkened, and the moon will not give its light, and
the stars will be falling from heaven, and the powers in
the heavens will be shaken. And then they will see the Son
of man coming in clouds with great power and glory. And
then he will send out the angels, and gather his elect from
the four winds, from the ends of the earth to the ends of
heaven. From the fig tree learn its lesson: as soon as its
branch becomes tender and puts forth its leaves, you
know that summer is near. So also, when you see these
things taking place, you know that he is near, at the very
gates. Truly, I say to you, this generation will not pass
away before all these things take place. Heaven and earth
will pass away, but my words will not pass away."

[*Jesus said,*] "Of that day or that hour no one knows, not
even the angels in heaven, nor the Son, but only the Father.

Take heed, watch; for you do not know when the time will come. It is like a man going on a journey, when he leaves home and puts his servants in charge, each with his work, and commands the doorkeeper to be on the watch. Watch therefore — for you do not know when the master of the house will come, in the evening, or at midnight, or at cockcrow, or in the morning — lest he come suddenly and find you asleep. And what I say to you I say to all: Watch."

Second Sunday of Advent

A Reading (Lesson) from the Book of Isaiah [40:1-11]

Comfort, comfort my people, says your God. Speak tenderly to Jerusalem, and cry to her that her warfare is ended, that her iniquity is pardoned, that she has received from the Lord's hand double for all her sins. A voice cries: "In the wilderness prepare the way of the Lord, make straight in the desert a highway for our God. Every valley shall be lifted up, and every mountain and hill be made low; the uneven ground shall become level, and the rough places a plain. And the glory of the Lord shall be revealed, and all flesh shall see it together, for the mouth of the Lord has spoken." A voice says, "Cry!" and I said, "What shall I cry?" All flesh is grass, and all its beauty is like the flower of the field. The grass withers, the flower fades, when the breath of the Lord blows upon it; surely the people is grass. The grass withers, the flower fades; but the word of our God will stand for ever. Get you up to a high mountain, O Zion, herald of good tidings; lift up your voice with strength, O Jerusalem, herald of good tidings, lift it up, fear not; say to the cities of Judah, "Behold your God!" Behold, the Lord God comes with might, and his arm rules for him; behold, his reward is with him, and his recompense before him. He will feed his flock like a shepherd, he will gather the lambs in his arms, he will carry them in his bosom, and gently lead those that are with young.

Psalm 85 [page 708]   or   Psalm 85:7-13 [page 709]

A Reading (Lesson) from the Second Letter of Peter
[3:8-15a,18]

Do not ignore this one fact, beloved, that with the Lord one day is as a thousand years, and a thousand years as one day. The Lord is not slow about his promise as some count slowness, but is forbearing toward you, not wishing that any should perish, but that all should reach repentance. But the day of the Lord will come like a thief, and then the heavens will pass away with a loud noise, and the elements will be dissolved with fire, and the earth and the works that are upon it will be burned up. Since all these things are thus to be dissolved, what sort of persons ought you to be in lives of holiness and godliness, waiting for and hastening the coming of the day of God, because of which the heavens will be kindled and dissolved, and the elements will melt with fire! But according to his promise we wait for new heavens and a new earth in which righteousness dwells. Therefore, beloved, since you wait for these, be zealous to be found by him without spot or blemish, and at peace. And count the forbearance of our Lord as salvation. But grow in the grace and knowledge of our Lord and Savior Jesus Christ. To him be the glory both now and to the day of eternity. Amen.

✝ *The Holy Gospel of Our Lord Jesus Christ*
According to Mark [1:1-8]

The beginning of the gospel of Jesus Christ, the Son of God. As it is written in Isaiah the prophet, "Behold, I send my messenger before thy face, who shall prepare thy way; the voice of one crying in the wilderness: Prepare the way of the Lord, make his paths straight—" John the baptizer appeared in the wilderness, preaching a baptism of repentance for the forgiveness of sins. And there went out to him all the country of Judea, and all the people of Jerusalem; and they were baptized by him in the river Jordan, confessing their sins. Now John was clothed with camel's hair, and had a leather girdle around his waist, and ate locusts and wild honey. And he preached, saying, "After me comes he who is mightier than I, the thong of whose sandals I am not worthy to stoop down and untie. I have baptized you with water; but he will baptize you with the Holy Spirit."

Third Sunday of Advent

A Reading (Lesson) from the Book of Isaiah [65:17-25]

Thus says the Lord, "Behold, I create new heavens and a new earth; and the former things shall not be remembered or come into mind. But be glad and rejoice for ever in that which I create; for behold, I create Jerusalem a rejoicing, and her people a joy. I will rejoice in Jerusalem, and be glad in my people; no more shall be heard in it the sound of weeping and the cry of distress. No more shall there be in it an infant that lives but a few days, or an old man who does not fill out his days, for the child shall die a hundred years old, and the sinner a hundred years old shall be accursed. They shall build houses and inhabit them; they shall plant vineyards and eat their fruit. They shall not build and another inhabit; they shall not plant and another eat; for like the days of a tree shall the days of my people be, and my chosen shall long enjoy the work of their hands. They shall not labor in vain, or bear children for calamity, for they shall be the offspring of the blessed of the Lord, and their children with them. Before they call I will answer, while they are yet speaking I will hear. The wolf and the lamb shall feed together, the lion shall eat straw like the ox; and dust shall be the serpent's food. They shall not hurt or destroy in all my holy mountain, says the Lord."

Psalm 126 [page 782]   or

The Magnificat, Canticle 3 or 15 [page 50 or 91]

A Reading (Lesson) from the First Letter of Paul to the Thessalonians [5:(12-15) 16-28]

> We beseech you, brethren, to respect those who labor among you and are over you in the Lord and admonish you, and to esteem them very highly in love because of their work. Be at peace among yourselves. And we exhort you, brethren, admonish the idlers, encourage the fainthearted, help the weak, be patient with them all. See that none of you repays evil for evil, but always seek to do good to one another and to all.

Rejoice always, pray constantly, give thanks in all circumstances; for this is the will of God in Christ Jesus for you. Do not quench the Spirit, do not despise prophesying, but test everything; hold fast what is good, abstain from every form of evil. May the God of peace himself sanctify you wholly; and may your spirit and soul and body be kept sound and blameless at the coming of our Lord Jesus Christ. He who calls you is faithful, and he will do it. Brethren, pray for us. Greet all the brethren with a holy kiss. I adjure you by the Lord that this letter be read to all the brethren. The grace of our Lord Jesus Christ be with you.

✝ *The Holy Gospel of Our Lord Jesus Christ According to John* [1:6-8, 19-28]

There was a man sent from God, whose name was John. He came for testimony, to bear witness to the light, that all might believe through him. He was not the light, but came to bear witness to the light. And this is the testimony of John, when the Jews sent priests and Levites from Jerusalem to ask him, "Who are you?" He confessed, he did not deny, but confessed, "I am not the Christ." And they asked him, "What then? Are you Eli'jah?" He said, "I am not." "Are you the prophet?" And he answered, "No." They said to him then, "Who are you? Let us have an answer for those who sent us. What do you say about yourself?" He said, "I am the voice of one crying in the wilderness, 'Make straight the way of the Lord,' as the prophet Isaiah said." Now they had been sent from the Pharisees. They asked him, "Then why are you baptizing, if you are neither the Christ, nor Eli'jah, nor the prophet?" John answered them, "I baptize with water; but among you stands one whom you do not know, even he who comes after me, the thong of whose sandal I am not worthy to untie." This took place in Bethany beyond the Jordan, where John was baptizing.

or this

✝ *The Holy Gospel of Our Lord Jesus Christ According to John* [3:23-30]

John was baptizing at Ae'non near Salim, because there was much water there; and people came and were baptized. For John had not yet been put in prison. Now a discussion arose between John's disciples and a Jew over purifying. And they came to John, and said to him, "Rabbi, he who was with you beyond the Jordan, to whom you bore witness, here he is, baptizing, and all are going to him." John answered, "No one can receive anything except what is given him from heaven. You yourselves bear me witness, that I said, I am not the Christ, but I have been sent before him. He who has the bride is the bridegroom; the friend of the bridegroom, who stands and hears him, rejoices greatly at the bridegroom's voice; therefore this joy of mine is now full. He must increase, but I must decrease."

Fourth Sunday of Advent

A Reading (Lesson) from the Second Book of Samuel [7:4, 8-16]

The word of the Lord came to Nathan the prophet, "Go and tell my servant David, 'Thus says the Lord of hosts: I took you from the pasture, from following the sheep, that you should be prince over my people Israel; and I have been with you wherever you went, and have cut off all your enemies from before you; and I will make for you a great name, like the name of the great ones of the earth. And I will appoint a place for my people Israel, and will plant them, that they may dwell in their own place, and be disturbed no more; and violent men shall afflict them no more, as formerly, from the time that I appointed judges over my people Israel; and I will give you rest from all your enemies. Moreover the Lord declares to you that the Lord will make you a house. When your days are fulfilled and you lie down with your fathers, I will raise up your offspring after you, who shall come forth from your body, and I will establish his kingdom. He shall build a house for my name, and I will establish the throne of his kingdom for ever. I will be his father, and he shall be my son. When he commits iniquity, I will chasten him with the rod of men, with the stripes of the sons of men; but I will not take my steadfast love from him, as I took it from Saul, whom I put away from before you. And your house and your kingdom shall be made sure for ever before me; your throne shall be established for ever.'"

Psalm 132 [page 785] or *Psalm 132:8-15* [page 786]

A Reading (Lesson) from the Letter of Paul to the Romans
[16:25-27]

Now to him who is able to strengthen you according to my gospel and the preaching of Jesus Christ, according to the revelation of the mystery which was kept secret for long ages, but is now disclosed and through the prophetic writings is made known to all nations, according to the command of the eternal God, to bring about the obedience of faith — to the only wise God be glory for evermore through Jesus Christ! Amen.

✝ *The Holy Gospel of Our Lord Jesus Christ According to Luke* [1:26-38]

In the sixth month the angel Gabriel was sent from God to a city of Galilee named Nazareth, to a virgin betrothed to a man whose name was Joseph, of the house of David; and the virgin's name was Mary. And he came to her and said, "Hail, O favored one, the Lord is with you!" But she was greatly troubled at the saying, and considered in her mind what sort of greeting this might be. And the angel said to her, "Do not be afraid, Mary, for you have found favor with God. And behold, you will conceive in your womb and bear a son, and you shall call his name Jesus. He will be great, and will be called the Son of the Most High; and the Lord God will give to him the throne of his father David, and he will reign over the house of Jacob for ever; and of his kingdom there will be no end." And Mary said to the angel, "How shall this be, since I have no husband?" And the angel said to her, "The Holy Spirit will come upon you, and the power of the Most High will overshadow you; therefore the child to be born will be called holy, the Son of God. And behold, your kinswoman Elizabeth in her old age has also conceived a son; and this is the sixth month with her who was called barren. For with God nothing will be impossible." And Mary said, "Behold, I am the handmaid of the Lord; let it be to me according to your word." And the angel departed from her.

The Nativity of Our Lord: Christmas Day I

A Reading (Lesson) from the Book of Isaiah [9:2-4, 6-7]

The people who walked in darkness have seen a great light; those who dwelt in a land of deep darkness, on them has light shined. Thou hast multiplied the nation, thou hast increased its joy; they rejoice before thee as with joy at the harvest, as men rejoice when they divide the spoil. For the yoke of his burden, and the staff for his shoulder, the rod of his oppressor, thou hast broken as on the day of Mid'ian. For to us a child is born, to us a son is given; and the government will be upon his shoulder, and his name will be called, "Wonderful Counselor, Mighty God, Everlasting Father, Prince of Peace." Of the increase of his government and of peace there will be no end, upon the throne of David, and over his kingdom, to establish it, and to uphold it with justice and with righteousness, from this time forth and for evermore. The zeal of the Lord of hosts will do this.

Psalm 96 [page 725]   or   *Psalm 96:1-4, 11-12* [page 725]

A Reading (Lesson) from the Letter of Paul to Titus
[2:11-14]

The grace of God has appeared for the salvation of all men, training us to renounce irreligion and worldly passions, and to live sober, upright, and godly lives in this world, awaiting our blessed hope, the appearing of the glory of our great God and Savior Jesus Christ, who gave himself for us to redeem us from all iniquity and to purify for himself a people of his own who are zealous for good deeds.

✝ *The Holy Gospel of Our Lord Jesus Christ*
According to Luke [2:1-14 (15-20)]

In those days a decree went out from Caesar Augustus that all the world should be enrolled. This was the first enrollment, when Quirin'i-us was governor of Syria. And all went to be enrolled, each to his own city. And Joseph also went up from Galilee, from the city of Nazareth, to Judea, to the city of David, which is called Bethlehem, because he was of the house and lineage of David, to be enrolled with Mary, his betrothed, who was with child. And while they were there, the time came for her to be delivered. And she gave birth to her first-born son and wrapped him in swaddling cloths, and laid him in a manger, because there was no place for them in the inn. And in that region there were shepherds out in the field, keeping watch over their flock by night. And an angel of the Lord appeared to them and the glory of the Lord shone around them and they were filled with fear. And the angel said to them, "Be not afraid; for behold, I bring you good news of a great joy which will come to all the people; for to you is born this day in the city of David a Savior, who is Christ the Lord. And this will be a sign for you: you will find a babe wrapped in swaddling clothes and lying in a manger." And suddenly there was with the angel a multitude of the heavenly host praising God and saying, "Glory to God in the highest, and on earth peace among men with whom he is pleased!"

When the angels went away from them into heaven, the shepherds said to one another, "Let us go over to Bethlehem and see this thing that has happened, which the Lord has made known to us." And they went with haste, and found Mary and Joseph, and the babe lying in a manger. And when they saw it they made known the saying which had been told them concerning this child; and all who heard it wondered at what the shepherds told them. But Mary kept all these things, pondering them in her heart. And the shepherds returned, glorifying and praising God for all they had heard and seen as it had been told them.

Christmas Day II

A Reading (Lesson) from the Book of Isaiah [62:6-7, 10-12]

Upon your walls, O Jerusalem, I have set watchmen; all the day and all the night they shall never be silent. You who put the Lord in remembrance, take no rest, and give him no rest until he establishes Jerusalem and makes it a praise in the earth. Go through, go through the gates, prepare the way for the people; build up, build up the highway, clear it of stones, lift up an ensign over the peoples. Behold, the Lord has proclaimed to the end of the earth: Say to the daughter of Zion, "Behold, your salvation comes; behold, his reward is with him, and his recompense before him." And they shall be called The holy people, The redeemed of the Lord; and you shall be called Sought out, a city not forsaken.

Psalm 97 [page 726]   or   *Psalm 97: 1-4, 11-12* [page 726]

A Reading (Lesson) from the Letter of Paul to Titus [3:4-7]

When the goodness and loving kindness of God our Savior appeared, he saved us, not because of deeds done by us in righteousness, but in virtue of his own mercy, by the washing of regeneration and renewal in the Holy Spirit, which he poured out upon us richly through Jesus Christ our Savior, so that we might be justified by his grace and become heirs in hope of eternal life.

✚ *The Holy Gospel of Our Lord Jesus Christ According to Luke* [2:(1-14)15-20]

In those days a decree went out from Caesar Augustus that all the world should be enrolled. This was the first enrollment, when Quirin'i-us was governor of Syria. And all went to be enrolled, each to his own city. And Joseph also went up from Galilee, from the city of Nazareth, to Judea, to the city of David, which is called Bethlehem, because he was of the house and lineage of David, to be enrolled with Mary, his bethrothed, who was with child. And while they were there, the time came for her to be delivered. And she gave birth to her first-born son and wrapped him in swaddling cloths, and laid him in a manger, because there was no place for them in the inn. And in that region there were shepherds out in the field, keeping watch over their flock by night. And an angel of the Lord appeared to them, and the glory of the Lord shone around them, and they were filled with fear. And the angel said to them, "Be not afraid; for behold, I bring you good news of a great joy which will come to all the people; for to you is born this day in the city of David a Savior, who is Christ the Lord. And this will be a sign for you: You will find a babe wrapped in swaddling cloths and lying in a manger." And suddenly there was with the angel a multitude of the heavenly host praising God and saying, "Glory to God in the highest, and on earth peace among men with whom he is pleased!"

When the angels went away from them into heaven, the shepherds said to one another, "Let us go over to Bethlehem and see this thing that has happened, which the Lord has made known to us." And they went with haste, and found Mary and Joseph, and the babe lying in a manger. And when they saw it they made known the saying which had been told them concerning this child; and all who heard it wondered at what the shepherds told them. But Mary kept all these things, pondering them in her heart. And the shepherds returned, glorifying and praising God for all they had heard and seen as it had been told them.

Christmas Day III

A Reading (Lesson) from the Book of Isaiah [52:7-10]

How beautiful upon the mountains are the feet of him who brings good tidings, who publishes peace, who brings good tidings of good, who publishes salvation, who says to Zion, "Your God reigns." Hark, your watchmen lift up their voice, together they sing for joy; for eye to eye they see the return of the Lord to Zion. Break forth together into singing, you waste places of Jerusalem; for the Lord has comforted his people, he has redeemed Jerusalem. The Lord has bared his holy arm before the eyes of all the nations; and all the ends of the earth shall see the salvation of our God.

Psalm 98 [page 727]   or   *Psalm 98: 1-6* [page 727]

A Reading (Lesson) from the Letter to the Hebrews [1:1-12]

In many and various ways God spoke of old to our fathers
by the prophets; but in these last days he has spoken to us by
a son, whom he appointed the heir of all things, through
whom also he created the world. He reflects the glory of
God and bears the very stamp of his nature, upholding the
universe by his word of power. When he had made
purification for sins, he sat down at the right hand of the
Majesty on high, having become as much superior to angels
as the name he has obtained is more excellent than theirs.
For to what angel did God ever say, "Thou art my Son,
today I have begotten thee"? Or again, "I will be to him a
father, and he shall be to me a son"? And again, when he
brings the firstborn into the world, he says, "Let all God's
angels worship him." Of the angels he says, "Who makes his
angels winds, and his servants flames of fire." But of the Son
he says, "Thy throne, O God, is for ever and ever, the
righteous scepter is the scepter of thy kingdom. Thou hast
loved righteousness and hated lawlessness; therefore God,
thy God, has anointed thee with the oil of gladness beyond
thy comrades." And, "Thou, Lord, didst found the earth in
the beginning, and the heavens are the work of thy hands;
they will perish, but thou remainest; they will all grow old
like a garment, like a mantle thou wilt roll them up, and they
will be changed. But thou art the same, and thy years will
never end."

✝ *The Holy Gospel of Our Lord Jesus Christ*
According to John [1:1-14]

In the beginning was the Word, and the Word was with God,
and the Word was God. He was in the beginning with God;
all things were made through him, and without him was not
anything made that was made. In him was life, and the life
was the light of men. The light shines in the darkness, and
the darkness has not overcome it. There was a man sent

from God, whose name was John. He came for testimony, to bear witness to the light, that all might believe through him. He was not the light, but came to bear witness to the light. The true light that enlightens every man was coming into the world. He was in the world, and the world was made through him, yet the world knew him not. He came to his own home, and his own people received him not. But to all who received him, who believed in his name, he gave power to become children of God; who were born, not of blood nor of the will of the flesh nor of the will of man, but of God. And the Word became flesh and dwelt among us, full of grace and truth; we have beheld his glory, glory as of the only Son from the Father.

First Sunday after Christmas

A Reading (Lesson) from the Book of Isaiah [61:10—62:3]

I will greatly rejoice in the Lord, my soul shall exult in my God; for he has clothed me with the garments of salvation, he has covered me with the robe of righteousness, as a bridegroom decks himself with a garland, and as a bride adorns herself with her jewels. For as the earth brings forth its shoots, and as a garden causes what is sown in it to spring up, so the Lord God will cause righteousness and praise to spring forth before all the nations. For Zion's sake I will not keep silent, and for Jerusalem's sake I will not rest, until her vindication goes forth as brightness, and her salvation as a burning torch. The nations shall see your vindication, and all the kings your glory; and you shall be called by a new name which the mouth of the Lord will give. You shall be a crown of beauty in the hand of the Lord, and a royal diadem in the hand of your God.

Psalm 147 [page 804]   or   *Psalm 147:13-21* [page 805]

A Reading (Lesson) from the Letter of Paul to the Galatians [3:23-25; 4:4-7]

Now before faith came, we were confined under the law, kept under restraint until faith should be revealed. So that the law was our custodian until Christ came, that we might be justified by faith. But now that faith has come, we are no longer under a custodian. But when the time had fully come, God sent forth his Son, born of woman, born under the law, to redeem those who were under the law, so that we might receive adoption as sons. And because you are sons, God has sent the Spirit of his Son into our hearts, crying, "Abba! Father!" So through God you are no longer a slave but a son, and if a son then an heir.

✝ *The Holy Gospel of Our Lord Jesus Christ According to John* [1:1-18]

In the beginning was the Word, and the Word was with God, and the Word was God. He was in the beginning with God; all things were made through him, and without him was not anything made that was made. In him was life, and the life was the light of men. The light shines in the darkness, and the darkness has not overcome it. There was a man sent from God, whose name was John. He came for testimony, to bear witness to the light, that all might believe through him. He was not the light, but came to bear witness to the light. The true light that enlightens every man was coming into the world. He was in the world, and the world was made through him, yet the world knew him not. He came to his own home, and his own people received him not. But to all who received him, who believed in his name, he gave power to become children of God; who were born, not of blood nor of the will of the flesh nor of the will of man, but of God. And the Word became flesh and dwelt among us, full of grace and truth; we have beheld his glory, glory as of the only Son from the Father. (John bore witness to him, and cried, "This was he of whom I said, 'He who comes after me ranks before me, for he was before me.'") And from his fullness have we all received, grace upon grace. For the law was given through Moses; grace and truth came through Jesus Christ. No one has ever seen God; the only Son, who is in the bosom of the Father, he has made him known.

The Holy Name of Our Lord Jesus Christ *January 1*

A Reading (Lesson) from the Book of Exodus [34:1-8]

The Lord said to Moses, "Cut two tables of stone like the first; and I will write upon the tables the words that were on the first tables, which you broke. Be ready in the morning, and come up in the morning to Mount Sinai, and present yourself there to me on the top of the mountain. No man shall come up with you, and let no man be seen throughout all the mountain; let no flocks or herds feed before that mountain." So Moses cut two tables of stone like the first; and he rose early in the morning and went up on Mount Sinai, as the Lord had commanded him, and took in his hand two tables of stone. And the Lord descended in the cloud and stood with him there, and proclaimed the name of the Lord. The Lord passed before him, and proclaimed, "The Lord, the Lord, a God merciful and gracious, slow to anger, and abounding in steadfast love and faithfulness, keeping steadfast love for thousands, forgiving iniquity and transgression and sin, but who will by no means clear the guilty, visiting the iniquity of the fathers upon the children and the children's children, to the third and the fourth generation." And Moses made haste to bow his head toward the earth, and worshiped.

Psalm 8 [page 592]

A Reading (Lesson) from the Letter of Paul to the Romans
[1:1-7]

Paul, a servant of Jesus Christ, called to be an apostle, set
apart for the gospel of God which he promised beforehand
through his prophets in the holy scriptures, the gospel
concerning his Son, who was descended from David
according to the flesh, and designated Son of God in power
according to the Spirit of holiness by his resurrection from
the dead, Jesus Christ our Lord, through whom we have
received grace and apostleship to bring about the obedience
of faith for the sake of his name among all the nations,
including yourselves who are called to belong to Jesus
Christ; to all God's beloved in Rome, who are called to be
saints: Grace to you and peace from God our Father and the
Lord Jesus Christ.

✝ *The Holy Gospel of Our Lord Jesus Christ
According to Luke* [2:15-21]

When the angels went away from them into heaven, the
shepherds said to one another, "Let us go over to Bethlehem
and see this thing that has happened, which the Lord has
made known to us." And they went with haste, and found
Mary and Joseph, and the babe lying in a manger. And
when they saw it they made known the saying which had
been told them concerning this child; and all who heard it
wondered at what the shepherds told them. But Mary kept
all these things, pondering them in her heart. And the
shepherds returned, glorifying and praising God for all they
had heard and seen, as it had been told them. And at the
end of eight days, when he was circumcised, he was called
Jesus, the name given by the angel before he was conceived
in the womb.

Second Sunday after Christmas Day

A Reading (Lesson) from the Book of Jeremiah [31:7-14]

Thus says the Lord: "Sing aloud with gladness for Jacob, and raise shouts for the chief of the nations; proclaim, give praise, and say, 'The Lord has saved his people, the remnant of Israel.' Behold, I will bring them from the north country, and gather them from the farthest parts of the earth, among them the blind and the lame, the woman with child and her who is in travail, together; a great company, they shall return here. With weeping they shall come, and with consolations I will lead them back, I will make them walk by brooks of water, in a straight path in which they shall not stumble; for I am a father to Israel, and E'phraim is my first-born. Hear the word of the Lord, O nations, and declare it in the coastlands afar off; say, 'He who scattered Israel will gather him, and will keep him as a shepherd keeps his flock.' For the Lord has ransomed Jacob, and has redeemed him from hands too strong for him. They shall come and sing aloud on the height of Zion, and they shall be radiant over the goodness of the Lord, over the grain, the wine, and the oil, and over the young of the flock and the herd; their life shall be like a watered garden, and they shall languish no more. Then shall the maidens rejoice in the dance, and the young men and the old shall be merry. I will turn their mourning into joy, I will comfort them and give them gladness for sorrow. I will feast the soul of the priests with abundance, and my people shall be satisfied with my goodness, says the Lord."

Psalm 84 [page 707]   or   *Psalm 84:1-8* [page 707]

A Reading (Lesson) from the Letter of Paul to the Ephesians [1:3-6, 15-19a]

Blessed be the God and Father of our Lord Jesus Christ, who has blessed us in Christ with every spiritual blessing in the heavenly places, even as he chose us in him before the foundation of the world, that we should be holy and blameless before him. He destined us in love to be his sons through Jesus Christ, according to the purpose of his will, to the praise of his glorious grace which he freely bestowed on us in the Beloved. For this reason, because I have heard of your faith in the Lord Jesus and your love toward all the saints, I do not cease to give thanks for you, remembering you in my prayers, that the God of our Lord Jesus Christ, the Father of glory, may give you a spirit of wisdom and of revelation in the knowledge of him, having the eyes of your hearts enlightened, that you may know what is the hope to which he has called you, what are the riches of his glorious inheritance in the saints, and what is the immeasurable greatness of his power in us who believe.

✝ *The Holy Gospel of Our Lord Jesus Christ According to Matthew* [2:13-15, 19-23]

Now when the wise men had departed, behold, an angel of the Lord appeared to Joseph in a dream and said, "Rise, take the child and his mother, and flee to Egypt, and remain there till I tell you; for Herod is about to search for the child, to destroy him." And he rose and took the child and his mother by night, and departed to Egypt, and remained there until the death of Herod. This was to fulfill what the Lord had spoken by the prophet, "Out of Egypt have I called my son." But when Herod died, behold, an angel of the Lord appeared in a dream to Joseph in Egypt, saying, "Rise, take the child and his mother, and go to the land of Israel, for those who sought the child's life are dead." And he rose and took the child and his mother, and went to the land of Israel. But when he heard that Archela'us reigned over Judea in place of his father Herod, he was afraid to go there, and being warned in a dream he withdrew to the district of Galilee. And he went and dwelt in a city called Nazareth, that what was spoken by the prophets might be fulfilled, "He shall be called a Nazarene."

or this

✝ *The Holy Gospel of Our Lord Jesus Christ*
According to Luke [2:41-52]

Now the parents of Jesus went to Jerusalem every year at the feast of the Passover. And when he was twelve years old, they went up according to custom; and when the feast was ended, as they were returning, the boy Jesus stayed behind in Jerusalem. His parents did not know it, but supposing him to be in the company they went a day's journey, and they sought him among their kinsfolk and acquaintances; and when they did not find him, they returned to Jerusalem, seeking him. After three days they found him in the temple, sitting among the teachers, listening to them and asking them questions; and all who heard him were amazed at his understanding and his answers. And when they saw him they were astonished; and his mother said to him, "Son, why have you treated us so? Behold, your father and I have been looking for you anxiously." And he said to them, "How is it that you sought me? Did you not know that I must be in my Father's house?" And they did not understand the saying which he spoke to them. And he went down with them and came to Nazareth, and was obedient to them; and his mother kept all these things in her heart. And Jesus increased in wisdom and in stature, and in favor with God and man.

or this

Matthew 2:1-12 [page 27 below]

The Epiphany *January 6*

A Reading (Lesson) from the Book of Isaiah [60:1-6,9]

Arise, shine; for your light has come, and the glory of the Lord has risen upon you. For behold, darkness shall cover the earth, and thick darkness the peoples; but the Lord will arise upon you, and his glory will be seen upon you. And nations shall come to your light, and kings to the brightness of your rising. Lift up your eyes round about, and see; they all gather together, they come to you; your sons shall come from far, and your daughters shall be carried in the arms. Then you shall see and be radiant, your heart shall thrill and rejoice; because the abundance of the sea shall be turned to you, the wealth of the nations shall come to you. A multitude of camels shall cover you, the young camels of Mid'ian and Ephah; all those from Sheba shall come. They shall bring gold and frankincense, and shall proclaim the praise of the Lord. For the coastlands shall wait for me, the ships of Tarshish first, to bring your sons from far, their silver and gold with them, for the name of the Lord your God, and for the Holy One of Israel, because he has glorified you.

Psalm 72 [page 685] or *Psalm 72:1-2, 10-17* [page 685]

A Reading (Lesson) from the Letter of Paul to the Ephesians [3:1-12]

I, Paul, a prisoner for Christ Jesus on behalf of you Gentiles, assume that you have heard of the stewardship of God's grace that was given to me for you, how the mystery was made known to me by revelation, as I have written briefly. When you read this you can perceive my insight into the mystery of Christ, which was not made known to the sons of men in other generations as it has now been revealed to his holy apostles and prophets by the Spirit; that is, how the Gentiles are fellow heirs, members of the same body, and partakers of the promise in Christ Jesus through the gospel. Of this gospel I was made a minister according to the gift of God's grace which was given me by the working of his power. To me, though I am the very least of all the saints, this grace was given, to preach to the Gentiles the unsearchable riches of Christ, and to make all men see what is the plan of the mystery hidden for ages in God who created all things; that through the church the manifold wisdom of God might now be made known to the principalities and powers in the heavenly places. This was according to the eternal purpose which he has realized in Christ Jesus our Lord, in whom we have boldness and confidence of access through our faith in him.

✝ *The Holy Gospel of Our Lord Jesus Christ
According to Matthew* [2:1-12]

Now when Jesus was born in Bethlehem of Judea in the days of Herod the king, behold, wise men from the East came to Jerusalem, saying, "Where is he who has been born king of the Jews? For we have seen his star in the East, and have come to worship him." When Herod the king heard this, he was troubled, and all Jerusalem with him; and assembling all the chief priests and scribes of the people, he inquired of them where the Christ was to be born. They told him, "In Bethlehem of Judea; for so it is written by the prophet: 'And you, O Bethlehem, in the land of Judah, are by no means least among the rulers of Judah; for from you shall come a ruler who will govern my people Israel.'" Then Herod summoned the wise men secretly and ascertained from them what time the star appeared; and he sent them to Bethlehem, saying, "Go and search diligently for the child, and when you have found him bring me word, that I too may come and worship him." When they had heard the king they went their way; and lo, the star which they had seen in the East went before them till it came to rest over the place where the child was. When they saw the star, they rejoiced exceedingly with great joy; and going into the house they saw the child with Mary his mother, and they fell down and worshiped him. Then, opening their treasures, they offered him gifts, gold and frankincense and myrrh. And being warned in a dream not to return to Herod, they departed to their own country by another way.

First Sunday after the Epiphany

A Reading (Lesson) from the Book of Isaiah [42:1-9]

Behold my servant, whom I uphold, my chosen, in whom my
soul delights; I have put my Spirit upon him, he will bring
forth justice to the nations. He will not cry or lift up his
voice, or make it heard in the street; a bruised reed he will
not break, and a dimly burning wick he will not quench; he
will faithfully bring forth justice. He will not fail or be
discouraged till he has established justice in the earth; and
the coastlands wait for his law. Thus says God, the Lord,
who created the heavens and stretched them out, who spread
forth the earth and what comes from it, who gives breath to
the people upon it and spirit to those who walk in it: "I am
the Lord, I have called you in righteousness, I have taken
you by the hand and kept you; I have given you as a
covenant to the people, a light to the nations, to open the
eyes that are blind, to bring out the prisoners from the
dungeon, from the prison those who sit in darkness. I am the
Lord, that is my name; my glory I give to no other, nor my
praise to graven images. Behold, the former things have
come to pass, and new things I now declare; before they
spring forth, I tell you of them."

Psalm 89:1-29 [page 713]   or   *Psalm 89:20-29* [page 715]

A Reading (Lesson) from the Acts of the Apostles [10:34-38]

Peter opened his mouth and said: "Truly I perceive that God
shows no partiality, but in every nation any one who fears
him and does what is right is acceptable to him. You know
the word which he sent to Israel, preaching good news of
peace by Jesus Christ (he is Lord of all), the word which was
proclaimed throughout all Judea, beginning from Galilee
after the baptism which John preached: how God anointed
Jesus of Nazareth with the Holy Spirit and with power; how

he went about doing good and healing all that were oppressed by the devil, for God was with him."

✝ *The Holy Gospel of Our Lord Jesus Christ According to Mark* [1:7-11]

John the Baptist preached, saying, "After me comes he who is mightier than I, the thong of whose sandals I am not worthy to stoop down and untie. I have baptized you with water; but he will baptize you with the Holy Spirit." In those days Jesus came from Nazareth of Galilee and was baptized by John in the Jordan. And when he came up out of the water, immediately he saw the heavens opened and the Spirit descending upon him like a dove; and a voice came from heaven, "Thou art my beloved Son; with thee I am well pleased."

Second Sunday after the Epiphany

A Reading (Lesson) from the First Book of Samuel [3:1-10 (11-20)]

Now the boy Samuel was ministering to the Lord under Eli. And the word of the Lord was rare in those days; there was no frequent vision. At that time Eli, whose eyesight had begun to grow dim, so that he could not see, was lying down in his own place; the lamp of God had not yet gone out, and Samuel was lying down within the temple of the Lord, where the ark of God was. Then the Lord called, "Samuel! Samuel!" and he said, "Here I am!" and ran to Eli, and said, "Here I am, for you called me." But he said, "I did not call; lie down again." So he went and lay down. And the Lord called again, "Samuel!" And Samuel arose and went to Eli and said, "Here I am, for you called me." But he said, "I did not call, my son; lie down again." Now Samuel did not yet know the Lord, and the word of the Lord had not yet been revealed to him. And the Lord called Samuel again the third time. And he arose and went to Eli, and said, "Here I am, for you called me." Then Eli perceived that the Lord was calling the boy. Therefore Eli said to Samuel, "Go, lie down; and if he calls you, you shall say, 'Speak Lord, for thy servant hears.' " So Samuel went and lay down in his place. And the Lord came and stood forth, calling as at other times, "Samuel! Samuel!" And Samuel said, "Speak, for thy servant hears."

Then the Lord said to Samuel, "Behold, I am about to do a thing in Israel, at which the two ears of every one that hears it will tingle. On that day I will fulfill against Eli all that I have spoken concerning his house, from beginning to end. And I tell him that I am about to punish his house for ever, for the iniquity which he knew, because his sons were blaspheming God, and he did not restrain them. Therefore I swear to the house of Eli that the iniquity of Eli's house shall not be expiated by sacrifice or offering for ever." Samuel lay until morning; then he opened the doors of the house of the Lord. And Samuel was afraid to tell the vision to Eli. But Eli called Samuel and said, "Samuel, my son." And he said, "Here I am." and Eli said, "What was it that he told you? Do not hide it from me. May God do so to you and more also, if you hide anything from me of all that he told you." So Samuel told him everything and hid nothing from him. And he said, "It is the Lord; let him do what seems good to him." And Samuel grew, and the Lord was with him and let none of his words fall to the ground. And all Israel from Dan to Beer-sheba knew that Samuel was established as a prophet of the Lord.

Psalm 63:1-8 [page 670]

A Reading (Lesson) from the First Letter of Paul to the Corinthians [6:11b-20]

You were washed, you were sanctified, you were justified in the name of the Lord Jesus Christ and in the Spirit of our

God. "All things are lawful for me," but not all things are helpful. "All things are lawful for me," but I will not be enslaved by anything. "Food is meant for the stomach and the stomach for food" — and God will destroy both one and the other. The body is not meant for immorality, but for the Lord, and the Lord for the body. And God raised the Lord and will also raise us up by his power. Do you not know that your bodies are members of Christ? Shall I therefore take the members of Christ and make them members of a prostitute? Never! Do you not know that he who joins himself to a prostitute becomes one body with her? For, as it is written, "The two shall become one flesh." But he who is united to the Lord becomes one spirit with him. Shun immorality. Every other sin which a man commits is outside the body; but the immoral man sins against his own body. Do you not know that your body is a temple of the Holy Spirit within you, which you have from God? You are not your own; you were bought with a price. So glorify God in your body.

✝ *The Holy Gospel of Our Lord Jesus Christ*
According to John [1:43-51]

The next day Jesus decided to go to Galilee. And he found Philip and said to him, "Follow me." Now Philip was from Beth-sa'ida, the city of Andrew and Peter. Philip found Nathan'a-el, and said to him, "We have found him of whom Moses, in the law and also the prophets wrote, Jesus of Nazareth, the son of Joseph." Nathan'a-el said to him, "Can anything good come out of Nazareth?" Philip said to him, "Come and see." Jesus saw Nathan'a-el coming to him, and said of him, "Behold, an Israelite indeed, in whom is no guile!" Nathan'a-el said to him, "How do you know me?" Jesus answered him, "Before Philip called you, when you were under the fig tree, I saw you." Nathan'a-el answered him, "Rabbi, you are the Son of God! You are the King of Israel!" Jesus answered him, "Because I said to you, I saw you under the fig tree, do you believe? You shall see greater things than these." And he said to him, "Truly, truly, I say to you, you will see heaven opened, and the angels of God ascending and descending upon the Son of man."

Third Sunday after the Epiphany

A Reading (Lesson) from the Book of Jeremiah [3:21 — 4:2]

A voice on the bare heights is heard, the weeping and pleading of Israel's sons, because they have perverted their way, they have forgotten the Lord their God. "Return, O faithless sons, I will heal your faithlessness." — "Behold, we come to thee; for thou art the Lord our God. Truly the hills are a delusion, the orgies on the mountains. Truly in the Lord our God is the salvation of Israel. But from our youth the shameful thing has devoured all for which our fathers labored, their flocks and their herds, their sons and their daughters. Let us lie down in our shame, and let our dishonor cover us; for we have sinned against the Lord our God, we and our fathers, from our youth even to this day; and we have not obeyed the voice of the Lord our God." — "If you return, O Israel, says the Lord, to me you should return. If you remove your abominations from my presence, and do not waver, and if you swear, 'As the Lord lives,' in truth, in justice, and in uprightness, then nations shall bless themselves in him, and in him shall they glory."

Psalm 130 [page 784]

A Reading (Lesson) from the First Letter of Paul to the Corinthians [7:17-23]

Let every one lead the life which the Lord has assigned to him, and in which God has called him. This is my rule in all the churches. Was any one at the time of his call already circumcised? Let him not seek to remove the marks of circumcision. Was any one at the time of his call uncircumcised? Let him not seek circumcision. For neither circumcision counts for anything nor uncircumcision, but keeping the commandments of God. Every one should remain in the state in which he was called. Were you a slave when called? Never mind. But if you can gain your freedom, avail yourself of the opportunity. For he who was called in the Lord as a slave is a freedman of the Lord. Likewise he who was free when called is a slave of Christ. You were bought with a price; do not become slaves of men.

✝ *The Holy Gospel of Our Lord Jesus Christ According to Mark* [1:14-20]

Now after John was arrested, Jesus came into Galilee, preaching the gospel of God, and saying, "The time is fulfilled, and the kingdom of God is at hand; repent, and believe in the gospel." And passing along by the Sea of Galilee, he saw Simon and Andrew the brother of Simon casting a net in the sea; for they were fishermen. And Jesus said to them, "Follow me and I will make you become fishers of men." And immediately they left their nets and followed him. And going on a little farther, he saw James the son of Zeb'edee and John his brother, who were in their boat mending the nets. And immediately he called them; and they left their father Zeb'edee in the boat with the hired servants, and followed him.

Fourth Sunday after the Epiphany

A Reading (Lesson) from Book of Deuteronomy [18:15-20]

Moses summoned all Israel and said to them, "The Lord your God will raise up for you a prophet like me from among you, from your brethren — him you shall heed — just as you desired of the Lord your God at Horeb on the day of the assembly, when you said, 'Let me not hear again the voice of the Lord my God, or see this great fire any more, lest I die.' And the Lord said to me, 'They have rightly said all that they have spoken. I will raise up for

them a prophet like you from among their brethren; and
I will put my words in his mouth, and he shall speak to them
all that I command him. And whoever will not give heed to
my words which he shall speak in my name, I myself will
require it of him. But the prophet who presumes to speak a
word in my name which I have not commanded him to
speak, or who speaks in the name of other gods, that same
prophet shall die."

Psalm 111 [page 754]

*A Reading (Lesson) from the First Letter of Paul to the
Corinthians* [8:1b-13]

"Knowledge" puffs up, but love builds up. If any one
imagines that he knows something, he does not yet know as
he ought to know. But if one loves God, one is known by
him. Hence, as to the eating of food offered to idols, we
know that "an idol has no real existence," and that "there is
no God but one." For although there may be so-called gods
in heaven or on earth — as indeed there are many "gods"
and many "lords" — yet for us there is one God, the Father,
from whom are all things and for whom we exist, and one
Lord, Jesus Christ, through whom are all things and
through whom we exist. However, not all possess this
knowledge. But some, through being hitherto accustomed
to idols, eat food as really offered to an idol; and their
conscience, being weak, is defiled. Food will not commend
us to God. We are no worse off if we do not eat, and no
better off if we do. Only take care lest this liberty of yours
somehow become a stumbling block to the weak. For if any
one sees you, a man of knowledge, at table in an idol's
temple, might he not be encouraged, if his conscience is
weak, to eat food offered to idols? And so by your
knowledge this weak man is destroyed, the brother for
whom Christ died. Thus, sinning against your brethren and
wounding their conscience when it is weak, you sin against

Christ. Therefore, if food is a cause of my brother's falling, I will never eat meat, lest I cause my brother to fall.

✝ *The Holy Gospel of Our Lord Jesus Christ According to Mark* [1:21-28]

Jesus and his disciples went into Caper'na-um; and immediately on the sabbath he entered the synagogue and taught. And the people were astonished at his teaching, for he taught them as one who had authority, and not as the scribes. And immediately there was in their synagogue a man with an unclean spirit; and he cried out, "What have you to do with us, Jesus of Nazareth? Have you come to destroy us? I know who you are, the Holy One of God." But Jesus rebuked him, saying, "Be silent, and come out of him!" And the unclean spirit, convulsing him and crying with a loud voice, came out of him. And they were all amazed, so that they questioned among themselves, saying, "What is this? A new teaching! With authority he commands even the unclean spirits, and they obey him." And at once his fame spread everywhere throughout all the surrounding region of Galilee.

Fifth Sunday after the Epiphany

A Reading (Lesson) from the Second Book of the Kings [4:(8-17) 18-21 (22-31) 32-37]

One day Eli'sha went on to Shunem, where a wealthy woman lived, who urged him to eat some food. So whenever he passed that way, he would turn in there to eat food. And she said to her husband, "Behold now, I perceive that this is a holy man of God, who is continually passing our way. Let us make a small roof chamber with walls, and put there for him a bed, a table, a chair, and a lamp, so that whenever he comes to us, he can go in there." One day he came there, and he turned into the chamber and rested there. And he said to Geha'zi his servant, "Call this Shu'nammite." When he had called her, she stood before him. And he said to him, "Say now to her, See, you have taken all this trouble for us; what is to be done for you? Would you have a word spoken on your behalf to the king or to the commander of the army?" She answered, "I dwell among my own people." And he said, "What then is to be done for her?" Geha'zi answered, "Well, she has no son, and her husband is old." He said, "Call her." And when he had called her, she stood in the doorway. And he said, "At this season, when the time comes round, you shall embrace a son." And she said, "No, my lord, O man of God; do not lie to your maidservant." But the woman conceived, and she bore a son about that time the following spring, as Eli'sha had said to her.

When the child [*born to the woman of Shunem according to Eli'sha's promise*] had grown, he went out one day to his father among the reapers. And he said to his father, "Oh, my head, my head!" The father said to his servant, "Carry him to his mother." And when he had lifted him, and brought him to his mother, the child sat on her lap till noon, and then he died. And she went up and laid him on the bed of the man of God, and shut the door upon him, and went out.

Then she called to her husband, and said, "Send me one of the servants and one of the asses, that I may quickly go to the man of God, and come back again." And he said, "Why will you go to him today? It is neither new moon nor sabbath." She said, "It will be well." Then she saddled the ass, and she said to her servant, "Urge the beast on; do not slacken the pace for me unless I tell you." So she set out, and came to the man of God at Mount Carmel. When the man of God saw her coming, he said to Geha'zi his servant, "Look, yonder is the Shu'nammite; run at once to meet her, and say to her, Is it well with you? Is it well with your husband? Is it well with the child?" And she answered, "It is well." And when she came to the mountain to the man of God, she caught hold of his feet. And Geha'zi came to thrust her away. But the man of God said, "Let her alone, for she is in bitter distress; and the Lord has hidden it from me, and has not told me." Then she said, "Did I ask my lord for a son? Did I not say, Do not deceive me?" He said to Geha'zi "Gird up your loins, and take my staff in your hand, and go. If you meet any one, do not salute him; and if any one salutes you, do not reply; and lay my staff upon the face of the child." Then the mother of the child said, "As the Lord lives, and as you yourself live, I will not leave you." So he arose and followed her. Geha'zi went on ahead and laid the staff upon the face of the child, but there was no sound or sign of life. Therefore he returned to meet him, and told him, "The child has not awaked."

When Eli'sha came into the house, he saw the child lying dead on his bed. So he went in and shut the door upon the two of them, and prayed to the Lord. Then he went up and lay upon the child, putting his mouth upon his mouth, his eyes upon his eyes, and his hands upon his hands; and as he stretched himself upon him, the flesh of the child became warm. Then he got up again, and walked once to and fro in the house, and went up, and stretched himself upon him; the child sneezed seven times, and the child opened his eyes. Then he summoned Geha'zi and said, "Call this Shu'nammite." So he called her. And when she came to him, he said, "Take up your son." She came and fell at his feet, bowing to the ground; then she took up her son and went out.

Psalm 142 [page 798]

A Reading (Lesson) from the First Letter of Paul to the Corinthians [9:16-23]

If I preach the gospel, that gives me no ground for boasting. For necessity is laid upon me. Woe to me if I do not preach the gospel! For if I do this of my own will, I have a reward; but if not of my own will, I am entrusted with a commission. What then is my reward? Just this: that in my preaching I may make the gospel free of charge, not making full use of my right in the gospel. For though I am free from all men, I have made myself a slave to all, that I might win the more. To the Jews I became as a Jew, in order to win Jews; to those under the law I became as one under the law — though not being myself under the law — that I might win those under the law. To those outside the law I became as one outside the law — not being without law toward God but under the law of Christ — that I might win those outside the law. To the weak I became weak, that I might win the weak. I have become all things to all men, that I might by all means save some. I do it all for the sake of the gospel, that I may share in its blessings.

✝ *The Holy Gospel of Our Lord Jesus Christ According to Mark* [1:29-39]

Jesus left the synagogue at Caper'na-um, and entered the house of Simon and Andrew, with James and John. Now Simon's mother-in-law lay sick with a fever, and immediately they told him of her. And he came and took her by the hand and lifted her up, and the fever left her; and she served them. That evening, at sundown, they brought to him all who were sick or possessed with demons. And the whole city was gathered together about the door. And he healed many who were sick with various diseases, and cast out many demons; and he would not permit the demons to speak, because they knew him. And in the morning, a great while before day, he rose and went out to a lonely place and there he prayed. And Simon and those who were with him pursued him, and they found him and said to him, "Every one is searching for you." And he said to them, "Let us go on to the next towns, that I may preach there also; for that is why I came out." And he went throughout all Galilee, preaching in their synagogues and casting out demons.

Sixth Sunday after the Epiphany

A Reading (Lesson) from the Second Book of the Kings
[5:1-15ab]

Na'aman, commander of the army of the king of Syria, was a
great man with his master and in high favor, because by him
the Lord had given victory to Syria. He was a mighty man of
valor, but he was a leper. Now the Syrians on one of their
raids had carried off a little maid from the land of Israel,
and she waited on Na'aman's wife. She said to her mistress,
"Would that my lord were with the prophet who is in
Samar'ia! He would cure him of his leprosy." So Na'aman
went in and told his lord, "Thus and so spoke the maiden
from the land of Israel." And the king of Syria said, "Go
now, and I will send a letter to the king of Israel." So he
went, taking with him ten talents of silver, six thousand
shekels of gold, and ten festal garments. And he brought the
letter to the king of Israel, which read, "When this letter
reaches you, know that I have sent to you Na'aman my
servant, that you may cure him of his leprosy." And when the
king of Israel read the letter, he rent his clothes and said,
"Am I God, to kill and to make alive, that this man sends
word to me to cure a man of his leprosy? Only consider, and
see how he is seeking a quarrel with me." But when Eli'sha
the man of God heard that the king of Israel had rent his
clothes, he sent to the king, saying, "Why have you rent your
clothes? Let him come now to me, that he may know that
there is a prophet in Israel." So Na'aman came with his
horses and chariots, and halted at the door of Eli'sha's house.
And Eli'sha sent a messenger to him, saying, "Go and wash
in the Jordan seven times, and your flesh shall be restored,
and you shall be clean." But Na'aman was angry, and went
away, saying, "Behold, I thought that he would surely come
out to me, and stand, and call on the name of the Lord his
God, and wave his hand over the place, and cure the leper.
Are not Aba'na and Pharpar, the rivers of Damascus, better

than all the waters of Israel? Could I not wash in them, and be clean?" So he turned and went away in a rage. But his servants came near and said to him, "My father, if the prophet had commanded you to do some great thing, would you not have done it? How much rather, then, when he says to you, 'Wash, and be clean'?" So he went down and dipped himself seven times in the Jordan, according to the word of the man of God; and his flesh was restored like the flesh of a little child, and he was clean. Then he returned to the man of God, he and all his company, and he came and stood before him; and he said, "Behold, I know that there is no God in all the earth but in Israel."

Psalm 42 [page 643]   or   *Psalm 42:1-7* [page 643]

A Reading (Lesson) from the First Letter of Paul to the Corinthians [9:24-27]

Do you not know that in a race all the runners compete, but only one receives the prize? So run that you may obtain it. Every athlete exercises self-control in all things. They do it to receive a perishable wreath, but we an imperishable. Well, I do not run aimlessly, I do not box as one beating the air; but I pommel my body and subdue it, lest after preaching to others I myself should be disqualified.

✝ *The Holy Gospel of Our Lord Jesus Christ According to Mark* [1:40-45]

A leper came to Jesus beseeching him, and kneeling said to him, "If you will, you can make me clean." Moved with pity, he stretched out his hand and touched him, and said to him, "I will; be clean." And immediately the leprosy left him, and he was made clean. And he sternly charged him, and sent him away at once, and said to him, "See that you say nothing to any one; but go, show yourself to the priest, and offer for your cleansing what Moses commanded, for a proof to the people." But he went out and began to talk freely about it, and to spread the news, so that Jesus could no longer openly enter a town, but was out in the country; and people came to him from every quarter.

Seventh Sunday after the Epiphany

A Reading (Lesson) from the Book of Isaiah [43:18-25]

Thus says the Lord, the Holy One of Israel: "Remember not the former things, nor consider the things of old. Behold, I am doing a new thing; now it springs forth, do you not perceive it? I will make a way in the wilderness and rivers in the desert. The wild beasts will honor me, the jackals and the ostriches; for I give water in the wilderness, rivers in the desert, to give drink to my chosen people, the people whom I formed for myself that they might declare my praise. Yet you did not call upon me, O Jacob; but you have been weary of me, O Israel! You have not brought me your sheep for burnt offerings, or honored me with your sacrifices. I have not burdened you with offerings, or wearied you with frankincense. You have not bought me sweet cane with money, or satisfied me with the fat of your sacrifices. But you have burdened me with your sins, you have wearied me with your iniquities. I, I am He who blots out your transgressions for my own sake, and I will not remember your sins."

Psalm 32 [page 624]   or   *Psalm 32:1-8* [page 624]

A Reading (Lesson) from the Second Letter of Paul to the Corinthians [1:18-22]

As surely as God is faithful, our word to you has not been Yes and No. For the Son of God, Jesus Christ, whom we preached among you, Silva'nus and Timothy and I, was not Yes and No; but in him it is always Yes. For all the promises of God find their Yes in him. That is why we utter the Amen through him, to the glory of God. But it is God who establishes us with you in Christ, and has commissioned us; he has put his seal upon us and given us his spirit in our hearts as a guarantee.

✝ *The Holy Gospel of Our Lord Jesus Christ According to Mark* [2:1-12]

When Jesus returned to Caper'na-um after some days, it was reported that he was at home. And many were gathered together, so that there was no longer room for them, not even about the door; and he was preaching the word to them. And they came, bringing to him a paralytic carried by four men. And when they could not get near him because of the crowd, they removed the roof above him; and when they had made an opening, they let down the pallet on which the paralytic lay. And when Jesus saw their faith, he said to the paralytic, "My son, your sins are forgiven." Now some of the scribes were sitting there, questioning in their hearts, "Why does this man speak thus? It is blasphemy! Who can forgive sins but God alone?" And immediately Jesus, perceiving in his spirit that they thus questioned within themselves, said to them, "Why do you question thus in your hearts? Which is easier, to say to a paralytic, 'Your sins are forgiven,' or to say, 'Rise, take up your pallet and walk'? But that you may know that the son of man has authority on earth to forgive sins" — he said to the paralytic — "I say to you, rise, take up your pallet and go home." And he rose, and immediately took up the pallet and went out before them all; so that they were all amazed and glorified God, saying, "We never saw anything like this!"

Eighth Sunday after the Epiphany

A Reading (Lesson) from the Book of Hosea [2:14-23]

The Lord said, "Behold, I will allure Israel, and bring her into the wilderness, and speak tenderly to her. And there I will give her her vineyards, and make the Valley of Achor a door of hope. And there she shall answer as in the days of her youth, as at the time when she came out of the land of Egypt. And in that day, says the Lord, you will call me, 'My husband,' and no longer will you call me, 'My Ba'al.' For I will remove the names of the Ba'als from her mouth, and they shall be mentioned by name no more. And I will make for you a covenant on that day with the beasts of the field, the birds of the air, and the creeping things of the ground; and I will abolish the bow, the sword, and war from the land; and I will make you lie down in safety. And I will betroth you to me for ever; I will betroth you to me in righteousness and in justice, in steadfast love, and in mercy. I will betroth you to me in faithfulness; and you shall know the Lord. And in that day, says the Lord, I will answer the heavens, and they shall answer the earth; and the earth shall answer the grain, the wine, and the oil, and they shall answer Jezreel; and I will sow him for myself in the land. And I will have pity on 'Not pitied', and I will say to 'Not my people', 'You are my people'; and he shall say, 'Thou art my God.'"

Psalm 103 [page 733] or *Psalm 103:1-6* [page 733]

A Reading (Lesson) from the Second Letter of Paul to the Corinthians [3:(4-11)17—4:2]

Such is the confidence that we have through Christ toward God. Not that we are competent of ourselves to claim anything as coming from us; our competence is from God, who has made us competent to be ministers of a new covenant, not in a written code but in the Spirit; for the written code kills, but the Spirit gives life. Now if the dispensation of death, carved in letters on stone, came with such splendor that the Israelites could not look at Moses' face because of its brightness, fading as this was, will not the dispensation of the Spirit be attended with greater splendor? For if there was splendor in the dispensation of condemnation, the dispensation of righteousness must far exceed it in splendor. Indeed, in this case, what once had splendor has come to have no splendor at all, because of the splendor that surpasses it. For if what faded away came with splendor, what is permanent must have much more splendor.

Now the Lord is the Spirit, and where the Spirit of the Lord is, there is freedom. And we all, with unveiled face, beholding the glory of the Lord, are being changed into his likeness from one degree of glory to another; for this comes from the Lord who is the Spirit. Therefore, having this ministry by the mercy of God, we do not lose heart. We have renounced disgraceful, underhanded ways; we refuse to practice cunning or to tamper with God's word, but by the open statement of the truth we would commend ourselves to every man's conscience in the sight of God.

✝ *The Holy Gospel of Our Lord Jesus Christ According to Mark* [2:18-22]

Now John's disciples and the Pharisees were fasting; and people came and said to Jesus, "Why do John's disciples and the disciples of the Pharisees fast, but your disciples do not fast?" And Jesus said to them, "Can the wedding guests fast while the bridegroom is with them? As long as they have the bridegroom with them, they cannot fast. The days will come, when the bridegroom is taken away from them and then they will fast in that day. No one sews a piece of unshrunk cloth on an old garment; if he does, the patch tears away from it, the new from the old, and a worse tear is made. And no one puts new wine into old wineskins; if he does, the wine will burst the skins, and the wine is lost, and so are the skins; but new wine is for fresh skins."

Last Sunday after the Epiphany

A Reading (Lesson) from the First Book of the Kings
[19:9-18]

Eli'jah fled to Mount Horeb, and there he came to a cave, and lodged there; and behold, the word of the Lord came to him, and he said to him, "What are you doing here, Eli'jah?" He said, "I have been very jealous for the Lord, the God of hosts; for the people of Israel have forsaken thy covenant, thrown down thy altars, and slain thy prophets with the sword; and I, even I only, am left; and they seek my life, to take it away." And he said, "Go forth, and stand upon the mount before the Lord." And behold, the Lord passed by, and a great and strong wind rent the mountains, and broke in pieces the rocks before the Lord, but the Lord was not in the wind; and after the wind an earthquake, but the Lord was not in the earthquake; and after the earthquake a fire, but the Lord was not in the fire; and after the fire a still small voice. And when Eli'jah heard it, he wrapped his face in his mantle and went out and stood at the entrance of the cave. And behold, there came a voice to him, and said, "What are you doing here, Eli'jah?" He said, "I have been very jealous for the Lord, the God of hosts; for the people of Israel have forsaken thy covenant, thrown down thy altars, and slain thy prophets with the sword; and I, even I only, am left; and they seek my life, to take it away." And the Lord said to him, "Go, return on your way to the wilderness of Damascus; and when you arrive, you shall anoint Haz'ael to be king over Syria; and Jehu the son of Nimshi you shall anoint to be king over Israel; and Eli'sha the son of Shaphat of A'bel-meho'lah you shall anoint to be prophet in your place. And him who escapes from the sword of Haza'el shall Jehu slay; and him who escapes from the sword of Jehu shall Eli'sha slay. Yet I will leave seven thousand in Israel, all the knees that have not bowed to Ba'al, and every mouth that has not kissed him."

Psalm 27 [page 617] or Psalm 27:5-11 [page 617]

A Reading (Lesson) from the Second Letter of Peter
[1:16-19(20-21)]

We did not follow cleverly devised myths when we made known to you the power and coming of our Lord Jesus Christ, but we were eyewitnesses of his majesty. For when he received honor and glory from God the Father and the voice was borne to him by the Majestic Glory, "This is my beloved Son, with whom I am well pleased," we heard this voice borne from heaven, for we were with him on the holy mountain. And we have the prophetic word made more sure. You will do well to pay attention to this as to a lamp shining in a dark place, until the day dawns and the morning star rises in your hearts.

First of all you must understand this, that no prophecy of scripture is a matter of one's own interpretation, because no prophecy ever came by the impulse of man, but men moved by the Holy Spirit spoke from God.

✝ *The Holy Gospel of Our Lord Jesus Christ According to Mark* [9:2-9]

After six days Jesus took with him Peter and James and John, and led them up a high mountain apart by themselves; and he was transfigured before them, and his garments became glistening, intensely white, as no fuller on earth could bleach them. And there appeared to them Eli'jah with Moses; and they were talking to Jesus. And Peter said to Jesus, "Master, it is well that we are here; let us make three booths, one for you and one for Moses and one for Eli'jah." For he did not know what to say, for they were exceedingly afraid. And a cloud overshadowed them, and a voice came out of the cloud, "This is my beloved Son; listen to him." And suddenly looking around they no longer saw any one with them but Jesus only. And as they were coming down the mountain, he charged them to tell no one what they had seen, until the Son of man should have risen from the dead.

Ash Wednesday

A Reading (Lesson) from the Book of Joel [2:1-2,12-17]

Blow the trumpet in Zion; sound the alarm on my holy mountain! Let all the inhabitants of the land tremble, for the day of the Lord is coming, it is near, a day of darkness and gloom, a day of clouds and thick darkness! Like blackness there is spread upon the mountains a great and powerful people; their like has never been from of old, nor will be again after them through the years of all generations. "Yet even now," says the Lord, "return to me with all your heart, with fasting, with weeping, and with mourning; and rend your hearts and not your garments." Return to the Lord, your God, for he is gracious and merciful, slow to anger, and abounding in steadfast love, and repents of evil. Who knows whether he will not turn and repent, and leave a blessing behind him, a cereal offering and a drink offering for the Lord, your God? Blow the trumpet in Zion; sanctify a fast; call a solemn assembly; gather the people. Sanctify the congregation; assemble the elders; gather the children, even nursing infants. Let the bridegroom leave his room, and the bride her chamber. Between the vestibule and the altar let the priests, the ministers of the Lord, weep and say, "Spare thy people, O Lord, and make not thy heritage a reproach, a byword among the nations. Why should they say among the peoples, 'Where is their God?'"

or this

A Reading (Lesson) from the Book of Isaiah [58:1-12]

Thus says the high and lofty One who inhabits eternity, whose name is Holy: "Cry aloud, spare not, lift up your voice like a trumpet; declare to my people their transgression, to the house of Jacob their sins. Yet they seek me daily, and delight to know my ways, as if they were a nation that did righteousness and did not forsake the ordinance of their God; they ask of me righteous judgments, they delight to draw near to God. 'Why have we fasted, and thou seest it not? Why have we humbled ourselves, and thou takest no knowledge of it?' Behold, in the day of your fast you seek your own pleasure, and oppress all your workers. Behold, you fast only to quarrel and to fight and to hit with wicked fist. Fasting like yours this day will not make your voice to be heard on high. Is such the fast that I choose, a day for a man to humble himself? Is it to bow down his head like a rush, and to spread sackcloth and ashes under him? Will you call this a fast, and a day acceptable to the Lord? Is not this the fast that I choose: to loose the bonds of wickedness, to undo the thongs of the yoke, to let the oppressed go free, and to break every yoke? Is it not to share your bread with the hungry, and bring the homeless poor into your house; when you see the naked, to cover him, and not to hide yourself from your own flesh? Then shall your light break forth like the dawn, and your healing shall spring up speedily; your righteousness shall go before you, the glory of the Lord shall be your rear guard. Then you shall call, and the Lord will answer; you shall cry, and he will say, Here I am. If you take away from the midst of you the yoke, the pointing of the finger, and speaking wickedness, if you pour yourself out for the hungry and satisfy the desire of the afflicted, then shall your light rise in the darkness and your gloom be as the noonday. And the Lord will guide you continually, and satisfy your desire with good things, and make your bones strong; and you shall be like a watered garden, like a spring of water, whose waters fail not. And your ancient ruins shall be rebuilt; you shall raise up the foundations of many generations; you shall be called the repairer of the breach, the restorer of streets to dwell in."

Psalm 103 [page 733]   or   *Psalm 103:8-14* [page 733]

A Reading (Lesson) from the Second Letter of Paul to the Corinthians [5:20b—6:10]

We beseech you on behalf of Christ, be reconciled to God. For our sake he made him to be sin who knew no sin, so that in him we might become the righteousness of God. Working together with him, then, we entreat you not to accept the grace of God in vain. For he says, "At the acceptable time I have listened to you, and helped you on the day of salvation." Behold, now is the acceptable time; behold, now is the day of salvation. We put no obstacle in any one's way, so that no fault may be found with our ministry, but as servants of God we commend ourselves in every way: through great endurance, in afflictions, hardships, calamities, beatings, imprisonments, tumults, labors, watching, hunger; by purity, knowledge, forbearance, kindness, the Holy Spirit, genuine love, truthful speech, and the power of God; with the weapons of righteousness for the right hand and for the left; in honor and dishonor, in ill repute and good repute. We are treated as impostors, and yet are true; as unknown, and yet well known; as dying, and behold we live; as punished, and yet not killed; as sorrowful, yet always rejoicing; as poor, yet making many rich; as having nothing, and yet possessing everything.

✝ *The Holy Gospel of Our Lord Jesus Christ According to Matthew* [6:1-6,16-21]

Jesus said, "Beware of practicing your piety before men in order to be seen by them; for then you will have no reward from your Father who is in heaven. Thus, when you give alms, sound no trumpet before you, as the hypocrites do in the synagogues and in the streets, that they may be praised by men. Truly, I say to you, they have received their reward. But when you give alms, do not let your left hand know what your right hand is doing, so that your alms may be in secret; and your Father who sees in secret will reward you. And when you pray, you must not be like the hypocrites; for they love to stand and pray in the synagogues and at the street corners, that they may be seen by men. Truly, I say to you, they have received their reward. But when you pray, go into your room and shut the door and pray to your Father who is in secret; and your Father who sees in secret will reward you. And when you fast, do not look dismal, like the hypocrites, for they disfigure their faces that their fasting may be seen by men. Truly, I say to you, they have received their reward. But when you fast, anoint your head and wash your face, that your fasting may not be seen by men but by your Father who is in secret; and your Father who sees in secret will reward you. Do not lay up for yourselves treasures on earth, where moth and rust consume and where thieves break in and steal, but lay up for yourselves treasure in heaven, where neither moth nor rust consumes and where thieves do not break in and steal. For where your treasure is, there will your heart be also."

First Sunday in Lent

A Reading (Lesson) from the Book of Genesis [9:8-17]

After the waters of the flood had subsided, God said to Noah and to his sons with him, "Behold, I establish my covenant with you and your descendants after you, and with every living creature that is with you, the birds, the cattle, and every beast of the earth with you, as many as came out of the ark. I establish my covenant with you, that never again shall all flesh be cut off by the waters of a flood, and never again shall there be a flood to destroy the earth." And God said, "This is the sign of the covenant which I make between me and you and every living creature that is with you, for all future generations: I set my bow in the cloud, and it shall be a sign of the covenant between me and the earth. When I bring clouds over the earth and the bow is seen in the clouds,

I will remember my covenant which is between me and you and every living creature of all flesh; and the waters shall never again become a flood to destroy all flesh. When the bow is in the clouds, I will look upon it and remember the everlasting covenant between God and every living creature of all flesh that is upon the earth." God said to Noah, "This is the sign of the covenant which I have established between me and all flesh that is upon the earth."

Psalm 25 [page 614]   or   *Psalm 25:3-9* [page 614]

A Reading (Lesson) from the First Letter of Peter [3:18-22]

Christ died for sins once for all, the righteous for the unrighteous, that he might bring us to God, being put to death in the flesh but made alive in the spirit; in which he went and preached to the spirits in prison, who formerly did not obey, when God's patience waited in the days of Noah, during the building of the ark, in which a few, that is, eight persons, were saved through water. Baptism, which corresponds to this, now saves you, not as a removal of dirt from the body but as an appeal to God for a clear conscience, through the resurrection of Jesus Christ, who has gone into heaven and is at the right hand of God, with angels, authorities, and powers subject to him.

✠ *The Holy Gospel of Our Lord Jesus Christ According to Mark* [1:9-13]

In those days Jesus came from Nazareth of Galilee and was baptized by John in the Jordan. And when he came up out of the water, immediately he saw the heavens opened and the Spirit descending upon him like a dove; and a voice came from heaven, "Thou art my beloved Son; with thee I am well pleased." The Spirit immediately drove him out into the wilderness. And he was in the wilderness forty days, tempted by Satan; and he was with the wild beasts; and the angels ministered to him.

Second Sunday in Lent

A Reading (Lesson) from the Book of Genesis [22:1-14]

God tested Abraham, and said to him, "Abraham!" And he said, "Here am I." He said, "Take your son, your only son Isaac, whom you love, and go to the land of Mori'ah, and offer him there as a burnt offering upon one of the mountains of which I shall tell you." So Abraham rose early in the morning, saddled his ass, and took two of his young men with him, and his son Isaac; and he cut the wood for the burnt offering, and arose and went to the place of which God had told him. On the third day Abraham lifted up his eyes and saw the place afar off. Then Abraham said to his young men, "Stay here with the ass; I and the lad will go yonder and worship, and come again to you." And Abraham took the wood of the burnt offering, and laid it on Isaac his son; and he took in his hand the fire and the knife. So they went both of them together. And Isaac said to his father Abraham, "My father!" And he said, "Here am I, my son." He said, "Behold, the fire and the wood; but where is the lamb for a burnt offering?" Abraham said, "God will provide himself the lamb for a burnt offering, my son." So they went both of them together. When they came to the place of which God had told him, Abraham built an altar there, and laid the wood in order, and bound Isaac his son, and laid him on the altar, upon the wood. Then Abraham put forth his hand, and took the knife to slay his son. But the angel of the Lord called to him from heaven, and said, "Abraham, Abraham!" And he said, "Here am I." He said, "Do not lay your hand on the lad or do anything to him; for now I know that you fear God, seeing you have not witheld your son, your only son, from me." And Abraham lifted up his eyes and looked, and behold, behind him was a ram, caught in a thicket by his horns; and Abraham went and took the ram, and offered it up as a burnt offering instead of his son. So Abraham called the name of that place The Lord will provide; as it is said to this day, "On the mount of the Lord it shall be provided."

Psalm 16 [page 599] or *Psalm 16:5-11* [page 600]

A Reading (Lesson) from the Letter of Paul to the Romans [8:31-39]

What then shall we say to this? If God is for us, who is against us? He who did not spare his own Son but gave him up for us all, will he not also give us all things with him? Who shall bring any charge against God's elect? It is God who justifies: who is to condemn? Is it Christ Jesus, who died, yes, who was raised from the dead, who is at the right hand of God, who indeed intercedes for us? Who shall separate us from the love of Christ? Shall tribulation, or distress, or persecution, or famine, or nakedness, or peril, or sword? As it is written, "For thy sake we are being killed all the day long; we are regarded as sheep to be slaughtered." No, in all these things we are more than conquerors through him who loved us. For I am sure that neither death, nor life, nor angels, nor principalities, nor things present, nor things to come, nor powers, nor height, nor depth, nor anything else in all creation, will be able to separate us from the love of God in Christ Jesus our Lord.

✝ *The Holy Gospel of Our Lord Jesus Christ According to Mark* [8:31-38]

Jesus began to teach his disciples that the Son of man must suffer many things, and be rejected by the elders and the chief priests and the scribes, and be killed, and after three days rise again. And he said this plainly. And Peter took him, and began to rebuke him. But turning and seeing his disciples, he rebuked Peter, and said, "Get behind me, Satan! For you are not on the side of God, but of men." And he called to him the multitude with his disciples, and said to them, "If any man would come after me, let him deny himself and take up his cross and follow me. For whoever would save his life will lose it; and whoever loses his life for my sake and the gospel's will save it. For what does it profit a man, to gain the whole world and forfeit his life? For what can a man give in return for his life? For whoever is ashamed of me and of my words in this adulterous and sinful generation, of him will the Son of man also be ashamed, when he comes in the glory of his Father with the holy angels."

Third Sunday in Lent

A Reading (Lesson) from the Book of Exodus [20:1-17]

God spoke to Moses on Mount Sinai, saying, "I am the Lord your God, who brought you out of the land of Egypt, out of the house of bondage. You shall have no other gods before me. You shall not make for yourself a graven image, or any likeness of anything that is in heaven above, or that is in the earth beneath, or that is in the water under the earth; you shall not bow down to them or serve them; for I the Lord your God am a jealous God, visiting the iniquity of the fathers upon the children to the third and the fourth generation of those who hate me, but showing steadfast love to thousands of those who love me and keep my commandments. You shall not take the name of the Lord your God in vain; for the Lord will not hold him guiltless who takes his name in vain. Remember the sabbath day, to keep it holy. Six days you shall labor, and do all your work; but the seventh day is a sabbath to the Lord your God; in it you shall not do any work, you, or your son, or your daughter, your manservant, or your maidservant, or your cattle, or the sojourner who is within your gates; for in six days the Lord made heaven and earth, the sea, and all that is in them, and rested the seventh day; therefore the Lord blessed the sabbath day and hallowed it. Honor your father and your mother, that your days may be long in the land which the Lord your God gives you. You shall not kill. You shall not commit adultery. You shall not steal. You shall not bear false witness against your neighbor. You shall not covet your neighbor's house; you shall not covet your neighbor's wife, or his manservant, or his maidservant, or his ox, or his ass, or anything that is your neighbor's."

Psalm 19:7-14 [page 607]

A Reading (Lesson) from the Letter of Paul to the Romans [7:13-25]

Did that which is good bring death to me? By no means! It was sin, working death in me through what is good, in order that sin might be shown to be sin, and through the commandment might become sinful beyond measure. We know that the law is spiritual; but I am carnal, sold under sin. I do not understand my own actions. For I do not do what I want, but I do the very thing I hate. Now if I do what I do not want, I agree that the law is good. So then it is no longer I that do it, but sin which dwells within me. For I know that nothing good dwells within me, that is, in my flesh. I can will what is right, but I cannot do it. For I do not do the good I want, but the evil I do not want is what I do. Now if I do what I do not want, it is no longer I that do it, but sin which dwells within me. So I find it to be a law that when I want to do right, evil lies close at hand. For I delight in the law of God, in my inmost self, but I see in my members another law at war with the law of my mind and making me captive to the law of sin which dwells in my members. Wretched man that I am! Who will deliver me from this body of death? Thanks be to God through Jesus Christ our Lord! So then, I of myself serve the law of God with my mind, but with my flesh I serve the law of sin.

✝ *The Holy Gospel of Our Lord Jesus Christ*
According to John [2:13-22]

The Passover of the Jews was at hand, and Jesus went up to Jerusalem. In the temple he found those who were selling oxen and sheep and pigeons, and the money-changers at their business. And making a whip of cords, he drove them all, with the sheep and oxen, out of the temple; and he poured out the coins of the money-changers and overturned their tables. And he told those who sold the pigeons, "Take these things away; you shall not make my Father's house a house of trade." His disciples remembered that it was written, "Zeal for thy house will consume me." The Jews then said to him, "What sign have you to show us for doing this?" Jesus answered them, "Destroy this temple, and in three days I will raise it up." The Jews then said, "It has taken forty-six years to build this temple, and will you raise it up in three days?" But he spoke of the temple of his body. When therefore he was raised from the dead, his disciples remembered that he had said this; and they believed the scripture and the word which Jesus had spoken.

Fourth Sunday in Lent

A Reading (Lesson) from the Second Book of the Chronicles [36:14-23]

King Zedeki'ah and all the leading priests and the people were exceedingly unfaithful, following all the abominations of the nations; and they polluted the house of the Lord, which the Lord had hallowed in Jerusalem. The Lord, the God of their fathers, sent persistently to them by his messengers, because he had compassion on his people and on his dwelling place; but they kept mocking the messengers of God, despising his words, and scoffing at his prophets, till the wrath of the Lord rose against his people, till there was no remedy. Therefore he brought up against them the king of the Chalde'ans, who slew their young men with the sword in the house of their sanctuary, and had no compassion on young man or virgin, old man or aged; he gave them all into his hand. And all the vessels of the house of God, great and small, and the treasures of the house of the Lord, and the treasures of the king and of his princes, all these he brought to Babylon. And they burned the house of God, and broke down the wall of Jerusalem, and burned all its palaces with fire, and destroyed all its precious vessels. He took into exile in Babylon those who had escaped from the sword, and they became servants to him and to his sons until the establishment of the kingdom of Persia, to fulfill the word of the Lord by the mouth of Jeremiah, until the land had enjoyed its sabbaths. All the days that it lay desolate it kept sabbath, to fulfill seventy years. Now in the first year of Cyrus king of Persia, that the word of the Lord by the mouth of Jeremiah might be accomplished, the Lord stirred up the spirit of Cyrus king of Persia so that he made a proclamation throughout all his kingdom and also put it in writing: "Thus says Cyrus king of Persia, 'The Lord, the God of heaven, has given me all the kingdoms of the earth, and he has charged me to build him a house at Jerusalem, which is in Judah. Whoever is among you of all his people, may the Lord his God be with him. Let him go up.'"

Psalm 122 [page 779]

A Reading (Lesson) from the Letter of Paul to the Ephesians [2:4-10]

God, who is rich in mercy, out of the great love with which he loved us, even when we were dead through our trespasses, made us alive together with Christ (by grace you have been saved), and raised us up with him, and made us sit with him in the heavenly places in Christ Jesus, that in the coming ages he might show the immeasurable riches of his grace in kindness toward us in Christ Jesus. For by grace you have been saved through faith; and this is not your own doing, it is the gift of God — not because of works, lest any man should boast. For we are his workmanship, created in Christ Jesus for good works, which God prepared beforehand, that we should walk in them.

✝ The Holy Gospel of Our Lord Jesus Christ According to John [6:4-15]

Now the Passover, the feast of the Jews, was at hand. Lifting up his eyes, then, and seeing that a multitude was coming to him, Jesus said to Philip, "How are we to buy bread, so that these people may eat?" This he said to test him, for he himself knew what he would do. Philip answered him, "Two hundred denarii would not buy enough bread for each of them to get a little." One of his disciples, Andrew, Simon Peter's brother, said to him, "There is a lad here who has five barley loaves and two fish; but what are they among so many?" Jesus said, "Make the people sit down." Now there was much grass in the place; so the men sat down, in number about five thousand. Jesus then took the loaves, and when he had given thanks, he distributed them to those who were seated; so also the fish, as much as they wanted. And when they had eaten their fill, he told his disciples, "Gather up the fragments left over, that nothing may be lost." So they gathered them up and filled twelve baskets with fragments from the five barley loaves, left by those who had eaten. When the people saw the sign which he had done, they said, "This is indeed the prophet who is to come into the world!" Perceiving then that they were about to come and take him by force to make him king, Jesus withdrew again to the mountain by himself.

Fifth Sunday in Lent

A Reading (Lesson) from the Book of Jeremiah [31:31-34]

Behold, the days are coming, says the Lord, when I will make a new covenant with the house of Israel and the house of Judah, not like the covenant which I made with their fathers when I took them by the hand to bring them out of the land of Egypt, my covenant which they broke, though I was their husband, says the Lord. But this is the covenant which I will make with the house of Israel after those days, says the Lord: I will put my law within them, and I will write it upon their hearts; and I will be their God, and they shall be my people. And no longer shall each man teach his neighbor and each his brother, saying, "Know the Lord," for they shall all know me, from the least of them to the greatest, says the Lord; for I will forgive their iniquity, and I will remember their sin no more.

Psalm 51 [page 656]   or   *Psalm 51:11-16* [page 657]

A Reading (Lesson) from the Letter to the Hebrews
[5:(1-4)5-10]

> Every high priest chosen from among men is appointed to act on behalf of men in relation to God, to offer gifts and sacrifices for sins. He can deal gently with the ignorant and wayward, since he himself is beset with weakness. Because of this he is bound to offer sacrifice for his own sins as well as for those of the people. And one does not take the honor upon himself, but he is called by God, just as Aaron was.

[*So also*] Christ did not exalt himself to be made a high priest, but was appointed by him who said to him, "Thou art my Son, today I have begotten thee"; as he says also in another place, "Thou art a priest for ever, after the order of Mel-chiz′edek." In the days of his flesh, Jesus offered up prayers and supplications, with loud cries and tears, to him who was able to save him from death, and he was heard for his godly fear. Although he was a Son, he learned obedience through what he suffered; and being made perfect he became the source of eternal salvation to all who obey him, being designated by God a high priest after the order of Mel-chiz'edek.

✝ *The Holy Gospel of Our Lord Jesus Christ According to John* [12:20-33]

Now among those who went up to worship at the feast were some Greeks. So these came to Philip, who was from Beth-sa'ida in Galilee, and said to him, "Sir, we wish to see Jesus." Philip went and told Andrew; Andrew went with Philip and they told Jesus. And Jesus answered them, "The hour has come for the Son of man to be glorified. Truly, truly, I say to you, unless a grain of wheat falls into the earth and dies, it remains alone; but if it dies, it bears much fruit. He who loves his life loses it, and he who hates his life in this world will keep it for eternal life. If any one serves me, he must follow me; and where I am, there shall my servant be also; if any one serves me, the Father will honor him. Now is my soul troubled. And what shall I say? 'Father, save me from this hour?' No, for this purpose I have come to this hour. Father, glorify thy name." Then a voice came from heaven, "I have glorified it, and I will glorify it again." The crowd standing by heard it and said that it had thundered. Others said, "An angel has spoken to him." Jesus answered, "This voice has come for your sake, not for mine. Now is the judgment of this world, now shall the ruler of this world be cast out; and I, when I am lifted up from the earth, will draw all men to myself." He said this to show by what death he was to die.

The Sunday of the Passion: Palm Sunday

At the Liturgy of the Palms

✝ *The Holy Gospel of Our Lord Jesus Christ*
According to Mark [11:1-11a]

When they drew near to Jerusalem, to Beth'phage and
Bethany, at the Mount of Olives, Jesus sent two of his
disciples, and said to them, "Go into the village opposite
you, and immediately as you enter it you will find a colt tied,
on which no one has ever sat; untie it and bring it. If any one
says to you, 'Why are you doing this?' say, 'The Lord has
need of it and will send it back here immediately.'" And they
went away, and found a colt tied at the door out in the open
street; and they untied it. And those who stood there said to
them, "What are you doing, untying the colt?" And they told
them what Jesus had said; and they let them go. And they
brought the colt to Jesus, and threw their garments on it;
and he sat upon it. And many spread their garments on the
road, and others spread leafy branches which they had cut
from the fields. And those who went before and those who
followed cried out, "Hosanna! Blessed is he who comes in
the name of the Lord! Blessed is the kingdom of our father
David that is coming! Hosanna in the highest!" And he
entered Jerusalem, and went into the temple.

The Blessing over the Branches follows [page 271 of the Prayer Book]

Processional Psalm 118:19-29 [page 762]

At the Liturgy of the Word

A Reading (Lesson) from the Book of Isaiah [45:21-25]

Thus says the Lord, "Declare and present your case; let them
take counsel together! Who told this long ago? Who

declared it of old? Was it not I, the Lord? And there is no other god besides me, a righteous God and a Savior; there is none besides me. Turn to me and be saved, all the ends of the earth! For I am God, and there is no other. By myself I have sworn, from my mouth has gone forth in righteousness a word that shall not return: 'To me every knee shall bow, every tongue shall swear.' Only in the Lord, it shall be said of me, are righteousness and strength; to him shall come and be ashamed, all who were incensed against him. In the Lord all the offspring of Israel shall triumph and glory."

or this

Isaiah 52:13—53:12 [page 82 below]

Psalm 22:1-21 [page 610] or *Psalm 22:1-11* [page 610]

A Reading (Lesson) from the Letter of Paul to the Philippians [2:5-11]

Have this mind among yourselves, which is yours in Christ Jesus, who, though he was in the form of God, did not count equality with God a thing to be grasped, but emptied himself, taking the form of a servant, being born in the likeness of men. And being found in human form he humbled himself and became obedient unto death, even death on a cross. Therefore God has highly exalted him and bestowed on him the name which is above every name, that at the name of Jesus every knee should bow, in heaven and on earth and under the earth, and every tongue confess that Jesus Christ is Lord, to the glory of God the Father.

The Passion of Our Lord Jesus Christ According to Mark
[14:32 — 15:39(40-47)]   or   [15:1-39(40-47)]

> *The customary responses before and after the Gospel are omitted.*
>
> *The shorter form of the Passion [Mark 15:1-39] begins on page 66.*
>
> *The Passion may be read by one or more persons.*
>
> *The congregation may be seated for the first part of the Passion. At the verse which mentions the arrival at Golgotha [Mark 15:22], page 68, all stand.*

Narrator   They went to a place which was called Gethsem'ane; and Jesus said to his disciples,

Jesus   Sit here, while I pray.

Narrator   And he took with him Peter and James and John, and began to be greatly distressed and troubled. And he said to them,

Jesus   My soul is very sorrowful, even to death; remain here, and watch.

Narrator   And going a little farther, he fell on the ground and prayed that, if it were possible, the hour might pass from him. And he said,

Jesus   Abba, Father, all things are possible to thee; remove this cup from me; yet not what I will, but what thou wilt.

Narrator   And he came and found them sleeping, and he said to Peter,

Jesus   Simon, are you asleep? Could you not watch one hour? Watch and pray that you may not enter into temptation; the spirit indeed is willing, but the flesh is weak.

Narrator	And again he went away and prayed, saying the same words. And again he came and found them sleeping for their eyes were very heavy; and they did not know what to answer him. And he came the third time, and said to them,
Jesus	Are you still sleeping and taking your rest? It is enough; the hour is come; the Son of man is betrayed into the hands of sinners. Rise, let us be going; see, my betrayer is at hand.
Narrator	And immediately, while he was still speaking, Judas came, one of the twelve, and with him a crowd with swords and clubs, from the chief priests and the scribes and the elders. Now the betrayer had given them a sign, saying,
Reader	The one I shall kiss is the man; seize him and lead him away under guard.
Narrator	And when he came, he went up to him at once, and said,
Reader	Hail, Master!
Narrator	And he kissed him. And they laid hands on him and seized him. But one of those who stood by drew his sword, and struck the slave of the high priest and cut off his ear. And Jesus said to them,
Jesus	Have you come out as against a robber, with swords and clubs to capture me? Day after day I was with you in the temple teaching, and you did not seize me. But let the scripture be fulfilled.
Narrator	And they all forsook him, and fled. And a young man followed him, with nothing but a linen cloth about his body; and they seized him, but he left the linen cloth and ran away naked. And they led Jesus to the high priest; and all the chief priests and the elders and the scribes were assembled.

And Peter had followed him at a distance, right into the courtyard of the high priest; and he was sitting with the guards, and warming himself at the fire. Now the chief priests and the whole council sought testimony against Jesus to put him to death; but they found none. For many bore false witness against him, and their witness did not agree. And some stood up and bore false witness against him, saying,

Reader(s)   We heard him say, "I will destroy this temple that is made with hands, and in three days I will build another, not made with hands."

Narrator   Yet not even so did their testimony agree. And the high priest stood up in the midst, and asked Jesus,

Reader   Have you no answer to make? What is it that these men testify against you?

Narrator   But he was silent and made no answer. Again the high priest asked him,

Reader   Are you the Christ, the Son of the Blessed?

Narrator   And Jesus said,

Jesus   I am; and you will see the Son of man seated at the right hand of Power, and coming with the clouds of heaven.

Narrator   And the high priest tore his garments, and said,

Reader   Why do we still need witnesses? You have heard his blasphemy. What is your decision?

Narrator   And they all condemned him as deserving death. And some began to spit on him, and to cover his face, and to strike him, saying to him,

Reader(s)   Prophesy!

Narrator	And the guards received him with blows. And as Peter was below in the courtyard, one of the maids of the high priest came; and seeing Peter warming himself, she looked at him and said,
Reader	You also were with the Nazarene, Jesus.
Narrator	But he denied it, saying,
Reader	I neither know nor understand what you mean.
Narrator	And he went out into the gateway. And the maid saw him, and began again to say to the bystanders,
Reader	This man is one of them.
Narrator	But again he denied it. And after a little while again the bystanders said to Peter,
Reader(s)	Certainly you are one of them; for you are a Galilean.
Narrator	But he began to invoke a curse on himself and to swear,
Reader	I do not know this man of whom you speak.
Narrator	And immediately the cock crowed a second time. And Peter remembered how Jesus had said to him, "Before the cock crows twice, you will deny me three times." And he broke down and wept.

The shorter form of the Passion begins here
[Mark 15:1-39(40-47)]

Narrator	And as soon as it was morning the chief priests, with the elders and scribes, and the whole council held a consultation; and they bound Jesus and led him away and delivered him to Pilate. And Pilate asked him,

Reader	Are you the King of the Jews?
Narrator	And he answered him,
Jesus	You have said so.
Narrator	And the chief priests accused him of many things. And Pilate again asked him,
Reader	Have you no answer to make? See how many charges they bring against you.
Narrator	But Jesus made no further answer, so that Pilate wondered. Now at the feast he used to release for them one prisoner for whom they asked. And among the rebels in prison, who had committed murder in the insurrection, there was a man called Barab'bas. And the crowd came up and began to ask Pilate to do as he was wont to do for them. And he answered them,
Reader	Do you want me to release for you the King of the Jews?
Narrator	For he perceived that it was out of envy that the chief priests had delivered him up. But the chief priests stirred up the crowd to have him release for them Barab'bas instead. And Pilate again said to them,
Reader	Then what shall I do with the man whom you call the King of the Jews?
Narrator	And they cried out again,
Crowd	Crucify him.
Narrator	And Pilate said to them,
Reader	Why, what evil has he done?
Narrator	But they shouted all the more,
Crowd	Crucify him.

Narrator	So Pilate, wishing to satisfy the crowd, released for them Barab'bas; and having scourged Jesus, he delivered him to be crucified. And the soldiers led him away inside the palace (that is, the praetorium); and they called together the whole battalion. And they clothed him in a purple cloak, and plaiting a crown of thorns they put it on him. And they began to salute him,
Reader(s)	Hail, King of the Jews!
Narrator	And they struck his head with a reed, and spat upon him, and they knelt down in homage to him. And when they had mocked him, they stripped him of the purple cloak, and put his own clothes on him. And they led him out to crucify him. And they compelled a passer-by, Simon of Cyre'ne, who was coming in from the country, the father of Alexander and Rufus, to carry his cross.

All stand.

Narrator	And they brought him to the place called Gol'gotha (which means the place of the skull). And they offered him wine mingled with myrrh; but he did not take it. And they crucified him, and divided his garments among them, casting lots for them, to decide what each should take. And it was the third hour, when they crucified him. And the inscription of the charge against him read "The King of the Jews." And with him they crucified two robbers, one on his right and one on his left. And those who passed by derided him, wagging their heads, and saying,
Reader(s)	Aha! You who would destroy the temple and build it in three days, save yourself, and come down from the cross!

Narrator	So also the chief priests mocked him to one another with the scribes, saying,
Reader(s)	He saved others; he cannot save himself. Let the Christ, the King of Israel, come down from the cross, that we may see and believe.
Narrator	Those who were crucified with him also reviled him. And when the sixth hour had come, there was darkness over the whole land until the ninth hour. And at the ninth hour, Jesus cried out with a loud voice, saying,
Jesus	E'lo-i, E'lo-i, la'ma, sabach-tha'ni?
Narrator	Which means,
Jesus	My God, my God, why hast thou forsaken me?
Narrator	And some of the bystanders hearing it said,
Reader(s)	Behold, he is calling Eli'jah.
Narrator	And one ran and, filling a sponge full of vinegar, put it on a reed and gave it to him to drink, saying,
Reader	Wait, let us see whether Eli'jah will come to take him down.
Narrator	And Jesus uttered a loud cry, and breathed his last.

Silence may be kept.

Narrator	And the curtain of the temple was torn in two, from top to bottom. And when the centurion, who stood facing him, saw that he thus breathed his last, he said,
Reader	Truly this man was the Son of God!

The following passage may be added [Mark 15:40–47]

Narrator There were also women looking on from afar, among whom were Mary Mag'dalene, and Mary the mother of James the younger and of Joses, and Salo'me, who, when he was in Galilee, followed him, and ministered to him; and also many other women who came up with him to Jerusalem. And when evening had come, since it was the day of Preparation, that is, the day before the sabbath, Joseph of Arimathe'a, a respected member of the council, who was also himself looking for the kingdom of God, took courage and went to Pilate, and asked for the body of Jesus. And Pilate wondered if he were already dead; and summoning the centurion, he asked him whether he was already dead. And when he learned from the centurion that he was dead, he granted the body to Joseph. And he bought a linen shroud, and taking him down, wrapped him in the linen shroud, and laid him in a tomb which had been hewn out of the rock; and he rolled a stone against the door of the tomb. Mary Mag'dalene and Mary the mother of Joses saw where he was laid.

Monday in Holy Week

A Reading (Lesson) from the Book of Isaiah [42:1-9]

Behold my servant, whom I uphold, my chosen, in whom my soul delights; I have put my Spirit upon him, he will bring forth justice to the nations. He will not cry or lift up his voice, or make it heard in the street; a bruised reed he will not break, and a dimly burning wick he will not quench; he will faithfully bring forth justice. He will not fail or be discouraged till he has established justice in the earth; and the coastlands wait for his law. Thus says God, the Lord, who created the heavens and stretched them out, who spread forth the earth and what comes from it, who gives breath to the people upon it and spirit to those who walk in it: "I am the Lord, I have called you in righteousness, I have taken you by the hand and kept you; I have given you as a covenant to the people, a light to the nations, to open the eyes that are blind, to bring out the prisoners from the dungeon, from the prison those who sit in darkness. I am the Lord, that is my name; my glory I give to no other, nor my praise to graven images. Behold, the former things have come to pass, and new things I now declare; before they spring forth I tell you of them."

Psalm 36:5-10 [page 632]

A Reading (Lesson) from the Letter to the Hebrews
[11:39 — 12:3]

All these, the patriarchs, prophets, and heroes of the Old Covenant, though well attested by their faith, did not receive what was promised, since God had foreseen something better for us, that apart from us they should not be made perfect. Therefore, since we are surrounded by so great a cloud of witnesses, let us also lay aside every weight, and sin which clings so closely, and let us run with perseverance the race that is set before us, looking to Jesus the pioneer and perfecter of our faith, who for the joy that was set before him endured the cross, despising the shame, and is seated at the right hand of the throne of God. Consider him who endured from sinners such hostility against himself, so that you may not grow weary or fainthearted.

✝ The Holy Gospel of Our Lord Jesus Christ
According to John [12:1-11]

Six days before the Passover, Jesus came to Bethany, where Laz'arus was, whom Jesus had raised from the dead. There they made him a supper; Martha served, and Laz'arus was one of those at table with him. Mary took a pound of costly ointment of pure nard and anointed the feet of Jesus and wiped his feet with her hair; and the house was filled with the fragrance of the ointment. But Judas Iscariot, one of the disciples (he who was to betray him), said, "Why was this ointment not sold for three hundred denarii and given to the poor?" This he said, not that he cared for the poor but because he was a thief, and as he had the money box he used to take what was put into it. Jesus said, "Let her alone, let her keep it for the day of my burial. The poor you always have with you, but you do not always have me." When the great crowd of the Jews learned that he was there, they came, not only on account of Jesus but also to see Laz'arus, whom he had raised from the dead. So the chief priests planned to put Laz'arus also to death, because on account of him many of the Jews were going away and believing in Jesus.

or this

✝ The Holy Gospel of Our Lord Jesus Christ
According to Mark [14:3-9]

While Jesus was at Bethany in the house of Simon the leper, as he sat at table, a woman came with an alabaster flask of ointment of pure nard, very costly, and she broke the flask and poured it over his head. But there were some who said to themselves indignantly, "Why was the ointment thus wasted? For this ointment might have been sold for more than three hundred denarii, and given to the poor." And they reproached her. But Jesus said, "Let her alone; why do you trouble her? She has done a beautiful thing to me. For you always have the poor with you, and whenever you will, you can do good to them; but you will not always have me. She has done what she could; she has anointed my body beforehand for burying. And truly, I say to you, wherever the gospel is preached in the whole world, what she has done will be told in memory of her."

Tuesday in Holy Week

A Reading (Lesson) from the Book of Isaiah [49:1-6]

Listen to me, O coastlands, and hearken, you peoples from afar. The Lord called me from the womb, from the body of my mother he named my name. He made my mouth like a sharp sword, in the shadow of his hand he hid me; he made me a polished arrow, in his quiver he hid me away. And he said to me, "You are my servant, Israel, in whom I will be glorified." But I said, "I have labored in vain, I have spent my strength for nothing and vanity; yet surely my right is with the Lord, and my recompense with my God." And now the Lord says, who formed me from the womb to be his servant, to bring Jacob back to him, and that Israel might be gathered to him, for I am honored in the eyes of the Lord, and my God has become my strength — he says: "It is too light a thing that you should be my servant to raise up the tribes of Jacob and to restore the preserved of Israel; I will give you as a light to the nations, that my salvation may reach to the end of the earth."

Psalm 71:1-12 [page 683]

A Reading (Lesson) from the First Letter of Paul to the Corinthians [1:18-31]

The word of the cross is folly to those who are perishing, but to us who are being saved it is the power of God. For it is written, "I will destroy the wisdom of the wise, and the cleverness of the clever I will thwart." Where is the wise man? Where is the scribe? Where is the debater of this age? Has not God made foolish the wisdom of the world? For since, in the wisdom of God, the world did not know God through wisdom, it pleased God through the folly of what we preach to save those who believe. For Jews demand signs and Greeks seek wisdom, but we preach Christ crucified, a stumbling block to Jews and folly to Gentiles, but to those who are called, both Jews and Greeks, Christ the power of God and the wisdom of God. For the foolishness of God is wiser than men, and the weakness of God is stronger than men. For consider your call, brethren; not many of you were wise according to worldly standards, not many were powerful, not many were of noble birth; but God chose what is foolish in the world to shame the wise, God chose what is weak in the world to shame the strong, God chose what is low and despised in the world, even things that are not, to bring to nothing things that are, so that no human being might boast in the presence of God. He is the source of your life in Christ Jesus, whom God made our wisdom, our righteousness and sanctification and redemption; therefore, as it is written, "Let him who boasts, boast of the Lord."

✝ The Holy Gospel of Our Lord Jesus Christ According to John [12:37-38, 42-50]

Though Jesus had done so many signs before the people, yet they did not believe in him; it was that the word spoken by the prophet Isaiah might be fulfilled, "Lord, who has believed our report, and to whom has the arm of the Lord been revealed?" Nevertheless many even of the authorities believed in him, but for fear of the Pharisees they did not confess it, lest they should be put out of the synagogue: for they loved the praise of men more than the praise of God. And Jesus cried out and said, "He who believes in me, believes not in me but in him who sent me. And he who sees me sees him who sent me. I have come as light into the world, that whoever believes in me may not remain in darkness. If any one hears my sayings and does not keep them I do not judge him; for I did not come to judge the world but to save the world. He who rejects me and does not receive my sayings has a judge; the word that I have spoken will be his judge on the last day. For I have not spoken on my own authority; the Father who sent me has himself given me commandment what to say and what to speak. And I know that his commandment is eternal life. What I say, therefore, I say as the Father has bidden me."

or this

✝ *The Holy Gospel of Our Lord Jesus Christ According to Mark* [11:15-19]

Jesus and those who followed came to Jerusalem. And Jesus entered the temple and began to drive out those who sold and those who bought in the temple, and he overturned the tables of the money-changers and the seats of those who sold pigeons; and he would not allow any one to carry anything through the temple. And he taught, and said to them, "Is it not written, 'My house shall be called a house of prayer for all nations'? But you have made it a den of robbers." And the chief priests and the scribes heard it and sought a way to destroy him; for they feared him, because all the multitude was astonished at his teaching. And when evening came they went out of the city.

Wednesday in Holy Week

A Reading (Lesson) from the Book of Isaiah [50:4-9a]

The Lord God has given me the tongue of those who are taught, that I may know how to sustain with a word him that is weary. Morning by morning he wakens, he wakens my ear to hear as those who are taught. The Lord God has opened my ear, and I was not rebellious, I turned not backward. I gave my back to the smiters, and my cheeks to those who pulled out the beard; I hid not my face from shame and spitting. For the Lord God helps me; therefore I have not been confounded; therefore I have set my face like a flint, and I know that I shall not be put to shame; he who vindicates me is near. Who will contend with me? Let us stand up together. Who is my adversary? Let him come near to me. Behold, the Lord God helps me; who will declare me guilty?

Psalm 69:7-15, 22-23 [page 679]

A Reading (Lesson) from the Letter to the Hebrews [9:11-15, 24-28]

When Christ appeared as a high priest of the good things that have come, then through the greater and more perfect tent (not made with hands, that is, not of this creation) he entered once for all into the Holy Place, taking not the blood of goats and calves but his own blood, thus securing an eternal redemption. For if the sprinkling of defiled persons with the blood of goats and bulls and with the ashes of a heifer sanctifies for the purification of the flesh, how much more shall the blood of Christ, who through the eternal Spirit offered himself without blemish to God, purify your conscience from dead works to serve the living God. Therefore he is the mediator of a new covenant, so that those who are called may receive the promised eternal inheritance, since a death has occurred which redeems them from the transgressions under the first covenant. For Christ has entered, not into a sanctuary made with hands, a copy of the true one, but into heaven itself, now to appear in the presence of God on our behalf. Nor was it to offer himself repeatedly, as the high priest enters the Holy Place yearly with blood not his own; for then he would have had to suffer repeatedly since the foundation of the world. But as it is, he has appeared once for all at the end of the age to put away sin by the sacrifice of himself. And just as it is appointed for men to die once, and after that comes judgment, so Christ, having been offered once to bear the sins of many, will appear a second time, not to deal with sin but to save those who are eagerly waiting for him.

✝ *The Holy Gospel of Our Lord Jesus Christ
According to John* [13:21-35]

At supper with his friends, Jesus was troubled in spirit, and testified, "Truly, truly, I say to you, one of you will betray me." The disciples looked at one another, uncertain of whom he spoke. One of his disciples, whom Jesus loved, was lying close to the breast of Jesus; so Simon Peter beckoned to him and said, "Tell us who it is of whom he speaks." So lying thus, close to the breast of Jesus, he said to him, "Lord, who is it?" Jesus answered, "It is he to whom I shall give this morsel when I have dipped it." So when he had dipped the morsel, he gave it to Judas, the son of Simon Iscariot. Then after the morsel, Satan entered into him. Jesus said to him, "What you are going to do, do quickly." Now no one at the table knew why he said this to him. Some thought that, because Judas had the money box, Jesus was telling him, "Buy what we need for the feast"; or, that he should give something to the poor. So, after receiving the morsel, he immediately went out; and it was night. When he had gone out, Jesus said "Now is the Son of man glorified, and in him God is glorified; if God is glorified in him, God will also glorify him in himself, and glorify him at once. Little children, yet a little while I am with you. You will seek me;

and as I said to the Jews so now I say to you, 'Where I am going you cannot come.' A new commandment I give to you, that you love one another; even as I have loved you, that you also love one another. By this all men will know that you are my disciples, if you have love for one another."

or this

✝ The Holy Gospel of Our Lord Jesus Christ
According to Matthew [26:1-5, 14-25]

Jesus said to his disciples, "You know that after two days the Passover is coming, and the Son of man will be delivered up to be crucified." Then the chief priests and the elders of the people gathered in the palace of the high priest, who was called Ca'iaphas, and took counsel together in order to arrest Jesus by stealth and kill him. But they said, "Not during the feast, lest there be a tumult among the people." Then one of the twelve, who was called Judas Iscariot, went to the chief priests, and said, "What will you give me if I deliver him to you?" And they paid him thirty pieces of silver. And from that moment he sought an opportunity to betray him. Now on the first day of Unleavened Bread the disciples came to Jesus, saying, "Where will you have us prepare for you to eat the passover?" He said, "Go into the city to a certain one, and say to him, 'The Teacher says, My time is at hand; I will keep the passover at your house with my disciples.'" And the disciples did as Jesus had directed them, and they prepared the passover. When it was evening, he sat at table with the twelve disciples; and as they were eating, he said, "Truly, I say to you, one of you will betray me." And they were very sorrowful, and began to say to him one after another, "Is it I, Lord?" He answered, "He who has dipped his hand in the dish with me, will betray me. The Son of man goes as it is written of him, but woe to that man by whom the Son of man is betrayed! It would have been better for that man if he had not been born." Judas, who betrayed him, said, "Is it I, Master?" He said to him, "You have said so."

Maundy Thursday

A Reading (Lesson) from the Book of Exodus [12:1-14a]

The Lord said to Moses and Aaron in the land of Egypt, "This month shall be for you the beginning of months; it shall be the first month of the year for you. Tell all the congregation of Israel that on the tenth day of this month they shall take every man a lamb according to their fathers' houses, a lamb for a household; and if the household is too small for a lamb, then a man and his neighbor next to his house shall take according to the number of persons; according to what each can eat you shall make your count for the lamb. Your lamb shall be without blemish, a male a year old; you shall take it from the sheep or from the goats; and you shall keep it until the fourteenth day of this month, when the whole assembly of the congregation of Israel shall kill their lambs in the evening. Then they shall take some of the blood, and put it on the two doorposts and the lintel of the houses in which they eat them. They shall eat the flesh that night, roasted; with unleavened bread and bitter herbs they shall eat it. Do not eat any of it raw or boiled with water, but roasted, its head with it legs and its inner parts. And you shall let none of it remain until the morning, anything that remains until the morning you shall burn. In this manner you shall eat it: your loins girded, your sandals on your feet, and your staff in your hand; and you shall eat it in haste. It is the Lord's passover. For I will pass through the land of Egypt that night, and I will smite all the first-born in the land of Egypt, both man and beast; and on all the gods of Egypt I will execute judgments: I am the Lord. The blood shall be a sign for you, upon the houses where you are; and when I see the blood, I will pass over you, and no plague shall fall upon you to destroy you, when I smite the land of Egypt. This day shall be for you a memorial day, and you shall keep it as a feast to the Lord."

Psalm 78:14-20, 23-25 [page 696]

A Reading (Lesson) from the First Letter of Paul to the Corinthians [11:23-26 (27-32)]

I received from the Lord what I also delivered to you, that the Lord Jesus on the night when he was betrayed took bread, and when he had given thanks, he broke it, and said, "This is my body which is for you. Do this in remembrance of me." In the same way also the cup, after supper, saying, "This cup is the new covenant in my blood. Do this, as often as you drink it, in remembrance of me." For as often as you eat this bread and drink the cup, you proclaim the Lord's death until he comes.

> Whoever, therefore, eats the bread or drinks the cup of the Lord in an unworthy manner will be guilty of profaning the body and blood of the Lord. Let a man examine himself, and so eat of the bread and drink of the cup. For any one who eats and drinks without discerning the body eats and drinks judgment upon himself. That is why many of you are weak and ill, and some have died. But if we judged ourselves truly, we should not be judged. But when we are judged by the Lord, we are chastened so that we may not be condemned along with the world.

✝ *The Holy Gospel of Our Lord Jesus Christ According to John* [13:1-15]

Now before the feast of the Passover, when Jesus knew that his hour had come to depart out of this world to the Father, having loved his own who were in the world, he loved them to the end. And during supper, when the devil had already put it into the heart of Judas Iscariot, Simon's son, to betray him, Jesus, knowing that the Father had given all things into his hands, and that he had come from God and was going to God, rose from supper, laid aside his garments, and girded himself with a towel. Then he poured water into a basin, and began to wash the disciples' feet, and to wipe them with the towel with which he was girded. He came to Simon Peter; and Peter said to him, "Lord, do you wash my feet?" Jesus answered him, "What I am doing you do not know now, but afterward you will understand." Peter said to him, "You shall never wash my feet." Jesus answered him, "If I do not wash you, you have no part in me." Simon Peter said to him, "Lord, not my feet only but also my hands and my head!" Jesus said to him, "He who has bathed does not need to wash, except for his feet, but he is clean all over; and you are clean, but not every one of you." For he knew who was to betray him; that was why he said, "You are not all clean." When he had washed their feet, and taken his garments, and resumed his place, he said to them, "Do you know what I have done to you? You call me Teacher and Lord; and you are right, for so I am. If I then, your Lord and Teacher, have washed your feet, you also ought to wash one another's feet. For I have given you an example, that you also should do as I have done to you."

or this

✝ *The Holy Gospel of Our Lord Jesus Christ According to Luke* [22:14-30]

And when the hour came, Jesus sat at table, and the apostles with him. And he said to them, "I have earnestly desired to eat this passover with you before I suffer; for I tell you I shall not eat it until it is fulfilled in the kingdom of God." And he took a cup, and when he had given thanks he said, "Take this, and divide it among yourselves; for I tell you that from now on I shall not drink of the fruit of the vine until the kingdom of God comes." And he took bread, and when he had given thanks he broke it, and gave it to them, saying, "This is my body which is given for you. Do this in remembrance of me." And likewise the cup after supper, saying, "This cup which is poured out for you is the new covenant in my blood. But behold the hand of him who betrays me is with me on the table. For the Son of man goes as it has been determined; but woe to that man by whom he is betrayed!" And they began to question one another, which of them it was that would do this. A dispute also arose among them, which of them was to be regarded as the greatest. And he said to them, "The kings of the Gentiles exercise lordship over them; and those in authority over them are called benefactors. But not so with you; rather let the greatest among you become as the youngest, and the leader as one who serves. For which is the greater, one who sits at table, or one who serves? Is it not the one who sits at table? But I am among you as one who serves. You are those who have continued with me in my trials; and I assign to you, as my Father assigned to me, a kingdom, that you may eat and drink at my table in my kingdom, and sit on thrones judging the twelve tribes of Israel."

Good Friday

A Reading (Lesson) from the Book of Isaiah [52:13 — 53:12]

Behold, my servant shall prosper, he shall be exalted and lifted up, and shall be very high. As many were astonished at him — his appearance was so marred, beyond human semblance, and his form beyond that of the sons of men — so shall he startle many nations; kings shall shut their mouths because of him; for that which has not been told them they shall see, and that which they have not heard they shall understand. Who has believed what we have heard? And to whom has the arm of the Lord been revealed? For he grew up before him like a young plant, and like a root out of dry ground; he had no form or comeliness that we should look at him, and no beauty that we should desire him. He was despised and rejected by men; a man of sorrows, and acquainted with grief; and as one from whom men hide their faces he was despised, and we esteemed him not. Surely he has borne our griefs and carried our sorrows; yet we esteemed him stricken, smitten by God, and afflicted. But he was wounded for our transgressions, he was bruised for our iniquities; upon him was the chastisement that made us whole, and with his stripes we are healed. All we like sheep have gone astray; we have turned every one to his own way; and the Lord has laid on him the iniquity of us all. He was oppressed, and he was afflicted, yet he opened not his mouth; like a lamb that is led to the slaughter, and like a sheep that before its shearers is dumb, so he opened not his mouth. By oppression and judgment he was taken away; and as for his generation, who considered that he was cut off out of the land of the living, stricken for the transgression of my people? And they made his grave with the wicked and with a rich man in his death, although he had done no violence, and there was no deceit in his mouth. Yet it was the will of the Lord to bruise him; he has put him to grief; when he makes himself an offering for sin, he shall see his offspring, he shall prolong his days; the will of the Lord shall prosper in his hand; he shall see the fruit of the travail of his soul and be satisfied; by his knowledge shall the righteous one, my servant, make many to be accounted righteous; and, he shall bear their iniquities. Therefore I will divide him a portion with the great, and he shall divide the spoil with the strong; because he poured out his soul to death, and was numbered with the transgressors; yet he bore the sin of many, and made intercession for the transgressors.

or this

A Reading (Lesson) from the Book of Genesis [22:1-18]

God tested Abraham, and said to him, "Abraham!" And he said, "Here am I." He said, "Take your son, your only son Isaac, whom you love, and go to the land of Mori'ah, and offer him there as a burnt offering upon one of the mountains of which I shall tell you." So Abraham rose early in the morning, saddled his ass, and took two of his young men with him, and his son Isaac; and he cut the wood for the burnt offering, and arose and went to the place of which God had told him. On the third day Abraham lifted up his eyes and saw the place afar off. Then Abraham said to his young men, "Stay here with the ass; I and the lad will go yonder and worship, and come again to you." And Abraham took the wood of the burnt offering, and laid it on Isaac his son; and he took in his hand the fire and the knife. So they went both of them together. And Isaac said to his father Abraham, "My father!" And he said, "Here am I, my son." He said, "Behold, the fire and the wood; but where is the lamb for a burnt offering?" Abraham said, "God will provide himself the lamb for a burnt offering, my son." So they went both of them together. When they came to the place of which God had told him, Abraham built an altar there, and laid the wood in order, and bound Isaac his son, and laid him on the altar, upon the wood. Then Abraham put forth his hand, and took the knife to slay his son. But the angel of the Lord called to him from heaven, and said, "Abraham, Abraham!" And he said, "Here am I." He said, "Do not lay your hand on the lad or do anything to him; for now I know that you fear God, seeing you have not withheld your son, your only son, from me." And Abraham lifted up his eyes and looked, and behold, behind him was a ram, caught in a thicket by his horns; and Abraham went and took the ram, and offered it up as a burnt offering instead of his son. So Abraham called the name of that place The Lord will provide; as it is said to this day, "On the mount of the Lord it shall be provided." And the angel of the Lord called to Abraham a second time from heaven, and said, "By myself I have sworn, says the Lord, because you have done this, and have not withheld your son, your only son, I will indeed bless you, and I will multiply your descendants as the

stars of heaven and as the sand which is on the seashore.
And your descendants shall possess the gate of their enemies,
and by your descendants shall all the nations of the earth
bless themselves, because you have obeyed my voice."

or this

A Reading (Lesson) from the Book of Wisdom [2:1,12-24]

The ungodly reasoned unsoundly, saying to themselves,
"Short and sorrowful is our life, and there is no remedy
when a man comes to his end, and no one has been known
to return from Hades. Let us lie in wait for the righteous
man, because he is inconvenient to us and opposes our
actions; he reproaches us for sins against the law, and
accuses us of sins against our training. He professes to have
knowledge of God, and calls himself a child of the Lord. He
became to us a reproof of our thoughts; the very sight of
him is a burden to us, because his manner of life is unlike
that of others, and his ways are strange. We are considered
by him as something base, and he avoids our ways as
unclean; he calls the last end of the righteous happy, and
boasts that God is his father. Let us see if his words are true,
and let us test what will happen at the end of his life; for if
the righteous man is God's son, he will help him, and will
deliver him from the hand of his adversaries. Let us test him
with insult and torture, that we may find out how gentle he
is, and make trial of his forbearance. Let us condemn him to
a shameful death, for, according to what he says, he will be
protected." Thus they reasoned, but they were led astray, for
their wickedness blinded them, and they did not know the
secret purposes of God, nor hope for the wages of holiness,
nor discern the prize for blameless souls; for God created
man for incorruption, and made him in the image of his own
eternity, but through the devil's envy death entered the
world, and those who belong to his party experience it.

Psalm 22:1-21 [page 610]   or   *Psalm 22:1-11* [page 610]   or
Psalm 40:1-14 [page 640]   or   *Psalm 69:1-23* [page 679]

A Reading (Lesson) from the Letter to the Hebrews [10:1-25]

Since the law has but a shadow of the good things to come
instead of the true form of these realities, it can never, by the
same sacrifices which are continually offered year after year,
make perfect those who draw near. Otherwise, would they
not have ceased to be offered? If the worshipers had once
been cleansed, they would no longer have any
consciousness of sin. But in these sacrifices there is a
reminder of sin year after year. For it is impossible that the
blood of bulls and goats should take away sins.
Consequently, when Christ came into the world, he said,
"Sacrifices and offerings thou has not desired, but a body
hast thou prepared for me; in burnt offerings and sin
offerings thou hast taken no pleasure. Then I said, 'Lo, I
have come to do thy will, O God,' as it is written of me in the
roll of the book." When he said above, "Thou hast neither
desired nor taken pleasure in sacrifices and offerings and
burnt offerings and sin offerings" (these are offered
according to the law), then he added, "Lo, I have to come to
do thy will." He abolishes the first in order to establish the
second. And by that will we have been sanctified through the
offering of the body of Jesus Christ once for all. And every
priest stands daily at his service, offering repeatedly the same
sacrifices, which can never take away sins. But when Christ
had offered for all time a single sacrifice for sins, he sat down
at the right hand of God, then to wait until his enemies
should be made a stool for his feet. For by a single offering
he has perfected for all time those who are sanctified. And
the Holy Spirit also bears witness to us; for after saying,
"This is the covenant that I will make with them after those
days, says the Lord: I will put my laws on their hearts, and

write them on their minds," then he adds, "I will remember their sins and their misdeeds no more." Where there is forgiveness of these, there is no longer any offering for sin. Therefore, brethren, since we have confidence to enter the sanctuary by the blood of Jesus, by the new and living way which he opened for us through the curtain, that is, through his flesh, and since we have a great priest over the house of God, let us draw near with a true heart in full assurance of faith, with our hearts sprinkled clean from an evil conscience and our bodies washed with pure water. Let us hold fast the confession of our hope without wavering, for he who promised is faithful; and let us consider how to stir up one another to love and good works, not neglecting to meet together, as is the habit of some, but encouraging one another, and all the more as you see the Day drawing near.

The Passion of Our Lord Jesus Christ According to John
[18:1—19:37] or [19:1-37]

The customary responses before and after the Gospel are omitted.

The shorter form of the Passion begins on page 92.

The Passion may be read by one or more persons.

The congregation may be seated for the first part of the Passion. At the verse which mentions the arrival at Golgotha [John 19:17], page 94, all stand.

Narrator   Jesus went forth with his disciples across the Kidron valley, where there was a garden, which he and his disciples entered. Now Judas, who betrayed him, also knew the place; for Jesus often met there with his disciples. So Judas, procuring a band of soldiers and some officers from the chief priests and the Pharisees, went there with lanterns and torches and weapons. Then Jesus, knowing all that was to befall him, came forward and said to them,

Jesus   Whom do you seek?

Narrator   They answered him,

Reader(s)   Jesus of Nazareth.

Narrator   Jesus said to them,

Jesus   I am he.

Narrator   Judas, who betrayed him, was standing with them. When he said to them, "I am he," they drew back and fell to the ground. Again he asked them,

Jesus   Whom do you seek?

Narrator	And they said,
Reader(s)	Jesus of Nazareth.
Narrator	Jesus answered them,
Jesus	I told you that I am he; so, if you seek me, let these men go.
Narrator	This was to fulfill the word which he had spoken, "Of those whom thou gavest me I lost not one." Then Simon Peter, having a sword, drew it and struck the high priest's slave and cut off his right ear. The slave's name was Malchus. Jesus said to Peter,
Jesus	Put your sword into its sheath; shall I not drink the cup which the Father has given me?
Narrator	So the band of soldiers and their captain and the officers of the Jews seized Jesus and bound him. First they led him to Annas; for he was the father-in-law of Ca'iaphas, who was high priest that year. It was Ca'iaphas who had given counsel to the Jews that it was expedient that one man should die for the people. Simon Peter followed Jesus, and so did another disciple. As this disciple was known to the high priest, he entered the court of the high priest along with Jesus, while Peter stood outside at the door. So the other disciple, who was known to the high priest, went out and spoke to the maid who kept the door, and brought Peter in. The maid who kept the door said to Peter,
Reader	Are not you also one of this man's disciples?
Narrator	And he said,
Reader	I am not.

Narrator	Now the servants and officers had made a charcoal fire, because it was cold, and they were standing and warming themselves; Peter also was with them, standing and warming himself. The high priest then questioned Jesus about his disciples and his teaching. Jesus answered him,
Jesus	I have spoken openly to the world; I have always taught in synagogues and in the temple, where all Jews come together; I have said nothing secretly. Why do you ask me? Ask those who have heard me, what I said to them; they know what I said.
Narrator	When he had said this, one of the officers standing by struck Jesus with his hand, saying,
Reader	Is that how you answer the high priest?
Narrator	Jesus answered him,
Jesus	If I have spoken wrongly, bear witness to the wrong; but if I have spoken rightly, why do you strike me?
Narrator	Annas then sent him bound to Ca'iaphas the high priest. Now Simon Peter was standing and warming himself. They said to him,
Reader(s)	Are not you also one of his disciples?
Narrator	He denied it and said,
Reader	I am not.
Narrator	One of the servants of the high priest, a kinsman of the man whose ear Peter had cut off, asked,
Reader	Did I not see you in the garden with him?
Narrator	Peter again denied it; and at once the cock crowed. Then they led Jesus from the house of Ca'iaphas to the praetorium. It was early. They themselves did not enter the praetorium, so that they might not be

defiled, but might eat the passover. So Pilate went out to them and said,

Reader   What accusation do you bring against this man?

Narrator   They answered him,

Reader(s)   If this man were not an evildoer, we would not have handed him over.

Narrator   Pilate said to them,

Reader   Take him yourselves and judge him by your own law.

Narrator   The Jews said to him,

Reader(s)   It is not lawful for us to put any man to death.

Narrator   This was to fulfill the word which Jesus had spoken to show by what death he was to die. Pilate entered the praetorium again and called Jesus, and he said to him,

Reader   Are you the King of the Jews?

Narrator   Jesus answered him,

Jesus   Do you say this of your own accord, or did others say it to you about me?

Narrator   Pilate answered,

Reader   Am I a Jew? Your own nation and the chief priests have handed you over to me; what have you done?

Narrator   Jesus answered him,

Jesus   My kingship is not of this world; if my kingship were of this world, my servants would fight, that I might not be handed over to the Jews; but my kingship is not from the world.

Narrator   Pilate said to him,

Reader   So you are a king?

Narrator	Jesus answered,
Jesus	You say that I am a king. For this I was born, and for this I have come into the world, to bear witness to the truth. Every one who is of the truth hears my voice.
Narrator	Pilate said to him,
Reader	What is truth?
Narrator	After he said this, he went out to the Jews again, and told them,
Reader	I find no crime in him. But you have a custom that I should release one man for you at the Passover; will you have me release for you the King of the Jews?
Narrator	They cried out again,
Crowd	Not this man, but Barab'bas!
Narrator	Now Barab'bas was a robber.

The shorter form of the Passion begins here [John 19:1-37]

Narrator	Pilate took Jesus and scourged him. And the soldiers plaited a crown of thorns, and put it on his head, and arrayed him in a purple robe; they came up to him, saying,
Readers(s)	Hail, King of the Jews!
Narrator	And struck him with their hands. Pilate went out again, and said to them,
Reader	See, I am bringing him out to you, that you may know that I find no crime in him.
Narrator	So Jesus came out, wearing the crown of thorns and the purple robe. Pilate said to them,

Reader	Behold the man!
Narrator	When the chief priests and the officers saw him, they cried out, saying,
Reader(s)	Crucify him, crucify him!
Narrator	Pilate said to them,
Reader	Take him yourselves and crucify him for I find no crime in him.
Narrator	The Jews answered him,
Reader(s)	We have a law, and by that law he ought to die, because he has made himself the Son of God.
Narrator	When Pilate heard these words, he was the more afraid; he entered the praetorium again and said to Jesus,
Reader	Where are you from?
Narrator	But Jesus gave no answer. Pilate therefore said to him,
Reader	You will not speak to me? Do you not know that I have power to release you, and power to crucify you?
Narrator	Jesus answered him,
Jesus	You would have no power over me unless it had been given you from above; therefore he who delivered me to you has the greater sin.
Narrator	Upon this Pilate sought to release him, but the Jews cried out,
Crowd	If you release this man, you are not Caesar's friend; every one who makes himself a king sets himself against Caesar.
Narrator	When Pilate heard these words, he brought Jesus out and sat down on the judgment seat at a place called the Pavement, and in Hebrew, Gab'batha.

Now it was the day of Preparation of the Passover; it was about the sixth hour. He said to the Jews,

Reader Behold your King!

Narrator They cried out,

Crowd Away with him, away with him, crucify him!

Narrator Pilate said to them,

Reader Shall I crucify your King?

Narrator The chief priests answered,

Reader(s) We have no king but Caesar.

Narrator Then he handed him over to them to be crucified.

All stand.

Narrator So they took Jesus, and he went out, bearing his own cross, to the place of a skull, which is called in Hebrew Gol′gotha. There they crucified him, and with him two others, one on either side, and Jesus between them. Pilate also wrote a title and put it on the cross; it read, "Jesus of Nazareth, the King of the Jews." Many of the Jews read this title, for the place where Jesus was crucified was near the city; and it was written in Hebrew, in Latin, and in Greek. The chief priests of the Jews then said to Pilate,

Reader(s) Do not write, "The King of the Jews," but, "This man said, I am King of the Jews."

Narrator Pilate answered,

Reader What I have written I have written.

Narrator When the soldiers had crucified Jesus they took his garments and made four parts, one for each soldier; also his tunic. But the tunic was without seam, woven from top to bottom; so they said to one another,

Reader(s)	Let us not tear it, but cast lots for it to see whose it shall be.
Narrator	This was to fulfill the scripture, "They parted my garments among them, and for my clothing they cast lots." So the soldiers did this. But standing by the cross of Jesus were his mother, and his mother's sister, Mary the wife of Clopas, and Mary Mag'dalene. When Jesus saw his mother, and the disciple whom he loved standing near, he said to his mother,
Jesus	Woman, behold your son!
Narrator	Then he said to the disciple,
Jesus	Behold your mother!
Narrator	And from that hour the disciple took her to his own home. After this, Jesus, knowing that all was now finished, to fulfill the scripture said,
Jesus	I thirst.
Narrator	A bowl full of vinegar stood there; so they put a sponge full of the vinegar on hyssop and held it to his mouth. When Jesus had received the vinegar, he said,
Jesus	It is finished.
Narrator	And he bowed his head and gave up his spirit.

Silence may be kept

| Narrator | Since it was the day of Preparation, in order to prevent the bodies from remaining on the cross on the sabbath (for that sabbath was a high day), the Jews asked Pilate that their legs might be broken, and that they might be taken away. So the soldiers came and broke the legs of the first, and of the other who had been crucified with him; but when |

they came to Jesus and saw that he was already dead, they did not break his legs. But one of the soldiers pierced his side with a spear, and at once there came out blood and water. He who saw it has borne witness — his testimony is true, and he knows that he tells the truth — that you also may believe. For these things took place that the scripture might be fulfilled, "Not a bone of him shall be broken." And again another scripture says, "They shall look on him whom they have pierced."

Holy Saturday

A Reading (Lesson) from the Book of Job [14:1-14]

Man that is born of a woman is of few days, and full of trouble. He comes forth like a flower, and withers; he flees like a shadow, and continues not. And dost thou open thy eyes upon such a one and bring him into judgment with thee? Who can bring a clean thing out of an unclean? There is not one. Since his days are determined, and the number of his months is with thee, and thou hast appointed his bounds that he cannot pass, look away from him, and desist, that he may enjoy, like a hireling, his day. For there is hope for a tree, if it be cut down, that it will sprout again, and that its shoots will not cease. Though its root grow old in the earth, and its stump die in the ground, yet at the scent of water it will bud and put forth branches like a young plant. But man dies, and is laid low; man breathes his last, and where is he? As waters fail from a lake, and a river wastes away and dries up, so man lies down and rises not again; till the heavens are no more he will not awake, or be roused out of his sleep. Oh that thou wouldest hide me in Sheol, that thou wouldest conceal me until thy wrath be past, that thou wouldest appoint me a set time, and remember me! If a man die, shall he live again? All the days of my service I would wait, till my release should come.

Psalm 130 [page 784]   or   *Psalm 31:1-5* [page 622]

A Reading (Lesson) from the First Letter of Peter [4:1-8]

Since Christ suffered in the flesh, arm yourselves with the same thought, for whoever has suffered in the flesh has ceased from sin, so as to live for the rest of the time in the flesh no longer by human passions but by the will of God. Let the time that is past suffice for doing what the Gentiles like to do, living in licentiousness, passions, drunkenness, revels, carousing, and lawless idolatry. They are surprised that you do not now join them in the same wild profligacy, and they abuse you; but they will give account to him who is ready to judge the living and the dead. For this is why the gospel was preached even to the dead, that though judged in the flesh like men, they might live in the spirit like God. The end of all things is at hand; therefore keep sane and sober for your prayers. Above all hold unfailing your love for one another, since love covers a multitude of sins.

✝ *The Holy Gospel of Our Lord Jesus Christ According to Matthew* [27:57-66]

When it was evening, there came a rich man from Arimathe′a, named Joseph, who also was a disciple of Jesus. He went to Pilate and asked for the body of Jesus. Then Pilate ordered it to be given to him. And Joseph took the body, and wrapped it in a clean linen shroud, and laid it in his own new tomb, which he had hewn in the rock; and he rolled a great stone to the door of the tomb, and departed. Mary Mag′dalene and the other Mary were there, sitting opposite the sepulchre. Next day, that is, after the day of Preparation, the chief priests and the Pharisees gathered before Pilate and said, "Sir, we remember how that impostor said, while he was still alive, 'After three days I will rise again.' Therefore order the sepulchre to be made secure until the third day, lest his disciples go and steal him away, and tell the people, 'He has risen from the dead,' and the last fraud will be worse than the first." Pilate said to them, "You have a guard of soldiers; go, make it as secure as you can." So they went and made the sepulchre secure by sealing the stone and setting a guard.

or this

✝ *The Holy Gospel of Our Lord Jesus Christ According to John* [19:38-42]

Joseph of Arimathe'a, who was a disciple of Jesus, but secretly, for fear of the Jews, asked Pilate that he might take away the body of Jesus, and Pilate gave him leave. So he came and took away his body. Nicode'mus also, who had at first come to him by night, came bringing a mixture of myrrh and aloes about a hundred pounds' weight. They took the body of Jesus, and bound it in linen cloths with the spices, as is the burial custom of the Jews. Now in the place where he was crucified there was a garden, and in the garden a new tomb where no one had ever been laid. So because of the Jewish day of Preparation, as the tomb was close at hand, they laid Jesus there.

The Great Vigil of Easter

At the Liturgy of the Word

At least two of the following Lessons are read, of which one is always the Lesson from Exodus. After each Lesson, the Psalm or Canticle listed, or some other suitable psalm, canticle, or hymn may be sung. A period of silence may be kept; and the Collect provided (pages 288-291 of the Prayer Book), or some other suitable Collect, may be said.

[The Story of Creation]

A Reading (Lesson) from the Book of Genesis [1:1 — 2:2]

In the beginning God created the heavens and the earth. The earth was without form and void, and darkness was upon the face of the deep; and the Spirit of God was moving over the face of the waters. And God said, "Let there be light"; and there was light. And God saw that the light was good; and God separated the light from the darkness. God called the light Day, and the darkness he called Night. And there was evening and there was morning, one day. And God said, "Let there be a firmament in the midst of the waters, and let it separate the waters from the waters." And God made the firmament and separated the waters which were under the firmament from the waters which were above the firmament. And it was so. And God called the firmament Heaven. And there was evening and there was morning, a second day. And God said, "Let the waters under the heavens be gathered together into one place, and let the dry land appear." And it was so. God called the dry land Earth, and the waters that were gathered together he called Seas. And God saw that it was good. And God said, "Let the earth put forth vegetation, plants yielding seed, and fruit trees bearing fruit in which is their seed, each according to its kind, upon the earth." And it was so. The earth brought forth vegetation, plants yielding seed according to their own kinds, and trees bearing fruit in which is their seed, each according to its kind. And God saw that it was good. And there was evening and there was morning, a third day. And God said, "Let there be lights in the firmament of the heavens to separate the day from the night; and let them be for signs and for seasons and for days and years, and let them be lights in the firmament of the heavens to give light upon the earth." And it was so. And God made the two great lights, the greater light to rule the day, and the lesser light to rule the night; he made the stars also. And God set them in the firmament of the heavens to give light upon the earth, to rule over the day and over the night, and to separate the light from the darkness. And God saw that it was good. And there was evening and there was morning, a fourth day. And God said, "Let the waters bring forth swarms of living creatures, and let birds fly above the earth across the firmament of the heavens." So God created the great sea monsters and every living creature that moves, with which the waters swarm, according to their kinds, and every winged bird according to its kind. And God saw that it was good. And God blessed them, saying, "Be fruitful and multiply and fill the waters in the seas, and let birds multiply on the earth." And there was evening and there was morning, a fifth day. And God said, "Let the earth bring forth living creatures according to their kinds: cattle and creeping things and beasts of the earth according to their kinds." And it was so. And God made the beasts of the earth according to their kinds and the cattle according to their kinds, and everything that creeps upon the ground according to its kind. And God saw that it was good. Then God said, "Let us make man in our image, after our likeness; and let them have dominion over the fish of the sea, and over the birds of the air, and over the cattle, and over all the earth, and over every creeping thing that creeps upon the earth." So God created man in his own image, in the image of God he created him; male and female he created them. And God blessed them, and God said to them, "Be fruitful and multiply, and fill the earth and subdue it; and have dominion over the fish of the sea and over the birds of the air and over every living thing that moves upon the earth." And God said, "Behold, I have given you every plant yielding seed which is upon the face of all the earth, and every tree with seed in its fruit; you shall have them for food. And to every beast of the earth, and to every bird of the air, and to everything that creeps on the earth, everything that has the breath of life, I have given every green plant for food." And it was so. And God saw everything that he had made, and behold, it was very good. And there was evening and there was morning, a sixth day. Thus the heavens and the earth were finished, and all the host of them. And on the seventh day God finished his work which he had done, and he rested on the seventh day from all his work which he had done.

Psalm 33:1-11 [page 626] or *Psalm 36:5-10* [page 632]

[The Flood]

A Reading (Lesson) from the Book of Genesis
[7:1-5, 11-18; 8:6-18; 9:8-13]

The Lord said to Noah, "Go into the ark, you and all your household, for I have seen that you are righteous before me in this generation. Take with you seven pairs of all clean animals, the male and his mate; and a pair of the animals that are not clean, the male and his mate; and seven pairs of the birds of the air also, male and female, to keep their kind alive upon the face of all the earth. For in seven days I will send rain upon the earth forty days and forty nights; and every living thing that I have made I will blot out from the face of the ground." And Noah did all that the Lord had commanded him. In the six hundredth year of Noah's life, in the second month, on the seventeenth day of the month, on that day all the fountains of the great deep burst forth, and the windows of the heavens were opened. And rain fell upon the earth forty days and forty nights. On the very same day Noah and his sons, Shem and Ham and Japheth, and Noah's wife and the three wives of his sons with them entered the ark, they and every beast according to its kind, and all the cattle according to their kinds, and every creeping thing that creeps on the earth according to its kind, and every bird according to its kind, every bird of every sort. They went into the ark with Noah, two and two of all flesh in which there was the breath of life. And they that entered, male and female of all flesh, went in as God had commanded him; and the Lord shut him in. The flood continued forty days upon the earth; and the waters increased, and bore up the ark, and it rose high above the earth. The waters prevailed and increased greatly upon the earth; and the ark floated on the face of the waters. At the end of forty days Noah opened the window of the ark which he had made, and sent forth a raven; and it went to and fro until the waters were dried up from the earth. Then he sent forth a dove from him, to see if the waters had subsided from the face of the ground; but the dove found no place to set her foot, and she returned to him to the ark, for the waters were still on the face of the whole earth. So he put forth his hand and took her and brought her into the ark with him. He waited another seven days, and again he sent forth the dove out of the ark; and the dove came back to him in the evening, and lo, in her mouth a freshly plucked olive leaf; so Noah knew that the waters had subsided from the earth. Then he waited another seven days, and sent forth the dove; and she did not return to him any more. In the six hundred and first year, in the first month, the first day of the month, the waters were dried from off the earth; and Noah removed the covering of the ark, and looked, and behold the face of the ground was dry. In the second month, on the twenty-seventh day of the month, the earth was dry. Then God said to Noah, "Go forth from the ark, you and your wife, and your sons and your sons' wives with you. Bring forth with you every living thing that is with you of all flesh — birds and animals and every creeping thing that creeps on the earth — that they may breed abundantly on the earth, and be fruitful and multiply upon the earth." So Noah went forth, and his sons and his wife and his sons' wives with him. Then God said to Noah and to his sons with him, "Behold, I establish my covenant with you and your descendants after you, and with every living creature that is with you, the birds, the cattle, and every beast of the earth with you, as many as came out of the ark. I establish my covenant with you, that never again shall all flesh be cut off by the waters of a flood, and never again shall there be a flood to destroy the earth." And God said, "This is the sign of the covenant which I make between me and you and every living creature that is with you, for all future generations: I set my bow in the cloud, and it shall be a sign of the covenant between me and the earth."

Psalm 46 [page 649]

[Abraham's sacrifice of Isaac]

A Reading (Lesson) from the Book of Genesis [22:1-18]

God tested Abraham, and said to him, "Abraham!" And he said, "Here am I." He said, "Take your son, your only son Isaac, whom you love, and go to the land of Mori'ah, and offer him there as a burnt offering upon one of the mountains of which I shall tell you." So Abraham rose early in the morning, saddled his ass, and took two of his young men with him, and his son Isaac; and he cut the wood for the burnt offering, and arose and went to the place of which God had told him. On the third day Abraham lifted up his eyes and saw the place afar off. Then Abraham said to his young men, "Stay here with the ass; I and the lad will go yonder and worship, and come again to you." And Abraham took the wood of the burnt offering, and laid it on Isaac his son; and he took in his hand the fire and the knife. So they went both of them together. And Isaac said to his father Abraham, "My father!" And he said, "Here am I, my son." He said, "Behold, the fire and the wood; but where is the lamb for a burnt offering?" Abraham said, "God will provide himself the lamb for a burnt offering, my son." So they went both of them together. When they came to the place of which God had told him, Abraham built an altar there, and laid the wood in order, and bound Isaac his son, and laid him on the altar, upon the wood. Then Abraham put forth his hand, and took the knife to slay his son. But the angel of the Lord called to him from heaven, and said, "Abraham, Abraham!" And he said, "Here am I." He said, "Do not lay your hand on the lad or do anything to him; for now I know that you fear God, seeing you have not withheld your son, your only son, from me." And Abraham lifted up his eyes and looked, and behold, behind him was a ram, caught in a thicket by his horns; and Abraham went and took the ram, and offered it up as a burnt offering instead of his son. So Abraham called the name of that place The Lord will provide; as it is said to this day, "On the mount of the Lord it shall be provided." And the angel of the Lord called to Abraham a second time from heaven, and said, "By myself I have sworn, says the Lord, because you have done this, and have not withheld your son, your only son, I will indeed bless you, and I will multiply your descendants as the stars of heaven and as the sand which is on the seashore. And your descendants shall possess the gate of their enemies, and by your descendants shall all the nations of the earth bless themselves, because you have obeyed my voice."

Psalm 33:12-22 [page 626] or *Psalm 16* [page 599]

[Israel's deliverance at the Red Sea]

A Reading (Lesson) from the Book of Exodus [14:10 — 15:1]

When Pharaoh drew near, the people of Israel lifted up
their eyes, and behold, the Egyptians were marching after
them; and they were in great fear. And the people of Israel
cried out to the Lord; and they said to Moses, "Is it because
there are no graves in Egypt that you have taken us away to
die in the wilderness? What have you done to us, in bringing
us out of Egypt? Is not this what we have said to you in
Egypt, 'Let us alone and let us serve the Egyptians'? For it
would have been better for us to serve the Egyptians than die
in the wilderness." And Moses said to the people, "Fear not,
stand firm, and see the salvation of the Lord, which he will
work for you today; for the Egyptians whom you see today,
you shall never see again. The Lord will fight for you, and
you have only to be still." The Lord said to Moses, "Why do
you cry to me? Tell the people of Israel to go forward. Lift up
your rod, and stretch out your hand over the sea and divide
it, that the people of Israel may go on dry ground through
the sea. And I will harden the hearts of the Egyptians so that
they shall go in after them, and I will get glory over Pharaoh
and all his host, his chariots, and his horsemen. And the
Egyptians shall know that I am the Lord, when I have gotten
glory over Pharaoh, his chariots, and his horsemen." Then
the angel of God who went before the host of Israel moved
and went behind them; and the pillar of cloud moved from
before them and stood behind them, coming between the
host of Egypt and the host of Israel. And there was the cloud
and the darkness; and the night passed without one coming
near the other all night. Then Moses stretched out his hand
over the sea; and the Lord drove the sea back by a strong
east wind all night, and made the sea dry land, and the
waters were divided. And the people of Israel went into the
midst of the sea on dry ground, the waters being a wall to
them on their right hand and on their left. The Egyptians

pursued, and went in after them into the midst of the sea, all Pharaoh's horses, his chariots, and his horsemen. And in the morning watch, the Lord in the pillar of fire and of cloud looked down upon the host of the Egyptians, and discomfited the host of the Egyptians, clogging their chariot wheels so that they drove heavily; and the Egyptians said, "Let us flee from before Israel; for the Lord fights for them against the Egyptians." Then the Lord said to Moses, "Stretch out your hand over the sea, that the water may come back upon the Egyptians, upon their chariots, and upon their horsemen." So Moses stretched forth his hand over the sea, and the sea returned to its wonted flow when the morning appeared; and the Egyptians fled into it, and the Lord routed the Egyptians in the midst of the sea. The waters returned and covered the chariots and the horsemen and all the host of Pharaoh that had followed them into the sea; not so much as one of them remained. But the people of Israel walked on dry ground through the sea, the waters being a wall to them on their right hand and on their left. Thus the Lord saved Israel that day from the hand of the Egyptians; and Israel saw the Egyptians dead upon the seashore. And Israel saw the great work which the Lord did against the Egyptians, and the people feared the Lord; and they believed in the Lord and in his servant Moses. Then Moses and the people of Israel sang this song to the Lord, saying, "I will sing to the Lord, for he has triumphed gloriously; the horse and his rider he has thrown into the sea."

Canticle 8, The Song of Moses [page 85]

[God's Presence in a renewed Israel]

A Reading (Lesson) from the Book of Isaiah [4:2-6]

In that day the branch of the Lord shall be beautiful and glorious, and the fruit of the land shall be the pride and glory of the survivors of Israel. And he who is left in Zion and remains in Jerusalem will be called holy, every one who has been recorded for life in Jerusalem, when the Lord shall have washed away the filth of the daughters of Zion, and cleansed the bloodstains of Jerusalem from its midst by a spirit of judgment and by a spirit of burning. Then the Lord will create over the whole site of Mount Zion and over her assemblies a cloud by day, and smoke and the shining of a flaming fire by night; for over all the glory there will be a canopy and a pavilion. It will be for a shade by day from the heat, and for a refuge and a shelter from the storm and rain.

Psalm 122 [page 779]

[Salvation offered freely to all]

A Reading (Lesson) from the Book of Isaiah [55:1-11]

Thus says the Lord: "Ho, every one who thirsts, come to the waters; and he who has no money, come, buy and eat! Come, buy wine and milk without money and without price. Why do you spend your money for that which is not bread, and your labor for that which does not satisfy? Hearken diligently to me, and eat what is good, and delight yourselves in fatness. Incline your ear, and come to me; hear, that your soul may live; and I will make with you an everlasting covenant, my steadfast, sure love for David. Behold, I made him a witness to the peoples, a leader and commander for the peoples. Behold, you shall call nations that you know not, and nations that knew you not shall run to you, because of the Lord your God, and of the Holy One of Israel, for he has glorified you. Seek the Lord while he may be found, call upon him while he is near; let the wicked forsake his way, and the unrighteous man his thoughts; let him return to the Lord, that he may have mercy on him, and to our God, for he will abundantly pardon. For my thoughts are not your thoughts, neither are your ways my ways, says the Lord. For as the heavens are higher than the earth, so are my ways higher than your ways and my thoughts than your thoughts. For as the rain and the snow come down from heaven, and return not thither but water the earth, making it bring forth and sprout, giving seed to the sower and bread to the eater, so shall my word be that goes forth from my mouth; it shall not return to me empty, but it shall accomplish that which I purpose, and prosper in the thing for which I sent it."

Canticle 9, The First Song of Isaiah [Page 86]   or

Psalm 42:1-7 [page 643]

[A new heart and a new spirit]

A Reading (Lesson) from the Book of Ezekiel [36:24-28]

Thus says the Lord God: "I will take you from the nations, and gather you from all the countries, and bring you into your own land. I will sprinkle clean water upon you, and you shall be clean from all your uncleannesses, and from all your idols I will cleanse you. A new heart I will give you, and a new spirit I will put within you; and I will take out of your flesh the heart of stone and give you a heart of flesh. And I will put my spirit within you, and cause you to walk in my statutes, and be careful to observe my ordinances. You shall dwell in the land which I gave to your fathers; and you shall be my people, and I will be your God."

Psalm 42:1-7 [page 643]   or

Canticle 9, The First Song of Isaiah [Page 86]

[The valley of dry bones]

A Reading (Lesson) from the Book of Ezekiel [37:1-14]

The hand of the Lord was upon me, and he brought me out by the Spirit of the Lord, and set me down in the midst of the valley; it was full of bones. And he led me round among them; and behold, there were very many upon the valley; and lo, they were very dry. And he said to me, "Son of man, can these bones live?" And I answered, "O Lord God, thou knowest." Again he said to me, "Prophesy to these bones, and say to them, O dry bones, hear the word of the Lord. Thus says the Lord God to these bones: Behold, I will cause breath to enter you, and you shall live. And I will lay sinews upon you, and will cause flesh to come upon you, and cover you with skin, and put breath in you, and you shall live; and you shall know that I am the Lord." So I prophesied as I was commanded; and as I prophesied, there was a noise, and behold, a rattling; and the bones came together, bone to its bone. And as I looked, there were sinews on them, and flesh had come upon them, and skin had covered them; but there was no breath in them. Then he said to me, "Prophesy to the breath, prophesy, son of man, and say to the breath, Thus says the Lord God: Come from the four winds, O breath, and breathe upon these slain, that they may live." So I prophesied as he commanded me, and the breath came into them, and they lived, and stood upon their feet, an exceedingly great host. Then he said to me, "Son of man, these bones are the whole house of Israel. Behold, they say, 'Our bones are dried up, and our hope is lost; we are clean cut off.' Therefore prophesy, and say to them, Thus says the Lord God: Behold, I will open your graves, and raise you from your graves, O my people; and I will bring you home into the land of Israel. And you shall know that I am the Lord, when I open your graves, and raise you from your graves, O my people. And I will put my Spirit within you, and you shall live, and I will place you in your own land;

then you shall know that I, the Lord, have spoken, and I have done it, says the Lord."

Psalm 30 [page 621] or *Psalm 143* [page 798]

[The gathering of God's people]

A Reading (Lesson) from the Book of Zephaniah [3:12-20]

Thus says the Lord: "I will leave in the midst of you a people humble and lowly. They shall seek refuge in the name of the Lord, those who are left in Israel; they shall do no wrong and utter no lies, nor shall there be found in their mouth a deceitful tongue. For they shall pasture and lie down, and none shall make them afraid." Sing aloud, O daughter of Zion; shout, O Israel! Rejoice and exult with all your heart, O daughter of Jerusalem! The Lord has taken away the judgments against you, he has cast out your enemies. The King of Israel, the Lord, is in your midst; you shall fear evil no more. On that day it shall be said to Jerusalem: "Do not fear, O Zion; let not your hands grow weak. The Lord, your God, is in your midst, a warrior who gives victory; he will rejoice over you with gladness, he will renew you in his love; he will exult over you with loud singing as on a day of festival. I will remove disaster from you, so that you will not bear reproach for it. Behold, at that time I will deal with all your oppressors. And I will save the lame, and gather the outcast, and I will change their shame into praise and renown in all the earth. At that time I will bring you home, at the time when I gather you together; yea, I will make you renowned and praised among all the peoples of the earth, when I restore your fortunes before your eyes," says the Lord.

Psalm 98 [page 727] or *Psalm 126* [page 782]

At the Eucharist

A Reading (Lesson) from the Letter of Paul to the Romans
[6:3-11]

Do you not know that all of us who have been baptized into
Christ Jesus were baptized into his death? We were buried
therefore with him by baptism into death, so that as Christ
was raised from the dead by the glory of the Father, we too
might walk in newness of life. For if we have been united
with him in a death like his, we shall certainly be united with
him in a resurrection like his. We know that our old self was
crucified with him so that the sinful body might be
destroyed, and we might no longer be enslaved to sin. For he
who has died is freed from sin. But if we have died with
Christ, we believe that we shall also live with him. For we
know that Christ being raised from the dead will never die
again; death no longer has dominion over him. The death he
died, he died to sin, once for all, but the life he lives, he lives
to God. So you also must consider yourselves dead to sin
and alive to God in Christ Jesus.

"Alleluia" may be sung and repeated.

*Psalm 114 [page 756], or some other suitable psalm or a hymn
may be sung.*

✝ *The Holy Gospel of Our Lord Jesus Christ
According to Matthew* [28:1-10]

After the sabbath, toward the dawn of the first day of the
week, Mary Mag'dalene and the other Mary went to see the
sepulchre. And behold, there was a great earthquake; for an
angel of the Lord descended from heaven and came and
rolled back the stone, and sat upon it. His appearance was
like lightning, and his raiment white as snow. And for fear of
him the guards trembled and became like dead men. But the
angel said to the women, "Do not be afraid; for I know that

you seek Jesus who was crucified. He is not here; for he has risen, as he said. Come, see the place where he lay. Then go quickly and tell his disciples that he has risen from the dead, and behold, he is going before you to Galilee; there you will see him. Lo, I have told you." So they departed quickly from the tomb with fear and great joy, and ran to tell his disciples. And behold, Jesus met them and said, "Hail!" And they came up and took hold of his feet and worshiped him. Then Jesus said to them, "Do not be afraid; go and tell my brethren to go to Galilee, and there they will see me."

Easter Day: Early Service

One of the Old Testament Lessons from the Vigil
[pages 99-110 above]
Psalm 114 [page 756]
The Epistle: Romans 6:3-11 [page 111 above]
The Holy Gospel: Matthew 28:1-10 [page 111 above]

Easter Day: Principal Service

A Reading (Lesson) from the Acts of the Apostles [10:34-43]

Peter opened his mouth and said, "Truly I perceive that God shows no partiality, but in every nation any one who fears him and does what is right is acceptable to him. You know the word which he sent to Israel, preaching good news of peace by Jesus Christ (he is Lord of all), the word which was proclaimed throughout all Judea, beginning from Galilee after the baptism which John preached: how God anointed Jesus of Nazareth with the Holy Spirit and with power; how he went about doing good and healing all that were oppressed by the devil, for God was with him. And we are witnesses to all that he did both in the country of the Jews and in Jerusalem. They put him to death by hanging him on a tree; but God raised him on the third day and made him manifest; not to all the people but to us who were chosen by God as witnesses, who ate and drank with him after he rose from the dead. And he commanded us to preach to the people, and to testify that he is the one ordained by God to be judge of the living and the dead. To him all the prophets bear witness that every one who believes in him receives forgiveness of sins through his name."

or this

A Reading (Lesson) from the Book of Isaiah [25:6-9]

On this mountain the Lord of hosts will make for all peoples a feast of fat things, a feast of wine on the lees, of fat things full of marrow, of wine on the lees well refined. And he will destroy on this mountain the covering that is cast over all peoples, the veil that is spread over all nations. He will swallow up death for ever, and the Lord God will wipe away tears from all faces, and the reproach of his people he will take away from all the earth; for the Lord has spoken. It will be said on that day, "Lo, this is our God; we have waited for him, that he might save us. This is the Lord; we have waited for him; let us be glad and rejoice in his salvation."

Psalm 118:14-29 [page 761] or *Psalm 118:14-17, 22-24* [page 761]

A Reading (Lesson) from the Letter of Paul to the Colossians [3:1-4]

Since you have been raised with Christ, seek the things that are above, where Christ is, seated at the right hand of God. Set your minds on things that are above, not on things that are on earth. For you have died, and your life is hid with Christ in God. When Christ who is our life appears, then you also will appear with him in glory.

or this

Acts 10:34-43 [page 112 above]

✝ *The Holy Gospel of Our Lord Jesus Christ*
According to Mark [16:1-8]

When the sabbath was past, Mary Mag'dalene, and Mary
the mother of James, and Salo'me, bought spices, so that they
might go and anoint him. And very early on the first day of
the week they went to the tomb when the sun had risen. And
they were saying to one another, "Who will roll away the
stone for us from the door of the tomb?" And looking up,
they saw that the stone was rolled back — it was very large.
And entering the tomb, they saw a young man sitting on the
right side, dressed in a white robe; and they were amazed.
And he said to them, "Do not be amazed; you seek Jesus of
Nazareth, who was crucified. He has risen, he is not here;
see the place where they laid him. But go, tell his disciples
and Peter that he is going before you to Galilee; there you
will see him, as he told you." And they went out and fled
from the tomb; for trembling and astonishment had come
upon them; and they said nothing to any one, for they were
afraid.

Easter Day: Evening Service

A Reading (Lesson) from the Acts of the Apostles [5:29a,30-32]

Peter and the apostles said to the high priest and the council,
"The God of our fathers raised Jesus whom you killed by
hanging him on a tree. God exalted him at his right hand
as Leader and Savior, to give repentance to Israel and
forgiveness of sins, and we are witnesses to these things, and
so is the Holy Spirit whom God has given to those who obey
him."

or the following

A Reading (Lesson) from the Book of Daniel [12:1-3]

The Lord spoke to Daniel in a vision and said, "At that time shall arise Michael, the great prince who has charge of your people. And there shall be a time of trouble, such as never has been since there was a nation till that time; but at that time your people shall be delivered, every one whose name shall be found written in the book. And many of those who sleep in the dust of the earth shall awake, some to everlasting life, and some to shame and everlasting contempt. And those who are wise shall shine like the brightness of the firmament; and those who turn many to righteousness, like the stars for ever and ever."

Psalm 114 [page 756]   or   *Psalm 136* [page 789]   or

Psalm 118:14-17, 22-24 [page 761]

A Reading (Lesson) from the First Letter of Paul to the Corinthians [5:6b-8]

Do you not know that a little leaven leavens the whole lump? Cleanse out the old leaven that you may be a new lump, as you really are unleavened. For Christ, our paschal lamb, has been sacrificed. Let us, therefore, celebrate the festival, not with the old leaven, the leaven of malice and evil, but with the unleavened bread of sincerity and truth.

or this

Acts 5:29a,30-32 [page 114 above]

✝ *The Holy Gospel of Our Lord Jesus Christ According to Luke* [24:13-35]

That very day, the first day of the week, two of the disciples were going to a village named Emmaus, about seven miles from Jerusalem, and talking with each other about all these things that had happened. While they were talking and discussing together, Jesus himself drew near and went with them. But their eyes were kept from recognizing him. And he said to them, "What is this conversation which you are holding with each other as you walk?" And they stood still, looking sad. Then one of them, named Cle'opas, answered him, "Are you the only visitor to Jerusalem who does not know the things that have happened there in these days?" And he said to them, "What things?" And they said to him, "Concerning Jesus of Nazareth, who was a prophet mighty in deed and word before God and all the people, and how our chief priests and rulers delivered him up to be condemned to death, and crucified him. But we had hoped that he was the one to redeem Israel. Yes, and besides all this, it is now the third day since this happened. Moreover, some women of our company amazed us. They were at the tomb early in the morning and did not find his body; and they came back saying that they had even seen a vision of angels, who said that he was alive. Some of those who were with us went to the tomb, and found it just as the women had said; but him they did not see." And he said to them, "O foolish men, and slow of heart to believe all that the prophets have spoken! Was it not necessary that the Christ should suffer these things and enter into his glory?" And beginning with Moses and all the prophets, he interpreted to them in all the scriptures the things concerning himself. So they drew near to the village to which they were going. He appeared to be going further, but they constrained him, saying, "Stay with us, for it is toward evening and the day is now far spent." So he went in to stay with them. When he was at table with them, he took the bread and blessed, and broke it, and gave it to them. And their eyes were opened and they recognized him; and he vanished out of their sight. They said to each other, "Did not our hearts burn within us while he talked to us on the road, while he opened to us the scriptures?" And they rose that same hour and returned to

Jerusalem; and they found the eleven gathered together and those who were with them, who said, "The Lord has risen indeed, and has appeared to Simon!" Then they told what had happened on the road, and how he was known to them in the breaking of the bread.

Monday in Easter Week

A Reading (Lesson) from the Acts of the Apostles
[2:14,22b-32]

Peter, standing with the eleven, lifted up his voice and addressed the multitude, "Men of Judea and all who dwell in Jerusalem, let this be known to you, and give ear to my words: Jesus of Nazareth, a man attested to you by God with mighty works and wonders and signs which God did through him in your midst, as you yourselves know — this Jesus, delivered up according to the definite plan and foreknowledge of God, you crucified and killed by the hands of lawless men. But God raised him up, having loosed the pangs of death, because it was not possible for him to be held by it. For David says concerning him, 'I saw the Lord always before me, for he is at my right hand that I may not be shaken; therefore my heart was glad, and my tongue rejoiced; moreover my flesh will dwell in hope. For thou wilt not abandon my soul to Hades, nor let thy Holy One see corruption. Thou hast made known to me the ways of life; thou wilt make me full of gladness with thy presence.' Brethren, I may say to you confidently of the patriarch David that he both died and was buried, and his tomb is with us to this day. Being therefore a prophet, and knowing that God had sworn with an oath to him that he would set one of his descendants upon his throne, he foresaw and spoke of the resurrection of the Christ, that he was not abandoned to Hades, nor did his flesh see corruption. This Jesus God raised up, and of that we all are witnesses."

Psalm 16:8-11 [page 600]   or   Psalm 118:19-24 [page 762]

✝ The Holy Gospel of Our Lord Jesus Christ
According to Matthew [28:9-15]

Behold, Jesus met Mary Mag'dalene and the other Mary and said, "Hail!" And they came up and took hold of his feet and worshiped him. Then Jesus said to them, "Do not be afraid; go and tell my brethren to go to Galilee, and there they will see me." While they were going, behold, some of the guard went into the city and told the chief priests all that had taken place. And when they had assembled with the elders and taken counsel, they gave a sum of money to the soldiers and said, "Tell people, 'His disciples came by night and stole him away while we were asleep.' And if this comes to the governor's ears, we will satisfy him and keep you out of trouble." So they took the money and did as they were directed; and this story has been spread among the Jews to this day.

Tuesday in Easter Week

A Reading (Lesson) from the Acts of the Apostles [2:36-41]

Peter said to the multitude, "Let all the house of Israel therefore know assuredly that God has made him both Lord and Christ, this Jesus whom you crucified." Now when they heard this they were cut to the heart, and said to Peter and the rest of the apostles, "Brethren, what shall we do?" And Peter said to them, "Repent, and be baptized every one of you in the name of Jesus Christ for the forgiveness of your sins; and you shall receive the gift of the Holy Spirit. For the promise is to you and to your children and to all that are far off, every one whom the Lord our God calls to him." And he testified with many other words and exhorted them, saying, "Save yourselves from this crooked generation." So those who received his word were baptized, and there were added that day about three thousand souls.

Psalm 33:18-22 [page 627]   or   *Psalm 118:19-24* [page 762]

✝ *The Holy Gospel of Our Lord Jesus Christ*
According to John [20:11-18]

Mary Mag'dalene stood weeping outside the tomb, and as she wept she stooped to look into the tomb; and she saw two angels in white, sitting where the body of Jesus had lain, one at the head and one at the feet. They said to her, "Woman, why are you weeping?" She said to them, "Because they have taken away my Lord, and I do not know where they have laid him." Saying this, she turned round and saw Jesus standing, but she did not know that it was Jesus. Jesus said to her, "Woman, why are you weeping? Whom do you seek?" Supposing him to be the gardener, she said to him, "Sir, if you have carried him away, tell me where you have laid him, and I will take him away." Jesus said to her, "Mary." She turned and said to him in Hebrew, "Rab-bo'ni!" (which means Teacher). Jesus said to her, "Do not hold me, for I have not yet ascended to the Father; but go to my brethren and say to them, I am ascending to my Father and your Father, to my God and your God." Mary Mag'dalene went and said to the disciples, "I have seen the Lord"; and she told them that he had said these things to her.

Wednesday in Easter Week

A Reading (Lesson) from the Acts of the Apostles [3:1-10]

Now Peter and John were going up to the temple at the hour of prayer, the ninth hour. And a man lame from birth was being carried, whom they laid daily at that gate of the temple which is called Beautiful to ask alms of those who entered the temple. Seeing Peter and John about to go into the temple, he asked for alms. And Peter directed his gaze at him, with John, and said, "Look at us." And he fixed his attention upon them, expecting to receive something from them. But Peter said, "I have no silver and gold, but I give you what I have; in the name of Jesus Christ of Nazareth, walk." And he took him by the right hand and raised him up; and immediately his feet and ankles were made strong. And leaping up he stood and walked and entered the temple with them, walking and leaping and praising God. And all the people saw him walking and praising God, and recognized him as the one who sat for alms at the Beautiful Gate of the temple; and they were filled with wonder and amazement at what had happened to him.

Psalm 105:1-8 [page 738]   or   *Psalm 118:19-24* [page 762]

✝ *The Holy Gospel of Our Lord Jesus Christ According to Luke* [24:13-35] [page 115 above]

Thursday in Easter Week

A Reading (Lesson) from the Acts of the Apostles [3:11-26]

While the lame man whom Peter and John had healed clung to them, all the people ran together to them in the portico called Solomon's, astounded. And when Peter saw it he addressed the people, "Men of Israel, why do you wonder at this, or why do you stare at us, as though by our own power or piety we had made him walk? The God of Abraham and of Isaac and of Jacob, the God of our fathers, glorified his servant Jesus, whom you delivered up and denied in the presence of Pilate, when he had decided to release him. But you denied the Holy and Righteous One, and asked for a murderer to be granted to you, and killed the Author of life, whom God raised from the dead. To this we are witnesses. And his name, by faith in his name, has made this man strong whom you see and know; and the faith which is through Jesus has given the man this perfect health in the presence of you all. And now, brethren, I know that you acted in ignorance, as did also your rulers. But what God foretold by the mouth of all the prophets, that his Christ should suffer, he thus fulfilled. Repent therefore, and turn again, that your sins may be blotted out, that times of refreshing may come from the presence of the Lord, and that he may send the Christ appointed for you, Jesus, whom heaven must receive until the time for establishing all that God spoke by the mouth of his holy prophets from of old. Moses said, 'The Lord God will raise up for you a prophet from your brethren as he raised me up. You shall listen to him in whatever he tells you. And it shall be that every soul that does not listen to that prophet shall be destroyed from the people.' And all the prophets who have spoken, from Samuel and those who came afterwards, also proclaimed these days. You are the sons of the prophets and of the covenant which God gave to your fathers, saying to Abraham, 'And in your posterity shall all the families of the earth be blessed.' God, having raised up his servant, sent him to you first, to bless you in turning every one of you from your wickedness."

Psalm 8 [page 592] or *Psalm 114* [page 756] or

Psalm 118:19-24 [page 762]

✝ *The Holy Gospel of Our Lord Jesus Christ According to Luke* [24:36b-48] [page 129 below]

Friday in Easter Week

A Reading (Lesson) from the Acts of the Apostles [4:1-12]

As Peter and John were speaking to the people, the priests and the captain of the temple and the Sad'ducees came upon them, annoyed because they were teaching the people and proclaiming in Jesus the resurrection from the dead. And they arrested them and put them in custody until the morrow, for it was already evening. But many of those who heard the word believed; and the number of the men came to about five thousand. On the morrow their rulers and elders and scribes were gathered together in Jerusalem, with Annas the high priest and Ca'iaphas and John and Alexander, and all who were of the high-priestly family. And when they had set them in the midst, they inquired, "By what power or by what name did you do this?" Then Peter, filled with the Holy Spirit, said to them, "Rulers of the people and elders, if we are being examined today concerning a good deed done to a cripple, by what means this man has been healed, be it known to you all, and to all the people of Israel, that by the name of Jesus Christ of Nazareth, whom you crucified, whom God raised from the dead, by him this man is standing before you well. This is the stone which was rejected by you builders, but which has become the head of the corner. And there is salvation in no one else, for there is no other name under heaven given among men by which we must be saved."

Psalm 116:1-8 [page 759] or *Psalm 118:19-24* [page 762]

✝ *The Holy Gospel of Our Lord Jesus Christ According to John* [21:1-14]

After this Jesus revealed himself again to the disciples by the Sea of Tibe'ri-as; and he revealed himself in this way. Simon Peter, Thomas called the Twin, Nathan'a-el of Cana in Galilee, the sons of Zeb'edee, and two others of his disciples were together. Simon Peter said to them, "I am going fishing." They said to him, "We will go with you." They went out and got into the boat; but that night they caught nothing. Just as day was breaking, Jesus stood on the beach; yet the disciples did not know that it was Jesus. Jesus said to them, "Children, have you any fish?" They answered him, "No." He said to them, "Cast the net on the right side of the boat, and you will find some." So they cast it, and now they were not able to haul it in, for the quantity of fish. That disciple whom Jesus loved said to Peter, "It is the Lord!" When Simon Peter heard that it was the Lord, he put on his clothes, for he was stripped for work, and sprang into the sea. But the other disciples came in the boat, dragging the net full of fish, for they were not far from the land, but about a hundred yards off. When they got out on land, they saw a charcoal fire there, with fish lying on it, and bread. Jesus said to them, "Bring some of the fish that you have just caught." So Simon Peter went aboard and hauled the net ashore, full of large fish, a hundred and fifty-three of them; and although there were so many, the net was not torn. Jesus said to them, "Come and have breakfast." Now none of the disciples dared ask him, "Who are you?" They knew it was the Lord. Jesus came and took the bread and gave it to them, and so with the fish. This was now the third time that Jesus was revealed to the disciples after he was raised from the dead.

Saturday in Easter Week

A Reading (Lesson) from the Acts of the Apostles [4:13-21]

Now when the rulers and elders and scribes saw the boldness of Peter and John, and perceived that they were uneducated, common men, they wondered; and they recognized that they had been with Jesus. But seeing the man that had been healed standing beside them, they had nothing to say in opposition. But when they had commanded them to go aside out of the council, they conferred with one another, saying, "What shall we do with these men? For that a notable sign has been performed through them is manifest to all the inhabitants of Jerusalem, and we cannot deny it. But in order that it may spread no further among the people, let us warn them to speak no more to any one in this name." So they called them and charged them not to speak or teach at all in the name of Jesus. But Peter and John answered them, "Whether it is right in the sight of God to listen to you rather than to God, you must judge; for we cannot but speak of what we have seen and heard." And when they had further threatened them, they let them go, finding no way to punish them, because of the people; for all men praised God for what had happened.

Psalm 118:14-18 [page 761]   or   *Psalm 118:19-24* [page 762]

✝ *The Holy Gospel of Our Lord Jesus Christ According to Mark* [16:9-15, 20]

Now when Jesus rose early on the first day of the week, he appeared first to Mary Mag'dalene, from whom he had cast out seven demons. She went out and told those who had been with him, as they mourned and wept. But when they heard that he was alive and had been seen by her, they would not believe it. After this he appeared in another form to two of them as they were walking into the country. And they went back and told the rest, but they did not believe them. Afterward he appeared to the eleven themselves as they sat at table; and he upbraided them for their unbelief and hardness of heart, because they had not believed those who saw him after he had risen. And he said to them, "Go into all the world and preach the gospel to the whole creation." And they went forth and preached everywhere, while the Lord worked with them and confirmed the message by the signs that attended it.

Second Sunday of Easter

A Reading (Lesson) from the Acts of the Apostles [3:12a, 13-15, 17-26]

When Peter saw the people running together to him and to John, he addressed them, saying, "Men of Israel, the God of

Abraham and of Isaac and of Jacob, the God of our fathers, glorified his servant Jesus, whom you delivered up and denied in the presence of Pilate, when he had decided to release him. But you denied the Holy and Righteous One, and asked for a murderer to be granted to you, and killed the Author of life, whom God raised from the dead. To this we are witnesses. And now, brethren, I know that you acted in ignorance, as did also your rulers. But what God foretold by the mouth of all the prophets, that his Christ should suffer, he thus fulfilled. Repent therefore, and turn again, that your sins may be blotted out, that times of refreshing may come from the presence of the Lord, and that he may send the Christ appointed for you, Jesus, whom heaven must receive until the time for establishing all that God spoke by the mouth of his holy prophets from of old. Moses said, 'The Lord God will raise up for you a prophet from your brethren as he raised me up. You shall listen to him in whatever he tells you. And it shall be that every soul that does not listen to that prophet shall be destroyed from the people.' And all the prophets who have spoken, from Samuel and those who came afterwards, also proclaimed these days. You are the sons of the prophets and of the covenant which God gave to your fathers, saying to Abraham, 'And in your posterity shall all the families of the earth be blessed.' God, having raised up his servant, sent him to you first, to bless you in turning every one of you from your wickedness."

or this

A Reading from the Book of Isaiah [26:2-9, 19]

Open the gates, that the righteous nation which keeps faith may enter in. Thou dost keep him in perfect peace, whose mind is stayed on thee, because he trusts in thee. Trust in the Lord for ever, for the Lord God is an everlasting rock. For he has brought low the inhabitants of the height, the lofty city. He lays it low, lays it low to the ground, casts it to the dust.

The foot tramples it, the feet of the poor, the steps of the needy. The way of the righteous is level; thou dost make smooth the path of the righteous. In the path of thy judgments, O Lord, we wait for thee; thy memorial name is the desire of our soul. My soul yearns for thee in the night, my spirit within me earnestly seeks thee. For when thy judgments are in the earth, the inhabitants of the world learn righteousness. Thy dead shall live, their bodies shall rise. O dwellers in the dust, awake and sing for joy! For thy dew is a dew of light, and on the land of the shades thou wilt let it fall.

Psalm 111 [page 754]   or   *Psalm 118:19-24* [page 762]

A Reading (Lesson) from the First Letter of John [5:1-6]

Every one who believes that Jesus is the Christ is a child of God, and every one who loves the parent loves the child. By this we know that we love the children of God, when we love God and obey his commandments. For this is the love of God, that we keep his commandments. And his commandments are not burdensome. For whatever is born of God overcomes the world; and this is the victory that overcomes the world, our faith. Who is it that overcomes the world but he who believes that Jesus is the Son of God? This is he who came by water and blood, Jesus Christ, not with the water only but with the water and the blood.

or this

Acts 3:12a, 13-15,17-26 [page 124 above]

✝ *The Holy Gospel of Our Lord Jesus Christ According to John* [20:19-31]

On the evening of that day, the first day of the week, the doors being shut where the disciples were, for fear of the Jews, Jesus came and stood among them and said to them,

"Peace be with you." When he had said this, he showed them his hands and his side. Then the disciples were glad when they saw the Lord. Jesus said to them again, "Peace be with you. As the Father has sent me, even so I send you." And when he had said this, he breathed on them and said to them, "Receive the Holy Spirit. If you forgive the sins of any, they are forgiven; if you retain the sins of any, they are retained." Now Thomas, one of the twelve, called the Twin, was not with them when Jesus came. So the other disciples told him, "We have seen the Lord." But he said to them, "Unless I see in his hands the print of the nails, and place my finger in the mark of the nails, and place my hand in his side, I will not believe." Eight days later, his disciples were again in the house, and Thomas was with them. The doors were shut, but Jesus came and stood among them, and said, "Peace be with you." Then he said to Thomas, "Put your finger here, and see my hands; and put out your hand, and place it in my side; do not be faithless, but believing." Thomas answered him, "My Lord and my God!" Jesus said to him, "Have you believed because you have seen me? Blessed are those who have not seen and yet believe." Now Jesus did many other signs in the presence of the disciples, which are not written in this book; but these are written that you may believe that Jesus is the Christ, the Son of God, and that believing you may have life in his name.

Third Sunday of Easter

A Reading (Lesson) from the Acts of the Apostles [4:5-12]

On the morning of the day after Peter and John healed the man lame from birth, the rulers and elders and scribes were gathered together in Jerusalem, with Annas the high priest and Ca'iaphas and John and Alexander, and all who were of the high-priestly family. And when they had set Peter and John in the midst, they inquired, "By what power or by what name did you this?" Then Peter, filled with the Holy Spirit, said to them, "Rulers of the people and elders, if we are being examined today concerning a good deed done to a cripple, by what means this man has been healed, be it known to you all, and to all the people of Israel, that by the name of Jesus Christ of Nazareth, whom you cruficied, whom God raised from the dead, by him this man is standing before you well. This is the stone which was rejected by you builders, but which has become the head of the corner. And there is salvation in no one else, for there is no other name under heaven given among men by which we must be saved."

or this

A Reading (Lesson) from the Book of Micah [4:1-5]

It shall come to pass in the latter days that the mountain of the house of the Lord shall be established as the highest of the mountains, and shall be raised up above the hills; and peoples shall flow to it, and many nations shall come, and say: "Come, let us go up to the mountain of the Lord, to the house of the God of Jacob; that he may teach us his ways and we may walk in his paths." For out of Zion shall go forth the law, and the word of the Lord from Jerusalem. He shall judge between many peoples, and shall decide for strong nations afar off; and they shall beat their swords into plowshares, and their spears into pruning hooks; nation shall not lift up sword against nation, neither shall they learn war any more; but they shall sit every man under his vine and under his fig tree, and none shall make them afraid; for the mouth of the Lord of hosts has spoken. For all the peoples walk each in the name of its god, but we will walk in the name of the Lord our God for ever and ever.

Psalm 98 [page 727]   or   *Psalm 98:1-5* [page 727]

A Reading (Lesson) from the First Letter of John [1:1—2:2]

That which was from the beginning, which we have heard, which we have seen with our eyes, which we have looked upon and touched with our hands, concerning the word of life — the life was made manifest, and we saw it, and testify to it, and proclaim to you the eternal life which was with the Father and was made manifest to us — that which we have seen and heard we proclaim also to you, so that you may have fellowship with us; and our fellowship is with the Father and with his Son Jesus Christ. And we are writing this that our joy may be complete. This is the message we have heard from him and proclaim to you, that God is light and in him is no darkness at all. If we say we have fellowship with him while we walk in darkness, we lie and do not live according to the truth; but if we walk in the light, as he is in the light, we have fellowship with one another, and the blood of Jesus his Son cleanses us from all sin. If we say we have no sin, we deceive ourselves, and the truth is not in us. If we confess our sins, he is faithful and just, and will forgive our sins and cleanse us from all unrighteousness. If we say we have not sinned, we make him a liar, and his word is not in us. My little children, I am writing this to you so that you may not sin; but if any one does sin, we have an advocate with the Father, Jesus Christ the righteous; and he is the expiation for our sins, and not for ours only but also for the sins of the whole world.

or this

Acts 4:5-12 [page 127 above]

✝ *The Holy Gospel of Our Lord Jesus Christ According to Luke* [24:36b-48]

While the disciples were telling how they had seen Jesus risen from the dead, Jesus himself stood among them. But they were startled and frightened, and supposed that they saw a spirit. And he said to them, "Why are you troubled, and why do questionings rise in your hearts? See my hands and my feet, that it is I myself; handle me, and see; for a spirit has not flesh and bones as you see that I have." And while they still disbelieved for joy, and wondered, he said to them, "Have you anything here to eat?" They gave him a piece of broiled fish, and he took it and ate before them. Then he said to them, "These are my words which I spoke to you, while I was still with you, that everything written about me in the law of Moses and the prophets and the psalms must be fulfilled." Then he opened their minds to understand the scriptures, and said to them, "Thus it is written, that the Christ should suffer and on the third day rise from the dead, and that repentance and forgiveness of sins should be preached in his name to all nations, beginning from Jersusalem. You are witnesses of these things."

Fourth Sunday of Easter

A Reading (Lesson) from the Acts of the Apostles
[4:(23-31) 32-37]

> When Peter and John were released they went to their friends and reported what the chief priests and the elders had said to them. And when they heard it, they lifted their voices together to God and said, "Sovereign Lord, who didst make the heaven and the earth and the sea and everything in them, who by the mouth of our father David, thy servant, didst say by the Holy Spirit, 'Why did the Gentiles rage, and the peoples imagine vain things? The kings of the earth set themselves in array, and the rulers were gathered together, against the Lord and against his Anointed'— for truly in this city there were gathered together against thy holy servant Jesus, whom thou didst anoint, both Herod and Pontius Pilate, with the Gentiles and the peoples of Israel, to do whatever thy

hand and thy plan had predestined to take place. And now, Lord, look upon their threats, and grant to thy servants to speak thy word with all boldness, while thou stretchest out thy hand to heal, and signs and wonders are performed through the name of thy holy servant Jesus." And when they had prayed, the place in which they were gathered together was shaken; and they were all filled with the Holy Spirit and spoke the word of God with boldness.

Now the company of those who believed were of one heart and soul, and no one said that any of the things which he possessed was his own, but they had everything in common. And with great power the apostles gave their testimony to the resurrection of the Lord Jesus, and great grace was upon them all. There was not a needy person among them, for as many as were possessors of lands or houses sold them, and brought the proceeds of what was sold and laid it at the apostles' feet; and distribution was made to each as any had need. Thus Joseph who was surnamed by the apostles Barnabas (which means, Son of encouragement), a Levite, a native of Cyprus, sold a field which belonged to him, and brought the money and laid it at the apostles' feet.

or this

A Reading (Lesson) from the Book of Ezekiel [34:1-10]

The word of the Lord came to me: "Son of man, prophesy against the shepherds of Israel, prophesy, and say to them, even to the shepherds, Thus says the Lord God: Ho, shepherds of Israel who have been feeding yourselves! Should not shepherds feed the sheep? You eat the fat, you clothe yourselves with the wool, you slaughter the fatlings; but you do not feed the sheep. The weak you have not strengthened, the sick you have not healed, the crippled you have not bound up, the strayed you have not brought back, the lost you have not sought, and with force and harshness you have ruled them. So they were scattered, because there was no shepherd; and they became food for all the wild beasts. My sheep were scattered, they wandered over all the mountains and on every high hill; my sheep were scattered over all the face of the earth, with none to search or seek for them. Therefore, you shepherds, hear the word of the Lord: As I live, says the Lord God, because my sheep have become a prey, and my sheep have become food for all the wild beasts, since there was no shepherd; and because my shepherds have not searched for my sheep, but the shepherds have fed themselves, and have not fed my sheep; therefore, you shepherds, hear the word of the Lord: Thus says the Lord God, Behold, I am against the shepherds; and I will require my sheep at their hand, and put a stop to their feeding the sheep; no longer shall the shepherds feed themselves. I will rescue my sheep from their mouths, that they may not be food for them."

Psalm 23 [page 612] or *Psalm 100* [page 729]

A Reading (Lesson) from the First Letter of John [3:1-8]

See what love the Father has given us, that we should be called children of God; and so we are. The reason why the world does not know us is that it did not know him. Beloved, we are God's children now; it does not yet appear what we shall be, but we know that when he appears we shall be like him, for we shall see him as he is. And every one who thus hopes in him purifies himself as he is pure. Every one who commits sin is guilty of lawlessness; sin is lawlessness. You know that he appeared to take away sins, and in him there is no sin. No one who abides in him sins; no one who sins has either seen him or known him. Little children, let no one deceive you. He who does right is righteous, as he is righteous. He who commits sin is of the devil; for the devil has sinned from the beginning. The reason the Son of God appeared was to destroy the works of the devil.

or this

Acts 4:(23-31) 32-37 [page 130 above]

✝ *The Holy Gospel of Our Lord Jesus Christ
According to John* [10:11-16]

Jesus said, "I am the good shepherd. The good shepherd lays
down his life for the sheep. He who is a hireling and not a
shepherd, whose own the sheep are not, sees the wolf
coming and leaves the sheep and flees; and the wolf snatches
them and scatters them. He flees because he is a hireling and
cares nothing for the sheep. I am the good shepherd; I know
my own and my own know me, as the Father knows me and
I know the Father; and I lay down my life for the sheep. And
I have other sheep, that are not of this fold; I must bring
them also, and they will heed my voice. So there shall be one
flock, one shepherd."

Fifth Sunday of Easter

A Reading (Lesson) from the Acts of the Apostles [8:26-40]

An angel of the Lord said to Philip, "Rise and go toward the
south to the road that goes down from Jerusalem to Gaza."
This is a desert road. And he rose and went. And behold, an
Ethiopian, a eunuch, a minister of the Canda'ce, queen of
the Ethiopians, in charge of all her treasure, had come to
Jerusalem to worship and was returning; seated in his
chariot, he was reading the prophet Isaiah. And the Spirit
said to Philip, "Go up and join this chariot." So Philip ran to
him, and heard him reading Isaiah the prophet, and asked,
"Do you understand what you are reading?" And he said,
"How can I, unless some one guides me?" And he invited
Philip to come up and sit with him. Now the passage of the
scripture which he was reading was this: "As a sheep led to
the slaughter or a lamb before its shearer is dumb, so he
opens not his mouth. In his humiliation justice was denied

him. Who can describe his generation? For his life is taken up from the earth." And the eunuch said to Philip, "About whom, pray, does the prophet say this, about himself or about some one else?" Then Philip opened his mouth, and beginning with this scripture he told him the good news of Jesus. And as they went along the road they came to some water, and the eunuch said, "See, here is water! What is to prevent my being baptized?" And he commanded the chariot to stop, and they both went down into the water, Philip and the eunuch, and he baptized him. And when they came up out of the water, the Spirit of the Lord caught up Philip; and the eunuch saw him no more, and went on his way rejoicing. But Philip was found at Azo′tus, and passing on he preached the gospel to all the towns till he came to Caesare′a.

or this

A Reading (Lesson) from the Book of Deuteronomy [4:32-40]

Ask now of the days that are past, which were before you, since the day that God created man upon the earth, and ask from one end of heaven to the other, whether such a great thing as this has ever happened or was ever heard of. Did any people ever hear the voice of a god speaking out of the midst of the fire, as you have heard, and still live? Or has any god ever attempted to go and take a nation for himself from the midst of another nation, by trials, by signs, by wonders, and by war, by a mighty hand and an outstretched arm, and by great terrors, according to all that the Lord your God did for you in Egypt before your eyes? To you it was shown, that you might know that the Lord is God; there is no other besides him. Out of heaven he let you hear his voice, that he might discipline you; and on earth he let you see his great fire, and you heard his words out of the midst of the fire. And because he loved your fathers and chose their descendants after them, and brought you out of Egypt with his own presence, by his great power, driving out before you nations greater and mightier than yourselves, to bring you in, to give you their land for an inheritance, as at this day; know therefore this day, and lay it to your heart, that the Lord is God in heaven above and on the earth beneath; there is no other. Therefore you shall keep his statutes and his commandments, which I command you this day, that it may go well with you, and with your children after you, and that you may prolong your days in the land which the Lord your God gives you for ever.

Psalm 66:1-11 [page 673] or *Psalm 66:1-8* [page 673]

A Reading (Lesson) from the First Letter of John [3:(14-17)18-24]

> We know that we have passed out of death into life, because we love the brethren. He who does not love abides in death. Any one who hates his brother is a murderer, and you know that no murderer has eternal life abiding in him. By this we know love, that he laid down his life for us; and we ought to lay down our lives for the brethren. But if any one has the world's goods and sees his brother in need, yet closes his heart against him, how does God's love abide in him?

Little children, let us not love in word or speech but in deed and in truth. By this we shall know that we are of the truth, and reassure our hearts before him whenever our hearts condemn us; for God is greater than our hearts, and he knows everything. Beloved, if our hearts do not condemn us, we have confidence before God; and we receive from him whatever we ask, because we keep his commandments and do what pleases him. And this is his commandment, that we should believe in the name of his Son Jesus Christ and love one another, just as he has commanded us. All who keep his commandments abide in him, and he in them. And by this we know that he abides in us, by the Spirit which he has given us.

or this

Acts 8:26-40 [page 133 above]

✟ *The Holy Gospel of Our Lord Jesus Christ*
According to John [14:15-21]

Jesus said to his disciples, "If you love me, you will keep my commandments. And I will pray the Father, and he will give you another Counselor, to be with you for ever, even the Spirit of truth, whom the world cannot receive, because it neither sees him nor knows him; you know him, for he dwells with you, and will be in you. I will not leave you desolate; I will come to you. Yet a little while, and the world will see me no more, but you will see me; because I live, you will live also. In that day you will know that I am in my Father, and you in me, and I in you. He who has my commandments and keeps them, he it is who loves me; and he who loves me will be loved by my Father, and I will love him and manifest myself to him."

Sixth Sunday of Easter

A Reading (Lesson) from the Acts of the Apostles [11:19-30]

Now those who were scattered because of the persecution that arose over Stephen traveled as far as Phoeni'cia and Cyprus and Antioch, speaking the word to none except Jews. But there were some of them, men of Cyprus and Cyre'ne, who on coming to Antioch spoke to the Greeks also, preaching the Lord Jesus. And the hand of the Lord was with them, and a great number that believed turned to the Lord. News of this came to the ears of the church in Jerusalem, and they sent Barnabas to Antioch. When he came and saw the grace of God, he was glad; and he exhorted them all to remain faithful to the Lord with steadfast purpose; for he was a good man, full of the Holy

Spirit and of faith. And a large company was added to the Lord. So Barnabas went to Tarsus to look for Saul; and when he had found him he brought him to Antioch. For a whole year they met with the church, and taught a large company of people; and in Antioch the disciples were for the first time called Christians. Now in these days prophets came down from Jerusalem to Antioch. And one of them named Ag'abus stood up and foretold by the Spirit that there would be a great famine over all the world; and this took place in the days of Claudius. And the disciples determined, every one according to his ability, to send relief to the brethren who lived in Judea; and they did so, sending it to the elders by the hand of Barnabas and Saul.

or this

A Reading (Lesson) from the Book of Isaiah [45:11-13,18-19]

Thus says the Lord, the Holy One of Israel, and his Maker: "Will you question me about my children, or command me concerning the work of my hands? I made the earth, and created man upon it; it was my hands that stretched out the heavens, and I commanded all their host. I have aroused him in righteousness, and I will make straight all his ways; he shall build my city and set my exiles free, not for price or reward," says the Lord of hosts. For thus says the Lord, who created the heavens (he is God!), who formed the earth and made it (he established it; he did not create it a chaos, he formed it to be inhabited!): "I am the Lord, and there is no other. I did not speak in secret, in a land of darkness; I did not say to the offspring of Jacob, 'Seek me in chaos.' I the Lord speak the truth, I declare what is right."

Psalm 33 [page 626]   or   *Psalm 33:1-8,18-22* [page 626]

A Reading (Lesson) from the First Letter of John [4:7-21]

Beloved, let us love one another; for love is of God, and he who loves is born of God and knows God. He who does not love does not know God; for God is love. In this the love of God was made manifest among us, that God sent his only Son into the world, so that we might live through him. In this is love, not that we loved God but that he loved us and sent his Son to be the expiation for our sins. Beloved, if God so loved us, we also ought to love one another. No man has ever seen God; if we love one another, God abides in us and his love is perfected in us. By this we know that we abide in him and he in us, because he has given us of his own Spirit. And we have seen and testify that the Father has sent his Son as the Savior of the world. Whoever confesses that Jesus is the Son of God, God abides in him, and he in God. So we know and believe the love God has for us. God is love, and he who abides in love abides in God, and God abides in him. In this is love perfected with us, that we may have confidence for the day of judgment, because as he is, so are we in this world. There is no fear in love, but perfect love casts out fear. For fear has to do with punishment, and he who fears is not perfected in love. We love, because he first loved us. If any one says, "I love God," and hates his brother, he is a liar; for he who does not love his brother whom he has seen, cannot love God whom he has not seen. And this commandment we have from him, that he who loves God should love his brother also.

or this

Acts 11: 19-30 [page 136 above]

✝ *The Holy Gospel of Our Lord Jesus Christ According to John* [15:9-17]

Jesus said to his disciples, "As the Father has loved me, so have I loved you; abide in my love. If you keep my commandments, you will abide in my love, just as I have kept my Father's commandments and abide in his love. These things I have spoken to you, that my joy may be in you, and that your joy may be full. This is my commandment, that you love one another as I have loved you. Greater love has no man than this, that a man lay down his life for his friends. You are my friends if you do what I command you. No longer do I call you servants, for the servant does not know what his master is doing; but I have called you friends, for all that I have heard from my Father I have made known to you. You did not choose me, but I chose you and appointed you that you should go and bear fruit and that your fruit should abide; so that whatever you ask the Father in my name, he may give it to you. This I command you, to love one another."

Ascension Day

A Reading (Lesson) from the Acts of the Apostles [1:1-11]

In the first book, O The-oph'ilus, I have dealt with all that Jesus began to do and teach, until the day when he was taken up, after he had given commandment through the Holy Spirit to the apostles whom he had chosen. To them he presented himself alive after his passion by many proofs, appearing to them during forty days, and speaking of the kingdom of God. And while staying with them he charged them not to depart from Jerusalem, but to wait for the promise of the Father, which, he said, "you heard from me, for John baptized with water, but before many days you shall be baptized with the Holy Spirit." So when they had come together, they asked him, "Lord, will you at this time restore the kingdom to Israel?" He said to them, "It is not for you to know times or seasons which the Father has fixed by his own authority. But you shall receive power when the Holy Spirit has come upon you; and you shall be my witnesses in Jerusalem and in all Judea and Samar'ia and to the end of the earth." And when he had said this, as they were looking on, he was lifted up, and a cloud took him out of their sight. And while they were gazing into heaven as he went, behold, two men stood by them in white robes, and said, "Men of Galilee, why do you stand looking into heaven? This Jesus, who was taken up from you into heaven, will come in the same way as you saw him go into heaven."

or this

A Reading (Lesson) from the Book of Ezekiel
[1:3-5a, 15-22, 26-28]

The word of the Lord came to Ezekiel the priest, the son of Buzi, in the land of the Chalde'ans by the river Chebar; and the hand of the Lord was upon him there. As I looked, behold, a stormy wind came out of the north, and a great cloud, with brightness round about it, and fire flashing forth continually, and in the midst of the fire, as it were gleaming bronze. And from the midst of it came the likeness of four living creatures. Now as I looked at the living creatures, I saw a wheel upon the earth beside the living creatures, one for each of the four of them. As for the appearance of the wheels and their construction: their appearance was like the gleaming of a chrysolite; and the four had the same likeness, their construction being as it were a wheel within a wheel. When they went, they went in any of their four directions without turning as they went. The four wheels had rims and they had spokes; and their rims were full of eyes round about. And when the living creatures went, the wheels went beside them; and when the living creatures rose from the earth, the wheels rose. Wherever the spirit would go, they went, and the wheels rose along with them; for the spirit of the living creatures was in the wheels. When those went, these went; and when those stood, these stood; and when those rose from the earth, the wheels rose along with them; for the spirit of the living creatures was in the wheels. Over the heads of the living creatures there was the likeness of a firmament, shining like crystal, spread out above their heads. And above the firmament over their heads there was the likeness of a throne, in appearance like sapphire; and seated above the likeness of a throne was a likeness as it were of a human form. And upward from what had the appearance of his loins I saw as it were gleaming bronze, like the appearance of fire enclosed round about; and downward from what had the appearance of his loins I saw as it were the appearance of fire, and there was brightness round about him. Like the appearance of the bow that is in the cloud on the day of rain, so was the appearance of the brightness round about. Such was the appearance of the likeness of the glory of the Lord. And when I saw it, I fell upon my face, and I heard the voice of one speaking.

Psalm 47 [page 650] or *Psalm 110:1-5* [page 753]

A Reading (Lesson) from the Letter of Paul to the Ephesians [1:15-23]

Because I have heard of your faith in the Lord Jesus and your love toward all the saints, I do not cease to give thanks for you, remembering you in my prayers, that the God of our Lord Jesus Christ, the Father of glory, may give you a spirit of wisdom and of revelation in the knowledge of him, having the eyes of your hearts enlightened, that you may know what is the hope to which he has called you, what are the riches of his glorious inheritance in the saints, and what is the immeasurable greatness of his power in us who believe, according to the working of his great might which he accomplished in Christ when he raised him from the dead and made him sit at his right hand in the heavenly places, far above all rule and authority and power and dominion, and above every name that is named, not only in this age but also in that which is to come; and he has put all things under his feet and has made him the head over all things for the church, which is his body, the fullness of him who fills all in all.

or this

Acts 1:1-11 [page 139 above]

✝ The Holy Gospel of Our Lord Jesus Christ
   According to Luke [24:49-53]

Jesus said to his disciples, "Behold, I send the promise of my Father upon you; but stay in the city, until you are clothed with power from on high." Then he led them out as far as Bethany, and lifting up his hands he blessed them. While he blessed them, he parted from them, and was carried up into heaven. And they returned to Jerusalem with great joy, and were continually in the temple blessing God.

or this

✝ The Holy Gospel of Our Lord Jesus Christ
   According to Mark [16:9-15, 19-20]

Now when Jesus rose early on the first day of the week, he appeared first to Mary Mag'dalene, from whom he had cast out seven demons. She went out and told those who had been with him, as they mourned and wept. But when they heard that he was alive and had been seen by her, they would not believe it. After this he appeared in another form to two of them, as they were walking into the country. And they went back and told the rest, but they did not believe them. Afterward he appeared to the eleven themselves as they sat at table; and he upbraided them for their unbelief and hardness of heart, because they had not believed those who saw him after he had risen. And he said to them, "Go into all the world and preach the gospel to the whole creation." So then the Lord Jesus, after he had spoken to them, was taken up into heaven, and sat down at the right hand of God. And they went forth and preached everywhere, while the Lord worked with them and confirmed the message by the signs that attended it.

Seventh Sunday of Easter

A Reading (Lesson) from the Acts of the Apostles [1:15-26]

In those days Peter stood up among the brethren (the company of persons was in all about a hundred and twenty), and said, "Brethren, the scripture had to be fulfilled, which the Holy Spirit spoke beforehand by the mouth of David, concerning Judas who was guide to those who arrested Jesus. For he was numbered among us, and was allotted his share in this ministry. (Now this man bought a field with the reward of his wickedness; and falling headlong he burst open in the middle and all his bowels gushed out. And it became known to all the inhabitants of Jerusalem, so that the field was called in their language Akel'dama, that is, Field of Blood.) For it is written in the book of Psalms, 'Let his habitation become desolate, and let there be no one to live in it'; and 'His office let another take.' So one of the men who have accompanied us during all the time that the Lord Jesus went in and out among us, beginning from the baptism of John until the day when he was taken up from us — one of these men must become with us a witness to his resurrection." And they put forward two, Joseph called Barsab'bas, who was surnamed Justus, and Matthi'as. And they prayed and said, "Lord, who knowest the hearts of all men, show which one of these two thou hast chosen to take the place in this ministry and apostleship from which Judas turned aside, to go to his own place." And they cast lots for them, and the lot fell on Matthi'as; and he was enrolled with the eleven apostles.

or this

A Reading (Lesson) from the Book of Exodus
[28:1-4, 9-10, 29-30]

The Lord said to Moses, "Bring near to you Aaron your brother, and his sons with him, from among the people of

Israel, to serve me as priests — Aaron and Aaron's sons, Nadab and Abi'hu, Elea'zar and Ith'amar. And you shall make holy garments for Aaron your brother, for glory and for beauty. And you shall speak to all who have ability, whom I have endowed with an able mind, that they make Aaron's garments to consecrate him for my priesthood. These are the garments which they shall make: a breastpiece, an ephod, a robe, a coat of checker work, a turban, and a girdle; they shall make holy garments for Aaron your brother and his sons to serve me as priests. And you shall take two onyx stones, and engrave on them the names of the sons of Israel, six of their names on the one stone, and the names of the remaining six on the other stone, in the order of their birth. So Aaron shall bear the names of the sons of Israel in the breastpiece of judgment upon his heart, when he goes into the holy place, to bring them to continual remembrance before the Lord. And in the breastpiece of judgment you shall put the Urim and the Thummim, and they shall be upon Aaron's heart, when he goes in before the Lord; thus Aaron shall bear the judgment of the people of Israel upon his heart before the Lord continually.

Psalm 68:1-20 [page 676] or *Psalm 47* [page 650]

A Reading (Lesson) from the First Letter of John [5:9-15]

If we receive the testimony of men, the testimony of God is greater; for this is the testimony of God that he has borne witness to his Son. He who believes in the Son of God has the testimony in himself. He who does not believe God, has made him a liar, because he has not believed in the testimony that God has borne to his Son. And this is the testimony, that God gave us eternal life, and this life is in his Son. He who has the Son has life; he who has not the Son of God has not life. I write this to you who believe in the name of the Son of God, that you may know that you have eternal life. And this is the confidence which we have in him, that if we ask

anything according to his will he hears us. And if we know
that he hears us in whatever we ask, we know that we have
obtained the requests made of him.

or this

Acts 1:15-26 [page 143 above]

✝ *The Holy Gospel of Our Lord Jesus Christ*
According to John [17:11b-19]

Jesus prayed for his disciples, saying, "Holy Father, keep
them in thy name, which thou hast given me, that they may
be one, even as we are one. While I was with them, I kept
them in thy name, which thou hast given me; I have guarded
them, and none of them is lost but the son of perdition, that
the scripture might be fulfilled. But now I am coming to
thee; and these things I speak in the world, that they may
have my joy fulfilled in themselves. I have given them thy
word; and the world has hated them because they are not of
the world, even as I am not of the world. I do not pray that
thou shouldst take them out of the world, but that thou
shouldst keep them from the evil one. They are not of the
world, even as I am not of the world. Sanctify them in the
truth; thy word is truth. As thou didst send me into the
world, so I have sent them into the world. And for their sake
I consecrate myself, that they also may be consecrated in
truth.

Day of Pentecost: Early or Vigil Service

A Reading (Lesson) from the Book of Genesis [11:1-9]

Now the whole earth had one language and few words. And
as men migrated from the east, they found a plain in the land
of Shinar and settled there. And they said to one another,
"Come, let us make bricks, and burn them thoroughly." And

they had brick for stone, and bitumen for mortar. Then they said, "Come, let us build ourselves a city, and a tower with its top in the heavens, and let us make a name for ourselves, lest we be scattered abroad upon the face of the whole earth." And the Lord came down to see the city and the tower, which the sons of men had built. And the Lord said, "Behold, they are one people, and they have all one language; and this is only the beginning of what they will do; and nothing that they propose to do will now be impossible for them. Come, let us go down, and there confuse their language, that they may not understand one another's speech." So the Lord scattered them abroad from there over the face of all the earth, and they left off building the city. Therefore its name was called Babel, because there the Lord confused the language of all the earth; and from there the Lord scattered them abroad over the face of all the earth.

Psalm 33:12-22 [page 626]

or this

A Reading (Lesson) from the Book of Exodus
[19:1-9a, 16-20a; 20:18-20]

On the third new moon after the people of Israel had gone forth out of the land of Egypt, on that day they came into the wilderness of Sinai. And when they set out from Reph'idim and came into the wilderness of Sinai, they encamped in the wilderness; and there Israel encamped before the mountain. And Moses went up to God, and the Lord called to him out of the mountain, saying, "Thus you shall say to the house of Jacob, and tell the people of Israel: You have seen what I did to the Egyptians, and how I bore you on eagles' wings and brought you to myself. Now therefore, if you will obey my voice and keep my covenant, you shall be my own possession among all peoples; for all the earth is mine, and you shall be to me a kingdom of priests and a holy nation. These are the words which you shall speak to the children of Israel." So Moses came and called the elders of the people, and set before them all these words which the Lord had commanded him. And all the people answered together and said, "All that the Lord has spoken we will do." And Moses reported the words of the people to the Lord. And the Lord said to Moses, "Lo, I am coming to you in a thick cloud, that the people may hear when I speak with you, and may also believe you for ever." On the morning of the third day there were thunders and lightnings, and a thick cloud upon the mountain, and a very loud trumpet blast, so that all the people who were in the camp trembled. Then Moses brought the people out of the camp to meet God; and they took their stand at the foot of the mountain. And Mount Sinai was wrapped in smoke, because the Lord descended upon it in fire; and the smoke of it went up like the smoke of a kiln, and the whole mountain quaked greatly. And as the sound of the trumpet grew louder and louder, Moses spoke, and God answered him in thunder. And the Lord came down upon Mount Sinai, to the top of the mountain. Now when all the people perceived the thunderings and the lightnings and the sound of the trumpet and the mountain smoking, the people were afraid and trembled; and they stood afar off, and said to Moses, "You speak to us, and we will hear; but let not God speak to us, lest we die." And Moses said to the people, "Do not fear; for God has come to prove you, and that the fear of him may be before your eyes, that you may not sin."

Canticle 2 or *13, A Song of Praise* [page 49 or 90]

or the following

A Reading (Lesson) from the Book of Ezekiel [37:1-14]

The hand of the Lord was upon me, and he brought me out by the Spirit of the Lord, and set me down in the midst of the valley; it was full of bones. And he led me round among them; and behold, there were very many upon the valley; and lo, they were very dry. And he said to me, "Son of man, can these bones live?" And I answered, "O Lord God, thou knowest." Again he said to me, "Prophesy to these bones, and say to them, O dry bones, hear the word of the Lord. Thus says the Lord God to these bones: Behold, I will cause breath to enter you, and you shall live. And I will lay sinews upon you, and will cause flesh to come upon you, and cover you with skin, and put breath in you, and you shall live; and you shall know that I am the Lord." So I prophesied as I was commanded; and as I prophesied, there was a noise and behold, a rattling; and the bones came together, bone to its bone. And as I looked, there were sinews on them, and flesh had come upon them, and skin had covered them; but there was no breath in them. Then he said to me, "Prophesy to the breath, prophesy, son of man, and say to the breath, Thus says the Lord God: Come from the four winds, O breath, and breathe upon these slain, that they may live." So I prophesied as he commanded me, and the breath came into them, and they lived, and stood upon their feet, an exceedingly great host. Then he said to me, "Son of man, these bones are the whole house of Israel. Behold, they say, 'Our bones are dried up, and our hope is lost; we are clean cut off.' Therefore prophesy, and say to them, Thus says the Lord God: Behold, I will open your graves and raise you from your graves, O my people; and I will bring you home into the land of Israel. And you shall know that I am the Lord, when I open your graves, and raise you from your graves, O my people. And I will put my Spirit within you, and you shall live, and I will place you in your own land; then you shall know that I, the Lord, have spoken, and I have done it, says the Lord."

Psalm 130 [page 784]

or this

A Reading (Lesson) from the Book of Joel [2:28-32]

The Lord said to his people, "It shall come to pass afterward, that I will pour out my spirit on all flesh; your sons and daughters shall prophesy, your old men shall dream dreams, and your young men shall see visions. Even upon the menservants and maidservants in those days, I will pour out my spirit. And I will give portents in the heavens and on the earth, blood and fire and columns of smoke. The sun shall be turned to darkness, and the moon to blood, before the great and terrible day of the Lord comes. And it shall come to pass that all who call upon the name of the Lord shall be delivered; for in Mount Zion and in Jerusalem there shall be those who escape, as the Lord has said, and among the survivors shall be those whom the Lord calls."

Canticle 9, The First Song of Isaiah [page 86]

or this

Acts 2:1-11 [page 150 below]

Psalm 104:25-32 [page 736]

or this

A Reading (Lesson) from the Letter of Paul to the Romans
[8:14-17,22-27]

All who are led by the Spirit of God are sons of God. For you did not receive the spirit of slavery to fall back into fear, but you have received the spirit of sonship. When we cry, "Abba! Father!" it is the Spirit himself bearing witness with our spirit that we are children of God, and if children, then heirs, heirs of God and fellow heirs with Christ, provided we suffer with him in order that we may also be glorified with him. We know that the whole creation has been groaning in travail together until now; and not only the creation, but we ourselves, who have the first fruits of the Spirit, groan inwardly as we wait for adoption as sons, the redemption of our bodies. For in this hope we were saved. Now hope that is seen is not hope. For who hopes for what he sees? But if we hope for what we do not see, we wait for it with patience. Likewise the Spirit helps us in our weakness; for we do not know how to pray as we ought, but the Spirit himself intercedes for us with sighs too deep for words. And he who searches the hearts of men knows what is in the mind of the Spirit, because the Spirit intercedes for the saints according to the will of God.

✝ *The Holy Gospel of Our Lord Jesus Christ According to John* [7:37-39a]

On the last day of the feast, the great day, Jesus stood up and proclaimed, "If any one thirst, let him come to me and drink. He who believes in me, as the scripture has said, 'Out of his heart shall flow rivers of living water.'" Now this he said about the Spirit, which those who believed in him were to receive.

Day of Pentecost: Principal Service

A Reading (Lesson) from the Acts of the Apostles [2:1-11]

When the day of Pentecost had come, the disciples were all together in one place. And suddenly a sound came from heaven like the rush of a mighty wind, and it filled all the house where they were sitting. And there appeared to them tongues as of fire, distributed and resting on each one of them. And they were all filled with the Holy Spirit and began to speak in other tongues, as the Spirit gave them utterance.

Now there were dwelling in Jerusalem Jews, devout men from every nation under heaven. And at this sound the multitude came together, and they were bewildered, because each one heard them speaking in his own language. And they were amazed and wondered, saying, "Are not all these who are speaking Galileans? And how is it that we hear, each of us in his own native language? Par'thians and Medes and Elamites and residents of Mesopota'mia, Judea and Cappado'cia, Pontus and Asia, Phryg'ia and Pamphyl'ia, Egypt and the parts of Libya belonging to Cyre'ne, and visitors from Rome, both Jews and proselytes, Cretans and Arabians, we hear them telling in our own tongues the mighty works of God."

or this

A Reading (Lesson) from the Book of Isaiah [44:1-8]

Thus says the Lord, "Now hear, O Jacob my servant, Israel whom I have chosen! Thus says the Lord who made you, who formed you from the womb and will help you: Fear not, O Jacob my servant, Jesh'urun whom I have chosen. For I will pour water on the thirsty land, and streams on the dry ground; I will pour my Spirit upon your descendants, and my blessing on your offspring. They shall spring up like grass amid waters, like willows by flowing streams. This one will say, 'I am the Lord's,' another will call himself by the name of Jacob, and another will write on his hand, 'The Lord's,' and surname himself by the name of Israel." Thus says the Lord, the King of Israel and his Redeemer, the Lord of hosts: "I am the first and I am the last; besides me there is no god. Who is like me? Let him proclaim it, let him declare and set it forth before me. Who has announced from of old the things to come? Let them tell us what is yet to be. Fear not, nor be afraid; have I not told you from of old and declared it? And you are my witnesses! Is there a God besides me? There is no Rock; I know not any."

Psalm 104:25-37 [page 736]   or   *Psalm 104:25-32* [page 736]

or   *Psalm 33:12-15, 18-22* [page 626]

A Reading (Lesson) From the First Letter of Paul to the Corinthians [12:4-13]

Now there are varieties of gifts, but the same Spirit; and there are varieties of service, but the same Lord; and there are varieties of working, but it is the same God who inspires them all in every one. To each is given the manifestation of the Spirit for the common good. To one is given through the Spirit the utterance of wisdom, and to another the utterance of knowledge according to the same Spirit, to another faith by the same Spirit, to another gifts of healing by the one Spirit, to another the working of miracles, to another prophecy, to another the ability to distinguish between spirits, to another various kinds of tongues, to another the interpretation of tongues. All these are inspired by one and the same Spirit, who apportions to each one individually as he wills. For just as the body is one and has many members, and all the members of the body, though many, are one body, so it is with Christ. For by one Spirit we were all baptized into one body — Jews or Greeks, slaves or free — and all were made to drink of one Spirit.

or this

Acts 2:1-11 [page 150 above]

✝ *The Holy Gospel of Our Lord Jesus Christ According to John* [20:19-23]

On the evening of that day, the first day of the week, the doors being shut where the disciples were, for fear of the Jews, Jesus came and stood among them and said to them, "Peace be with you." When he had said this, he showed them his hands and his side. Then the disciples were glad when they saw the Lord. Jesus said to them again, "Peace be with you. As the Father has sent me, even so I send you." And when he had said this, he breathed on them, and said to them, "Receive the Holy Spirit. If you forgive the sins of any, they are forgiven; if you retain the sins of any, they are retained."

or this

✝ *The Holy Gospel of Our Lord Jesus Christ According to John* [14:8-17]

Philip said to Jesus, "Lord, show us the Father, and we shall be satisfied." Jesus said to him, "Have I been with you so long, and yet you do not know me, Philip? He who has seen me has seen the Father; how can you say, 'Show us the Father'? Do you not believe that I am in the Father and the Father in me? The words that I say to you I do not speak on my own authority; but the Father who dwells in me does his works. Believe me that I am in the Father and the Father in me; or else believe me for the sake of the works themselves. Truly, truly, I say to you, he who believes in me will also do the works that I do; and greater works than these will he do, because I go to the Father. Whatever you ask in my name, I will do it, that the Father may be glorified in the Son; if you ask anything in my name, I will do it. If you love me, you will keep my commandments. And I will pray the Father, and he will give you another Counselor, to be with you for ever, even the Spirit of truth, whom the world cannot receive, because it neither sees him nor knows him; you know him, for he dwells with you, and will be in you."

Trinity Sunday

A Reading (Lesson) from the Book of Exodus [3:1-6]

Now Moses was keeping the flock of his father-in-law, Jethro, the priest of Mid'ian; and he led his flock to the west side of the wilderness, and came to Horeb, the mountain of God. And the angel of the Lord appeared to him in a flame of fire out of the midst of a bush; and he looked, and lo, the bush was burning, yet it was not consumed. And Moses said, "I will turn aside and see this great sight, why the bush is not burnt." When the Lord saw that he turned aside to see, God called to him out of the bush, "Moses, Moses!" And he said, "Here am I." Then he said, "Do not come near; put off your shoes from your feet, for the place on which you are standing is holy ground." And he said, "I am the God of your father, the God of Abraham, the God of Isaac, and the God of Jacob." And Moses hid his face, for he was afraid to look at God.

Psalm 93 [page 722]   or

Benedictus es, Canticle 2 or 13 [page 49 or 90]

A Reading (Lesson) from the Letter of Paul to the Romans [8:12-17]

So then, brethren, we are debtors, not to the flesh, to live according to the flesh — for if you live according to the flesh you will die, but if by the Spirit you put to death the deeds of the body you will live. For all who are led by the Spirit of God are sons of God. For you did not receive the spirit of slavery to fall back into fear, but you have received the spirit of sonship. When we cry, "Abba! Father!" it is the Spirit himself bearing witness with our spirit that we are children of God, and if children, then heirs, heirs of God and fellow heirs with Christ, provided we suffer with him in order that we may also be glorified with him.

✝ *The Holy Gospel of Our Lord Jesus Christ According to John* [3:1-16]

Now there was a man of the Pharisees, named Nicode'mus, a ruler of the Jews. This man came to Jesus by night and said to him, "Rabbi, we know that you are a teacher come from God; for no one can do these signs that you do, unless God is with him." Jesus answered him, "Truly, truly, I say to you, unless one is born anew, he cannot see the kingdom of God." Nicode′mus said to him, "How can a man be born when he is old? Can he enter a second time into his mother's womb and be born?" Jesus answered, "Truly, truly, I say to you, unless one is born of water and the Spirit, he cannot enter the kingdom of God. That which is born of the flesh is flesh, and that which is born of the Spirit is spirit. Do not marvel that I said to you, 'You must be born anew.' The wind blows where it wills, and you hear the sound of it, but you do not know whence it comes or whither it goes; so it is with every one who is born of the Spirit." Nicode′mus said to him, "How can this be?" Jesus answered him, "Are you a teacher of Israel, and yet you do not understand this? Truly, truly, I say to you, we speak of what we know, and bear witness to what we have seen; but you do not receive our testimony. If I have told you earthly things and you do not believe, how can you believe if I tell you heavenly things? No one has ascended into heaven but he who descended from heaven, the Son of man. And as Moses lifted up the serpent in the wilderness, so must the Son of man be lifted up, that whoever believes in him may have eternal life." For God so loved the world that he gave his only Son, that whoever believes in him should not perish but have eternal life.

Proper 1   *The Sunday Closest to May 11*
[*Same as on the Sixth Sunday after the Epiphany, pages 39-40*]

Proper 2   *The Sunday Closest to May 18*
[*Same as on the Seventh Sunday after the Epiphany, pages 41-42*]

Proper 3   *The Sunday Closest to May 25*
[*Same as on the Eighth Sunday after the Epiphany, pages 42-44*]

Proper 4 *The Sunday Closest to June 1*

A Reading (Lesson) from the Book of Deuteronomy [5:6-21]

The Lord said these words to all Israel, "I am the Lord your God, who brought you out of the land of Egypt, out of the house of bondage. You shall have no other gods before me. You shall not make for yourself a graven image, or any likeness of anything that is in heaven above, or that is on the earth beneath, or that is in the water under the earth; you shall not bow down to them or serve them; for I the Lord your God am a jealous God, visiting the iniquity of the fathers upon the children of the third and fourth generation of those who hate me, but showing steadfast love to thousands of those who love me and keep my commandments. You shall not take the name of the Lord your God in vain: for the Lord will not hold him guiltless who takes his name in vain. Observe the sabbath day, to keep it holy, as the Lord your God commanded you. Six days you shall labor, and do all your work; but the seventh day is a sabbath to the Lord your God; in it you shall not do any work, you, or your son, or your daughter, or your manservant, or your maidservant, or your ox, or your ass, or any of your cattle, or the sojourner who is within your gates, that your manservant and your maidservant may rest as well as you. You shall remember that you were a servant in the land of Egypt, and the Lord your God brought you out thence with a mighty hand and an outstretched arm; therefore the Lord your God commanded you to keep the sabbath day. Honor your father and your mother, as the Lord your God commanded you; that your days may be prolonged, and that it may go well with you, in the land which the Lord your God gives you. You shall not kill. Neither shall you commit adultery. Neither shall you steal. Neither shall you bear false witness against your neighbor. Neither shall you covet your neighbor's wife; and you shall not desire your neighbor's house, his field, or his manservant, or his maidservant, his ox, or his ass, or anything that is your neighbor's."

Psalm 81 [page 704] or *Psalm 81:1-10* [page 704]

A Reading (Lesson) from the Second Letter of Paul to the Corinthians [4:5-12]

What we preach is not ourselves, but Jesus Christ as Lord, with ourselves as your servants for Jesus' sake. For it is the God who said, "Let light shine out of darkness," who has shone in our hearts to give the light of the knowledge of the glory of God in the face of Christ. But we have this treasure in earthen vessels, to show that the transcendent power belongs to God and not to us. We are afflicted in every way, but not crushed; perplexed, but not driven to despair; persecuted, but not forsaken; struck down, but not destroyed; always carrying in the body the death of Jesus, so that the life of Jesus may also be manifested in our bodies. For while we live we are always being given up to death for Jesus' sake, so that the life of Jesus may be manifested in our mortal flesh. So death is at work in us, but life in you.

✝ *The Holy Gospel of Our Lord Jesus Christ According to Mark* [2:23-28]

On a sabbath day, Jesus and his disciples were going through the grainfields; and as they made their way his disciples began to pluck heads of grain. And the Pharisees said to him, "Look, why are they doing what is not lawful on the sabbath?" And he said to them, "Have you never read what David did, when he was in need and was hungry, he and those who were with him: how he entered the house of God, when Abi'athar was high priest, and ate the bread of the Presence, which it is not lawful for any but the priests to eat, and also gave it to those who were with him?" And he said to them, "The sabbath was made for man, not man for the sabbath; so the Son of man is lord even of the sabbath."

Proper 5   *The Sunday Closest to June 8*

A Reading (Lesson) from the Book of Genesis [3:(1-7)8-21]

Now the serpent was more subtle than any other wild creature that the Lord God had made. He said to the woman, "Did God say, 'You shall not eat of any tree of the garden'?" And the woman said to the serpent, "We may eat of the fruit of the trees of the garden; but God said, 'You shall not eat of the fruit of the tree which is in the midst of the garden, neither shall you touch it, lest you die.'" But the serpent said to the woman, "You will not die. For God knows that when you eat of it your eyes will be opened, and you will be like God, knowing good and evil." So when the woman saw that the tree was good for food, and that it was a delight to the eyes, and that the tree was to be desired to make one wise, she took of its fruit and ate; and she also gave some to her husband, and he ate. Then the eyes of both were opened, and they knew that they were naked; and they sewed fig leaves together and made themselves aprons.

And the man and his wife heard the sound of the Lord God walking in the garden in the cool of the day, and they hid themselves from the presence of the Lord God among the trees of the garden. But the Lord God called to the man, and said to him, "Where are you?" And he said, "I heard the sound of thee in the garden, and I was afraid, because I was naked; and I hid myself." He said, "Who told you that you were naked? Have you eaten of the tree of which I commanded you not to eat?" The man said, "The woman whom thou gavest to be with me, she gave me fruit of the tree, and I ate." Then the Lord God said to the woman, "What is this that you have done?" The woman said, "The serpent beguiled me, and I ate." The Lord God said to the serpent, "Because you have done this, cursed are you above all cattle, and above all wild animals; upon your belly you shall go, and dust you shall eat all the days of your life. I will put enmity between you and the woman, and between your seed and her seed; he shall bruise your head, and you shall bruise his heel." To the woman he said, "I will greatly multiply your pain in childbearing; in pain you shall bring forth children, yet your desire shall be for your husband, and he shall rule over you." And to Adam he said, "Because you have listened to the voice of your wife, and have eaten of the tree of which I commanded you, 'You shall not eat of it,' cursed is the ground because of you; in toil you shall eat of it all the days of your life; thorns and thistles it shall bring forth to you; and you shall eat the plants of the field. In the sweat of your face you shall eat bread till you return to the ground, for out of it you were taken; you are dust, and to dust you shall return." The man called his wife's name Eve, because she was the mother of all living. And the Lord God made for Adam and for his wife garments of skins, and clothed them.

Psalm 130 [page 784]

A Reading (Lesson) from the Second Letter of Paul to the Corinthians [4:13-18]

Since we have the same spirit of faith as he had who wrote, "I believed, and so I spoke," we too believe, and so we speak, knowing that he who raised the Lord Jesus will raise us also with Jesus and bring us with you into his presence. For it is all for your sake, so that as grace extends to more and more people it may increase thanksgiving, to the glory of God. So we do not lose heart. Though our outer nature is wasting away, our inner nature is being renewed every day. For this slight momentary affliction is preparing for us an eternal weight of glory beyond all comparison, because we look not to the things that are seen but to the things that are unseen; for the things that are seen are transient, but the things that are unseen are eternal.

✝ *The Holy Gospel of Our Lord Jesus Christ According to Mark* [3:20-35]

The crowd came together again, so that Jesus and his disciples could not even eat. And when his family heard it, they went out to seize him, for people were saying, "He is beside himself." And the scribes who came down from Jerusalem said, "He is possessed by Be-el'zebul, and by the prince of demons he casts out the demons." And he called them to him, and said to them in parables, "How can Satan cast out Satan? If a kingdom is divided against itself, that kingdom cannot stand. And if a house is divided against itself, that house will not be able to stand. And if Satan has risen up against himself and is divided, he cannot stand, but is coming to an end. But no one can enter a strong man's house and plunder his goods, unless he first binds the strong man; then indeed he may plunder his house. Truly, I say to you, all sins will be forgiven the sons of men, and whatever blasphemies they utter; but whoever blasphemes against the Holy Spirit never has forgiveness, but is guilty of an eternal sin" — for they had said, "He has an unclean spirit." And his mother and his brothers came; and standing outside they sent to him and called him. And a crowd was sitting about him; and they said to him, "Your mother and your brothers are outside, asking for you." And he replied, "Who are my mother and my brothers?" And looking around on those who sat about him, he said, "Here are my mother and my brothers! Whoever does the will of God is my brother, and sister, and mother."

Proper 6 *The Sunday Closest to June 15*

A Reading (Lesson) from the Book of Ezekiel [31:1-6, 10-14]

In the eleventh year, in the third month, on the first day of
the month, the word of the Lord came to me: "Son of man,
say to Pharaoh king of Egypt and to his multitude: 'Whom
are you like in your greatness? Behold, I will liken you to a
cedar in Lebanon, with fair branches and forest shade, and
of great height, its top among the clouds. The waters
nourished it, the deep made it grow tall, making its rivers
flow round the place of its planting, sending forth its streams
to all the trees of the forest. So it towered high above all the
trees of the forest; its boughs grew large and its branches
long, from abundant water in its shoots. All the birds of the
air made their nests in its boughs; under its branches all the
beasts of the field brought forth their young; and under its
shadow dwelt all great nations. Therefore thus says the Lord
God: Because it towered high and set its top among the
clouds, and its heart was proud of its height, I will give it
into the hand of a mighty one of the nations; he shall surely
deal with it as its wickedness deserves. I have cast it out.
Foreigners, the most terrible of the nations, will cut it down
and leave it. On the mountains and in all the valleys its
branches will fall, and its boughs will lie broken in all the
water-courses of the land; and all the peoples of the earth
will go from its shadow and leave it. Upon its ruin will dwell
all the birds of the air, and upon its branches will be all the
beasts of the field. All this is in order that no trees by the
waters may grow to lofty height or set their tops among the
clouds, and that no trees that drink water may reach up to
them in height; for they are all given over to death, to the
nether world among mortal men, with those who go down
to the Pit.'"

Psalm 92 [page 720]   or   *Psalm 92:1- 4, 11-14* [page 720]

*A Reading (Lesson) from the Second Letter of Paul to the
Corinthians* [5:1-10]

We know that if the earthly tent we live in is destroyed, we
have a building from God, a house not made with hands,
eternal in the heavens. Here indeed we groan, and long to
put on our heavenly dwelling, so that by putting it on we
may not be found naked. For while we are still in this tent,
we sigh with anxiety; not that we would be unclothed, but
that we would be further clothed, so that what is mortal may
be swallowed up by life. He who has prepared us for this
very thing is God, who has given us the Spirit as a guarantee.
So we are always of good courage; we know that while we
are at home in the body we are away from the Lord, for we
walk by faith, not by sight. We are of good courage, and we
would rather be away from the body and at home with the
Lord. So whether we are at home or away, we make it our
aim to please him. For we must all appear before the
judgment seat of Christ, so that each one may receive good
or evil, according to what he has done in the body.

✝ *The Holy Gospel of Our Lord Jesus Christ
According to Mark* [4:26-34]

Jesus said, "The kingdom of God is as if a man should
scatter seed upon the ground, and should sleep and rise
night and day, and the seed should sprout and grow, he
knows not how. The earth produces of itself, first the blade,
then the ear, then the full grain in the ear. But when the grain
is ripe, at once he puts in the sickle, because the harvest has
come." And he said, "With what can we compare the
kingdom of God, or what parable shall we use for it? It is
like a grain of mustard seed, which, when sown upon the
ground, is the smallest of all the seeds on earth; yet when it
is sown it grows up and becomes the greatest of all shrubs,
and puts forth large branches, so that the birds of the air can
make nests in its shade." With many such parables he spoke

the word to them, as they were able to hear it; he did not speak to them without a parable, but privately to his own disciples he explained everything.

Proper 7 *The Sunday Closest to June 22*

A Reading (Lesson) from the Book of Job [38:1-11, 16-18]

Then the Lord answered Job out of the whirlwind, "Who is this that darkens counsel by words without knowledge? Gird up your loins like a man, I will question you, and you shall declare to me. Where were you when I laid the foundation of the earth? Tell me, if you have understanding. Who determined its measurements — surely you know! Or who stretched the line upon it? On what were its bases sunk, or who laid its cornerstone, when the morning stars sang together, and all the sons of God shouted for joy? Or who shut in the sea with doors, when it burst forth from the womb; when I made clouds its garment, and thick darkness its swaddling band, and prescribed bounds for it, and set bars and doors, and said, 'Thus far shall you come, and no farther, and here shall your proud waves be stayed'? Have you entered into the springs of the sea, or walked in the recesses of the deep? Have the gates of death been revealed to you, or have you seen the gates of deep darkness? Have you comprehended the expanse of the earth? Declare, if you know all this."

Psalm 107:1-32 [page 746]   or
Psalm 107:1-3, 23-32 [page 746]

A Reading (Lesson) from the Second Letter of Paul to the Corinthians [5:14-21]

The love of Christ controls us, because we are convinced that one has died for all; therefore all have died. And he died for all, that those who live might live no longer for themselves, but for him who for their sake died and was raised. From now on, therefore, we regard no one from a human point of view; even though we once regarded Christ from a human point of view, we regard him thus no longer. Therefore, if any one is in Christ, he is a new creation; the old has passed away, behold, the new has come. All this is from God, who through Christ reconciled us to himself and gave us the ministry of reconciliation; that is, in Christ God was reconciling the world to himself, not counting their trespasses against them, and entrusting to us the message of reconciliation. So we are ambassadors for Christ, God making his appeal through us. We beseech you on behalf of Christ, be reconciled to God. For our sake he made him to be sin who knew no sin, so that in him we might become the righteousness of God.

✝ *The Holy Gospel of Our Lord Jesus Christ According to Mark* [4:35-41 (5:1-20)]

When evening had come, Jesus said to his disciples, "Let us go across to the other side." And leaving the crowd, they took him with them in the boat, just as he was. And other boats were with him. And a great storm of wind arose, and the waves beat into the boat, so that the boat was already filling. But he was in the stern, asleep on the cushion; and they woke him and said to him, "Teacher, do you not care if we perish?" And he awoke and rebuked the wind, and said to the sea, "Peace! Be still!" and the wind ceased, and there was a great calm. He said to them, "Why are you afraid? Have you no faith?" And they were filled with awe, and said to one another, "Who then is this, that even wind and sea obey him?"

They came to the other side of the sea, to the country of the Ger'asenes. And when he had come out of the boat, there met him out of the tombs a man with an unclean spirit, who lived among the tombs; and no one could bind him any more, even with a chain; for he had often been bound with fetters and chains, but the chains he wrenched apart, and the fetters he broke in pieces; and no one had the strength to subdue him. Night and day among the tombs and on the mountains he was always crying out, and bruising himself with stones. And when he saw Jesus from afar, he ran and worshiped him; and crying out with a loud voice, he said, "What have you to do with me, Jesus, Son of the Most High God? I adjure you by God, do not torment me." For he had said to him, "Come out of the man, you unclean spirit!" And Jesus asked him, "What is your name?" He replied, "My name is Legion; for we are many." And he begged him eagerly not to send them out of the country. Now a great herd of swine was feeding there on the hillside; and they begged him, "Send us to the swine, let us enter them." So he gave them leave. And the unclean spirits came out, and entered the swine; and the herd, numbering about two thousand, rushed down the steep bank into the sea, and were drowned in the sea. The herdsmen fled, and told it in the city and in the country. And people came to see what it was that had happened. And they came to Jesus, and saw the demoniac sitting there, clothed and in his right mind, the man who had had the legion; and they were afraid. And those who had seen it told what had happened to the demoniac and to the swine. And they began to beg Jesus to depart from their neighborhood. And as he was getting into the boat, the man who had been possessed with demons begged him that he might be with him. But he refused, and said to him, "Go home to your friends, and tell them how much the Lord has done for you, and how he has had mercy on you." And he went away and began to proclaim in the Decap'olis how much Jesus had done for him; and all men marveled.

Proper 8 *The Sunday Closest to June 29*

A Reading (Lesson) from the Book of Deuteronomy
[15:7-11]

Moses said to the people, "If there is among you a poor man, one of your brethren, in any of your towns within your land which the Lord your God gives you, you shall not harden your heart or shut your hand against your poor brother, but you shall open your hand to him, and lend him sufficient for his need, whatever it may be. Take heed lest there be a base thought in your heart, and you say, 'The seventh year, the year of release is near,' and your eye be hostile to your poor brother, and you give him nothing, and he cry to the Lord against you, and it be sin in you. You shall give to him freely, and your heart shall not be grudging when you give to him; because for this the Lord your God will bless you in all your work and in all that you undertake. For the poor will never cease out of the land; therefore I command you, You shall open wide your hand to your brother, to the needy and to the poor, in the land."

Psalm 112 [page 755]

A Reading (Lesson) from the Second Letter of Paul to the Corinthians [8:1-9, 13-15]

We want you to know, brethren, about the grace of God which has been shown in the churches of Macedo'nia, for in a severe test of affliction, their abundance of joy and their extreme poverty have overflowed in a wealth of liberality on their part. For they gave according to their means, as I can testify, and beyond their means, of their own free will, begging us earnestly for the favor of taking part in the relief of the saints — and this, not as we expected, but first they gave themselves to the Lord and to us by the will of God. Accordingly we have urged Titus that as he had already made a beginning, he should also complete among you this gracious work. Now as you excel in everything — in faith, in utterance, in knowledge, in all earnestness, and in your love for us — see that you excel in this gracious work also. I say this not as a command, but to prove by the earnestness of others that your love also is genuine. For you know the grace of our Lord Jesus Christ, that though he was rich, yet for your sake he became poor, so that by his poverty you might become rich. I do not mean that others should be eased and you burdened, but that as a matter of equality your abundance at the present time should supply their want, so that their abundance may supply your want, that there may be equality. As it is written, "He who gathered much had nothing over, and he who gathered little had no lack."

✝ *The Holy Gospel of Our Lord Jesus Christ
According to Mark* [5:22-24, 35b-43]

Then came one of the rulers of the synagogue, Ja'irus by name; and seeing Jesus, he fell at his feet, and besought him, saying, "My little daughter is at the point of death. Come and lay your hands on her, so that she may be made well, and live." And he went with him. And a great crowd followed him and thronged about him. There came from the ruler's house some who said, "Your daughter is dead. Why trouble the Teacher any further?" But ignoring what they said, Jesus said to the ruler of the synagogue, "Do not fear, only believe." And he allowed no one to follow him except Peter and James and John the brother of James. When they came to the house of the ruler of the synagogue, he saw a tumult, and people weeping and wailing loudly. And when he had entered, he said to them, "Why do you make a tumult and weep? The child is not dead but sleeping." And they laughed at him. But he put them all outside, and took the child's father and mother and those who were with him, and went in where the child was. Taking her by the hand he said to her, "Tal'itha cu'mi"; which means, "Little girl, I say to you, arise." And immediately the girl got up and walked (she was twelve years of age), and they were immediately overcome with amazement. And he strictly charged them that no one should know this, and told them to give her something to eat.

Proper 9   *The Sunday Closest to July 6*

A Reading (Lesson) from the Book of Ezekiel [2:1-7]

The Lord said to me, "Son of man, stand upon your feet, and I will speak with you." And when he spoke to me, the Spirit entered into me and set me upon my feet; and I heard him speaking to me. And he said to me, "Son of man, I send you to the people of Israel, to a nation of rebels, who have rebelled against me; they and their fathers have transgressed against me to this very day. The people also are impudent and stubborn; I send you to them; and you shall say to them, 'Thus says the Lord God.' And whether they hear or refuse to hear (for they are a rebellious house) they will know that there has been a prophet among them. And you, son of man, be not afraid of them, nor be afraid of their words, though briers and thorns are with you and you sit upon scorpions; be not afraid of their words, nor be dismayed at their looks for they are a rebellious house. And you shall speak my words to them, whether they hear or refuse to hear; for they are a rebellious house."

Psalm 123 [page 780]

A Reading (Lesson) from the Second Letter of Paul to the Corinthians [12:2-10]

I know a man in Christ who fourteen years ago was caught up to the third heaven — whether in the body or out of the body I do not know, God knows. And I know that this man was caught up into Paradise — whether in the body or out of the body I do not know, God knows — and he heard things that cannot be told, which man may not utter. On behalf of this man I will boast, but on my own behalf I will not boast, except of my weaknesses. Though if I wish to boast, I shall not be a fool, for I shall be speaking the truth. But I refrain from it, so that no one may think more of me than he sees in me or hears from me. And to keep me from being too elated by the abundance of revelations, a thorn was given me in the flesh, a messenger of Satan, to harass me, to keep me from being too elated. Three times I besought the Lord about this, that it should leave me; but he said to me, "My grace is sufficient for you, for my power is made perfect in weakness." I will all the more gladly boast of my weaknesses, that the power of Christ may rest upon me. For the sake of Christ, then, I am content with weaknesses, insults, hardships, persecutions, and calamities; for when I am weak, then I am strong.

✝ *The Holy Gospel of Our Lord Jesus Christ According to Mark* [6:1-6]

Jesus came to his own country; and his disciples followed him. And on the sabbath he began to teach in the synagogue; and many who heard him were astonished, saying, "Where did this man get all this? What is the wisdom given to him? What mighty works are wrought by his hands! Is not this the carpenter, the son of Mary and the brother of James and Joses and Judas and Simon, and are not his sisters here with us?" And they took offense at him. And Jesus said to them, "A prophet is not without honor, except in his own country, and among his own kin, and in his own house." And he could do no mighty work there, except that he laid his hands upon a few sick people and healed them. And he marveled because of their unbelief. And he went about among the villages teaching.

Proper 10   *The Sunday Closest to July 13*

A Reading (Lesson) from the Book of Amos [7:7-15]

Thus the Lord God showed me: behold, the Lord was standing beside a wall built with a plumb line, with a plumb line in his hand. And the Lord said to me, "Amos, what do you see?" And I said, "A plumb line." Then the Lord said, "Behold, I am setting a plumb line in the midst of my people Israel; I will never again pass by them; the high places of Isaac shall be made desolate, and the sanctuaries of Israel shall be laid waste, and I will rise against the house of Jerobo'am with the sword." Then Amazi'ah the priest of Bethel sent to Jerobo'am king of Israel, saying, "Amos has conspired against you in the midst of the house of Israel; the land is not able to bear all his words. For thus Amos has said, 'Jerobo'am shall die by the sword, and Israel must go into exile away from his land.' " And Amazi'ah said to Amos, "O seer, go, flee away to the land of Judah, and eat bread there, and prophesy there; but never again prophesy at Bethel, for it is the king's sanctuary, and it is a temple of the kingdom." Then Amos answered Amazi'ah, "I am no prophet, nor a prophet's son; but I am a herdsman, and a dresser of sycamore trees, and the Lord took me from following the flock, and the Lord said to me, 'Go, prophesy to my people Israel.' "

Psalm 85 [page 708]   or   *Psalm 85:7-13* [page 709]

A Reading (Lesson) from the Letter of Paul to the Ephesians [1:1-14]

Paul, an apostle of Christ Jesus by the will of God, to the saints who are also faithful in Christ Jesus: Grace to you and peace from God our Father and the Lord Jesus Christ. Blessed be the God and Father of our Lord Jesus Christ, who has blessed us in Christ with every spiritual blessing in the heavenly places, even as he chose us in him before the foundation of the world, that we should be holy and blameless before him. He destined us in love to be his sons through Jesus Christ, according to the purpose of his will, to the praise of his glorious grace which he freely bestowed on us in the Beloved. In him we have redemption through his blood, the forgiveness of our trespasses, according to the riches of his grace which he lavished upon us. For he has made known to us in all wisdom and insight the mystery of his will, according to his purpose which he set forth in Christ as a plan for the fullness of time, to unite all things in him, things in heaven and things on earth. In him, according to the purpose of him who accomplishes all things, according to the counsel of his will, we who first hoped in Christ have been destined and appointed to live for the praise of his glory. In him you also, who have heard the word of truth, the gospel of your salvation, and have believed in him, were sealed with the promised Holy Spirit, which is the guarantee of our inheritance until we acquire possession of it, to the praise of his glory.

✝ *The Holy Gospel of Our Lord Jesus Christ According to Mark* [6:7-13]

Jesus called to him the twelve, and began to send them out two by two, and gave them authority over the unclean spirits. He charged them to take nothing for their journey except a staff; no bread, no bag, no money in their belts; but to wear sandals and not put on two tunics. And he said to them, "Where you enter a house, stay there until you leave the place. And if any place will not receive you and they refuse to hear you, when you leave, shake off the dust that is on your feet for a testimony against them." So they went out and preached that men should repent. And they cast out many demons, and anointed with oil many that were sick and healed them.

Proper 11 *The Sunday Closest to July 20*

A Reading (Lesson) from the Book of Isaiah [57:14b-21]

"Build up, build up, prepare the way, remove every obstruction from my people's way." For thus says the high and lofty One who inhabits eternity, whose name is Holy: "I dwell in the high and holy place, and also with him who is of a contrite and humble spirit, to revive the spirit of the humble, and to revive the heart of the contrite. For I will not contend for ever, nor will I always be angry; for from me proceeds the spirit, and I have made the breath of life. Because of the iniquity of his covetousness I was angry, I smote him, I hid my face and was angry; but he went on backsliding in the way of his own heart. I have seen his ways, but I will heal him; I will lead him and requite him with comfort, creating for his mourners the fruit of the lips. Peace, peace, to the far and to the near, says the Lord; and I will heal him. But the wicked are like the tossing sea; for it cannot rest, and its waters toss up mire and dirt. There is no peace, says my God, for the wicked."

Psalm 22:22-30 [page 611]

A Reading (Lesson) from the Letter of Paul to the Ephesians [2:11-22]

Remember that at one time you Gentiles in the flesh, called the uncircumcision by what is called the circumcision, which is made in the flesh by hands — remember that you were at that time separated from Christ, alienated from the commonwealth of Israel, and strangers to the covenants of promise, having no hope and without God in the world. But now in Christ Jesus you who once were far off have been brought near in the blood of Christ. For he is our peace, who has made us both one, and has broken down the dividing wall of hostility, by abolishing in his flesh the law of commandments and ordinances, that he might create in himself one new man in place of the two, so making peace, and might reconcile us both to God in one body through the cross, thereby bringing the hostility to an end. And he came and preached peace to you who were far off and peace to those who were near; for through him we both have access in one Spirit to the Father. So then you are no longer strangers and sojourners, but you are fellow citizens with the saints and members of the household of God, built upon the foundation of the apostles and prophets, Christ Jesus himself being the cornerstone, in whom the whole structure is joined together and grows into a holy temple in the Lord; in whom you also are built into it for a dwelling place of God in the Spirit.

✝ *The Holy Gospel of Our Lord Jesus Christ According to Mark* [6:30-44]

The apostles returned to Jesus, and told him all that they had done and taught. And he said to them, "Come away by yourselves to a lonely place, and rest a while." For many were coming and going, and they had no leisure even to eat. And they went away in the boat to a lonely place by themselves. Now many saw them going, and knew them, and they ran there on foot from all the towns, and got there ahead of them. As he went ashore he saw a great throng, and he had compassion on them, because they were like sheep without a shepherd; and he began to teach them many things. And when it grew late, his disciples came to him and said, "This is a lonely place, and the hour is now late; send them away, to go into the country and villages round about and buy themselves something to eat." But he answered them, "You give them something to eat." And they said to him, "Shall we go and buy two hundred denarii worth of bread, and give it to them to eat?" And he said to them, "How many loaves have you? Go and see." And when they had found out, they said, "Five, and two fish." Then he commanded them all to sit down by companies upon the green grass. So they sat down in groups, by hundreds and by fifties. And taking the five loaves and the two fish he looked up to heaven, and blessed, and broke the loaves, and gave them to the disciples to set before the people; and he divided the two fish among them all. And they all ate and were satisfied. And they took up twelve baskets full of broken pieces and of the fish. And those who ate the loaves were five thousand men.

Proper 12 *The Sunday Closest to July 27*

A Reading (Lesson) from the Second Book of the Kings
[2:1-15]

Now when the Lord was about to take Eli'jah up to heaven by a whirlwind, Eli'jah and Eli'sha were on their way from Gilgal. And Eli'jah said to Eli'sha, "Tarry here, I pray you; for the Lord has sent me as far as Bethel." But Eli'sha said, "As the Lord lives, and as you yourself live, I will not leave you." So they went down to Bethel. And the sons of the prophets who were in Bethel came out to Eli'sha, and said to him, "Do you know that today the Lord will take away your master from over you?" And he said, "Yes, I know it; hold your peace." Eli'jah said to him, "Eli'sha, tarry here, I pray you; for the Lord has sent me to Jericho." But he said, "As the Lord lives, and as you yourself live, I will not leave you." So they came to Jericho. The sons of the prophets who were at Jericho drew near to Eli'sha, and said to him, "Do you know that today the Lord will take away your master from over you?" And he answered, "Yes, I know it; hold your peace." Then Eli'jah said to him, "Tarry here, I pray you; for the Lord has sent me to the Jordan." But he said, "As the Lord lives, and as you yourself live, I will not leave you." So the two of them went on. Fifty men of the sons of the prophets also went, and stood at some distance from them, as they both were standing by the Jordan. Then Eli'jah took his mantle, and rolled it up, and struck the water, and the water was parted to the one side and to the other, till the two of them could go over on dry ground. When they had crossed, Eli'jah said to Eli'sha, "Ask what I shall do for you, before I am taken from you." And Eli'sha said, "I pray you, let me inherit a double share of your spirit." And he said, "You have asked a hard thing; yet, if you see me as I am being taken from you, it shall be so for you; but if you do not see me, it shall not be so." And as they still went on and talked, behold, a chariot of fire and horses of fire separated the two of them. And Eli'jah went up by a whirlwind into heaven. And Eli'sha saw it and he cried, "My father, my father! the chariots of Israel and its horsemen!" And he saw him no more. Then he took hold of his own clothes and rent them in two pieces. And he took up the mantle of Eli'jah that had fallen from him, and went back and stood on the bank of the Jordan. Then he took the mantle of Eli'jah that had fallen from him, and struck the water, saying, "Where is the Lord, the God of Eli'jah?" And when he had struck the water, the water was parted to the one side and to the other; and Eli'sha went over. Now when the sons of the prophets who were at Jericho saw him over against them, they said, "The spirit of Eli'jah rests on Eli'sha." And they came to meet him, and bowed to the ground before him.

Psalm 114 [page 756]

A Reading (Lesson) from the Letter of Paul to the Ephesians [4:1-7, 11-16]

I, Paul, a prisoner for the Lord, beg you to lead a life worthy of the calling to which you have been called, with all lowliness and meekness, with patience, forbearing one another in love, eager to maintain the unity of the Spirit in the bond of peace. There is one body and one Spirit, just as you were called to the one hope that belongs to your call, one Lord, one faith, one baptism, one God and Father of us all, who is above all and through all and in all. But grace was given to each of us according to the measure of Christ's gift. And his gifts were that some should be apostles, some prophets, some evangelists, some pastors and teachers, to equip the saints for the work of ministry, for building up the body of Christ, until we all attain to the unity of the faith and of the knowledge of the Son of God, to mature manhood, to the measure of the stature of the fullness of Christ; so that we may no longer be children, tossed to and fro and carried about with every wind of doctrine, by the cunning of men, by their craftiness in deceitful wiles. Rather, speaking the truth in love, we are to grow up in every way into him who is the head, into Christ, from whom the whole body, joined and knit together by every joint with which it is supplied, when each part is working properly, makes bodily growth and upbuilds itself in love.

✠ *The Holy Gospel of Our Lord Jesus Christ*
According to Mark [6:45-52]

Immediately after the feeding of the five thousand, Jesus made his disciples get into the boat and go before him to the other side, to Beth-sa'ida, while he dismissed the crowd. And after he had taken leave of them, he went up on the mountain to pray. And when evening came, the boat was out on the sea, and he was alone on the land. And he saw that they were making headway painfully, for the wind was against them. And about the fourth watch of the night he came to them, walking on the sea. He meant to pass by them, but when they saw him walking on the sea they thought it was a ghost, and cried out; for they all saw him, and were terrified. But immediately he spoke to them and said, "Take heart, it is I; have no fear." And he got into the boat with them and the wind ceased. And they were utterly astounded, for they did not understand about the loaves, but their hearts were hardened.

A Reading (Lesson) from the Book of Exodus [16:2-4, 9-15]

And the whole congregation of the people of Israel murmured against Moses and Aaron in the wilderness, and said to them, "Would that we had died by the hand of the Lord in the land of Egypt, when we sat by the fleshpots and ate bread to the full; for you have brought us out into the wilderness to kill this whole assembly with hunger." Then the Lord said to Moses, "Behold, I will rain bread from heaven for you; and the people shall go out and gather a day's portion every day, that I may prove them, whether they will walk in my law or not. And Moses said to Aaron, "Say to the whole congregation of the people of Israel, 'Come near before the Lord, for he has heard your murmurings.'" And as Aaron spoke to the whole congregation of the people of Israel, they looked toward the wilderness, and behold, the glory of the Lord appeared in the cloud. And the Lord said to Moses, "I have heard the murmurings of the people of Israel; say to them, 'At twilight you shall eat flesh, and in the morning you shall be filled with bread; then you shall know that I am the Lord your God.'" In the evening quails came up and covered the camp; and in the morning dew lay round about the camp. And when the dew had gone up, there was on the face of the wilderness a fine, flake-like thing, fine as hoarfrost on the ground. When the people of Israel saw it, they said to one another, "What is it?" For they did not know what it was. And Moses said to them, "It is the bread which the Lord has given you to eat."

Psalm 78:1-25 [page 694]   or

Psalm 78:14-20, 23-25 [page 696]

A Reading (Lesson) from the Letter of Paul to the Ephesians
[4:17-25]

Now this I affirm and testify in the Lord, that you must no longer live as the Gentiles do, in the futility of their minds; they are darkened in their understanding, alienated from the life of God because of the ignorance that is in them, due to their hardness of heart; they have become callous and have given themselves up to licentiousness, greedy to practice every kind of uncleanness. You did not so learn Christ! — assuming that you have heard about him and were taught in him, as the truth is in Jesus. Put off your old nature which belongs to your former manner of life and is corrupt through deceitful lusts, and be renewed in the spirit of your minds, and put on the new nature, created after the likeness of God in true righteousness and holiness. Therefore, putting away falsehood, let every one speak the truth with his neighbor, for we are members one of another.

✝ *The Holy Gospel of Our Lord Jesus Christ*
According to John [6:24-35]

On the next day, when the people who remained after the feeding of the five thousand saw that Jesus was not there, nor his disciples, they themselves got into the boats and went to Caper'na-um, seeking Jesus. When they found him on the other side of the sea, they said to him, "Rabbi, when did you come here?" Jesus answered them, "Truly, truly, I say to you, you seek me, not because you saw signs, but because you ate your fill of the loaves. Do not labor for the food which perishes, but for the food which endures to eternal life, which the Son of man will give to you; for on him has God the Father set his seal." Then they said to him, "What must we do, to be doing the works of God?" Jesus answered them, "This is the work of God, that you believe in him whom he has sent." So they said to him, "Then what sign do you do, that we may see, and believe you? What work do you perform? Our fathers ate the manna in the wilderness; as it is written, 'He gave them bread from heaven to eat.'" Jesus then said to them, "Truly, truly, I say to you, it was not Moses who gave you the bread from heaven; my Father gives you the true bread from heaven. For the bread of God is that which comes down from heaven, and gives life to the world." They said to him, "Lord, give us this bread always." Jesus said to them, "I am the bread of life; he who comes to me shall not hunger, and he who believes in me shall never thirst."

Proper 14 *The Sunday Closest to August 10*

A Reading (Lesson) from the Book of Deuteronomy [8:1-10]

Moses said to the people, "All the commandments which I command you this day you shall be careful to do, that you may live and multiply, and go in and possess the land which the Lord swore to give to your fathers. And you shall remember all the way which the Lord your God has led you these forty years in the wilderness, that he might humble you, testing you to know what was in your heart, whether you would keep his commandments, or not. And he humbled you and let you hunger and fed you with manna, which you did not know, nor did your fathers know; that he might make you know that man does not live by bread alone, but that man lives by everything that proceeds out of the mouth of the Lord. Your clothing did not wear out upon you, and your foot did not swell, these forty years. Know then in your heart that, as a man disciplines his son, the Lord your God disciplines you. So you shall keep the commandments of the Lord your God, by walking in his ways and by fearing him. For the Lord your God is bringing you into a good land, a land of brooks of water, of fountains and springs, flowing forth in valleys and hills, a land of wheat and barley, of vines and fig trees and pomegranates, a land of olive trees and honey, a land in which you will eat bread without scarcity, in which you will lack nothing, a land whose stones are iron, and out of whose hills you can dig copper. And you shall eat and be full, and you shall bless the Lord your God for the good land he has given you."

Psalm 34 [page 627]   or   *Psalm 34:1-8* [page 627]

A Reading (Lesson) from the Letter of Paul to the Ephesians
[4:(25-29)30—5:2]

> Putting away falsehood, let everyone speak the truth with his neighbor, for we are members one of another. Be angry but do not sin; do not let the sun go down on your anger, and give no opportunity to the devil. Let the thief no longer steal, but rather let him labor, doing honest work with his hands, so that he may be able to give to those in need. Let no evil talk come out of your mouths, but only such as is good for edifying, as fits the occasion, that it may impart grace to those who hear.

Do not grieve the Holy Spirit of God, in whom you were sealed for the day of redemption. Let all bitterness and wrath and anger and clamor and slander be put away from you, with all malice, and be kind to one another, tenderhearted, forgiving one another, as God in Christ forgave you. Therefore be imitators of God, as beloved children. And walk in love, as Christ loved us and gave himself up for us, a fragrant offering and sacrifice to God.

✝ *The Holy Gospel of Our Lord Jesus Christ*
According to John [6:37-51]

Jesus said to the people, "All that the Father gives me will come to me; and him who comes to me I will not cast out. For I have come down from heaven, not to do my own will, but the will of him who sent me; and this is the will of him who sent me, that I should lose nothing of all that he has given me, but raise it up at the last day. For this is the will of my Father, that every one who sees the Son and believes in him should have eternal life; and I will raise him up at the last day." The Jews then murmured at him, because he said, "I am the bread which came down from heaven." They said, "Is not this Jesus, the son of Joseph, whose father and mother we know? How does he now say, 'I have come down from heaven'?" Jesus answered them, "Do not murmur among yourselves. No one can come to me unless the Father who sent me draws him; and I will raise him up at the last day. It is written in the prophets, 'And they shall all be taught by God.' Every one who has heard and learned from the Father comes to me. Not that any one has seen the Father except him who is from God; he has seen the Father. Truly, truly, I say to you, he who believes has eternal life. I am the bread of life. Your fathers ate the manna in the wilderness, and they died. This is the bread which comes down from heaven, that a man may eat of it and not die. I am the living bread which came down from heaven; if any one eats of this bread, he will live for ever; and the bread which I shall give for the life of the world is my flesh."

Proper 15 *The Sunday Closest to August 17*

A Reading (Lesson) from the Book of Proverbs [9:1-6]

Wisdom has built her house, she has set up her seven pillars. She has slaughtered her beasts, she has mixed her wine, she has also set her table. She has sent out her maids to call from the highest places in the town, "Whoever is simple let him turn in here!" To him who is without sense she says, "Come, eat of my bread and drink of the wine I have mixed. Leave simpleness, and live, and walk in the way of insight."

Psalm 147 [page 804]   or   *Psalm 34:9-14* [page 628]

A Reading (Lesson) from the Letter of Paul to the Ephesians [5:15-20]

Look carefully how you walk, not as unwise men but as wise, making the most of the time, because the days are evil.

Therefore do not be foolish, but understand what the will of the Lord is. And do not get drunk with wine, for that is debauchery; but be filled with the Spirit, addressing one another in psalms and hymns and spiritual songs, singing and making melody to the Lord with all your heart, always and for everything giving thanks in the name of our Lord Jesus Christ to God the Father.

✝ *The Holy Gospel of Our Lord Jesus Christ According to John* [6:53-59]

Jesus said, "Truly, truly, I say to you, unless you eat the flesh of the Son of man and drink his blood, you have no life in you; he who eats my flesh and drinks my blood has eternal life, and I will raise him up at the last day. For my flesh is food indeed, and my blood is drink indeed. He who eats my flesh and drinks my blood abides in me, and I in him. As the living Father sent me, and I live because of the Father, so he who eats me will live because of me. This is the bread which came down from heaven, not such as the fathers ate and died; he who eats this bread will live for ever." This he said in the synagogue, as he taught at Caper′na-um.

Proper 16   *The Sunday Closest to August 24*

A Reading (Lesson) from the Book of Joshua [24:1-2a, 14-25]

Joshua gathered all the tribes of Israel to Shechem, and summoned the elders, the heads, the judges, and the officers of Israel; and they presented themselves before God. And Joshua said to all the people, "Thus says the Lord, the God of Israel, 'Fear the Lord, and serve him in sincerity and in faithfulness; put away the gods which your fathers served beyond the River, and in Egypt, and serve the Lord. And if you be unwilling to serve the Lord, choose this day whom you will serve, whether the gods your fathers served in the region beyond the River, or the gods of the Amorites in whose land you dwell.' But as for me and my house, we will serve the Lord." Then the people answered, "Far be it from us that we should forsake the Lord, to serve other gods; for it is the Lord our God who brought us and our fathers up from the land of Egypt, out of the house of bondage, and who did those great signs in our sight, and preserved us in all the way that we went, and among all the peoples through whom we passed; and the Lord drove out before us all the peoples, the Amorites who lived in the land; therefore we also will serve the Lord, for he is our God." But Joshua said to the people, "You cannot serve the Lord; for he is a holy God; he is a jealous God; he will not forgive your transgressions or your sins. If you forsake the Lord and serve foreign gods, then he will turn and do you harm, and consume you, after having done you good." And the people said to Joshua, "Nay; but we will serve the Lord." Then Joshua said to the people, "You are witnesses against yourselves that you have chosen the Lord, to serve him." And they said, "We are witnesses." He said, "Then put away the foreign gods which are among you, and incline your heart to the Lord, the God of Israel." And the people said to Joshua, "The Lord our God we will serve, and his voice we will obey." So Joshua made a covenant with the people that day, and made statutes and ordinances for them at Shechem.

Psalm 16 [page 599]   or   *Psalm 34:15-22* [page 628]

A Reading (Lesson) from the Letter of Paul to the Ephesians
[5:21-33]

Be subject to one another out of reverence for Christ. Wives, be subject to your husbands, as to the Lord. For the husband is the head of the wife as Christ is the head of the church, his body, and is himself its Savior. As the church is subject to Christ, so let wives also be subject in everything to their husbands. Husbands, love your wives, as Christ loved the church and gave himself up for her, that he might sanctify her, having cleansed her by the washing of water with the word, that he might present the church to himself in splendor, without spot or wrinkle or any such thing, that she might be holy and without blemish. Even so husbands should love their wives as their own bodies. He who loves his wife loves himself. For no man ever hates his own flesh, but nourishes and cherishes it, as Christ does the church, because we are members of his body. "For this reason a man shall leave his father and mother and be joined to his wife, and the two shall become one flesh." This mystery is a profound one, and I am saying that it refers to Christ and the church; however, let each one of you love his wife as himself, and let the wife see that she respects her husband.

✝ *The Holy Gospel of Our Lord Jesus Christ According to John* [6:60-69]

Jesus said, "I am the living bread which came down from heaven . . . he who eats this bread will live for ever." Many of his disciples, when they heard it, said, "This is a hard saying; who can listen to it?" But Jesus, knowing in himself that his disciples murmured at it, said to them, "Do you take offense at this? Then what if you were to see the Son of man ascending where he was before? It is the spirit that gives life, the flesh is of no avail; the words that I have spoken to you are spirit and life. But there are some of you that do not believe." For Jesus knew from the first who those were that did not believe, and who it was that would betray him. And he said, "This is why I told you that no one can come to me unless it is granted him by the Father." After this many of his disciples drew back and no longer went about with him. Jesus said to the twelve, "Do you also wish to go away?" Simon Peter answered him, "Lord, to whom shall we go? You have the words of eternal life; and we have believed, and have come to know, that you are the Holy One of God."

A Reading (Lesson) from the Book of Deuteronomy [4:1-9]

Moses said, "And now, O Israel, give heed to the statutes and the ordinances which I teach you, and do them; that you may live, and go in and take possession of the land which the Lord, the God of your fathers, gives you. You shall not add to the word which I command you, nor take from it; that you may keep the commandments of the Lord your God which I command you. Your eyes have seen what the Lord did at Ba'al-pe'or; for the Lord your God destroyed from among you all the men who followed the Ba'al of Pe'or; but you who held fast to the Lord your God are all alive this day. Behold, I have taught you statutes and ordinances, as the Lord my God commanded me, that you should do them in the land which you are entering to take possession of it. Keep them and do them; for that will be your wisdom and your understanding in the sight of the peoples, who, when they hear all these statutes, will say, 'Surely this great nation is a wise and understanding people.' For what great nation is there that has a god so near to it as the Lord our God is to us, whenever we call upon him? And what great nation is there, that has statutes and ordinances so righteous as all this law which I set before you this day? Only take heed, and keep your soul diligently, lest you forget the things which your eyes have seen, and lest they depart from your heart all the days of your life; make them known to your children and your children's children."

Psalm 15 [page 599]

A Reading (Lesson) from the Letter of Paul to the Ephesians
[6:10-20]

Be strong in the Lord and in the strength of his might. Put on the whole armor of God, that you may be able to stand against the wiles of the devil. For we are not contending against flesh and blood, but against the principalities, against the powers, against the world rulers of this present darkness, against the spiritual hosts of wickedness in the heavenly places. Therefore take the whole armor of God, that you may be able to withstand in the evil day, and having done all, to stand. Stand therefore, having girded your loins with truth, and having put on the breastplate of righteousness, and having shod your feet with the equipment of the gospel of peace; besides all these, taking the shield of faith, with which you can quench all the flaming darts of the evil one. And take the helmet of salvation, and the sword of the Spirit, which is the word of God. Pray at all times in the Spirit, with all prayer and supplication. To that end keep alert with all perseverance, making supplication for all the saints, and also for me, that utterance may be given me in opening my mouth boldly to proclaim the mystery of the gospel, for which I am an ambassador in chains; that I may declare it boldly, as I ought to speak.

✝ *The Holy Gospel of Our Lord Jesus Christ
According to Mark* [7:1-8, 14-15, 21-23]

Now when the Pharisees gathered together to Jesus with some of the scribes, who had come from Jerusalem, they saw that some of his disciples ate with hands defiled, that is, unwashed. (For the Pharisees, and all the Jews, do not eat unless they wash their hands, observing the tradition of the elders; and when they come from the market place, they do not eat unless they purify themselves; and there are many other traditions which they observe, the washing of cups and pots and vessels of bronze.) And the Pharisees and the scribes asked him, "Why do your disciples not live according to the tradition of the elders, but eat with hands defiled?" And he said to them, "Well did Isaiah prophesy of you hypocrites, as it is written, 'This people honors me with their lips, but their heart is far from me; in vain do they worship me, teaching as doctrines the precepts of men.' You leave the

commandment of God, and hold fast the tradition of men."
And he called the people to him again, and said to them,
"Hear me, all of you, and understand: there is nothing
outside a man which by going into him can defile him; but
the things which come out of a man are what defile him. For
from within, out of the heart of man, come evil thoughts,
fornication, theft, murder, adultery, coveting, wickedness,
deceit, licentiousness, envy, slander, pride, foolishness. All
these evil things come from within, and they defile a man."

Proper 18 *The Sunday Closest to September 7*

A Reading (Lesson) from the Book of Isaiah [35:4-7a]

Say to those who are of a fearful heart, "Be strong, fear not!
Behold, your God will come with vengeance, with the
recompense of God. He will come and save you." Then the
eyes of the blind shall be opened, and the ears of the deaf
unstopped; then shall the lame man leap like a hart, and the
tongue of the dumb sing for joy. For waters shall break forth
in the wilderness, and streams in the desert; the burning
sand shall become a pool, and the thirsty ground springs of
water.

Psalm 146 [page 803]   or   *Psalm 146:4-9* [page 803]

A Reading (Lesson) from the Letter of James [1:17-27]

Every good endowment and every perfect gift is from above,
coming down from the Father of lights with whom there is
no variation or shadow due to change. Of his own will he
brought us forth by the word of truth that we should be a
kind of first fruits of his creatures. Know this, my beloved
brethren. Let every man be quick to hear, slow to speak,
slow to anger, for the anger of man does not work the
righteousness of God. Therefore put away all filthiness and
rank growth of wickedness and receive with meekness the
implanted word, which is able to save your souls. But be

doers of the word, and not hearers only, deceiving yourselves. For if any one is a hearer of the word and not a doer, he is like a man who observes his natural face in a mirror; for he observes himself and goes away and at once forgets what he was like. But he who looks into the perfect law, the law of liberty, and perseveres, being no hearer that forgets but a doer that acts, he shall be blessed in his doing. If any one thinks he is religious, and does not bridle his tongue but deceives his heart, this man's religion is vain. Religion that is pure and undefiled before God and the Father is this: to visit orphans and widows in their affliction, and to keep oneself unstained from the world.

✝ **The Holy Gospel of Our Lord Jesus Christ**
According to Mark [7:31-37]

Jesus returned from the region of Tyre, and went through Sidon to the Sea of Galilee, through the region of the Decap'olis. And they brought to him a man who was deaf and had an impediment in his speech; and they besought him to lay his hand upon him. And taking him aside from the multitude privately, he put his fingers into his ears, and he spat and touched his tongue; and looking up to heaven he sighed, and said to him, "Eph'phatha," that is, "Be opened." And his ears were opened, his tongue was released, and he spoke plainly. And he charged them to tell no one; but the more he charged them, the more zealously they proclaimed it. And they were astonished beyond measure, saying, "He has done all things well; he even makes the deaf hear and the dumb speak."

Proper 19 *The Sunday Closest to September 14*

A Reading (Lesson) from the Book of Isaiah [50:4-9]

The Lord God has given me the tongue of those who are taught, that I may know how to sustain with a word him that is weary. Morning by morning he wakens, he wakens my ear to hear as those who are taught. The Lord God has opened my ear, and I was not rebellious, I turned not backward. I gave my back to the smiters, and my cheeks to those who pulled out the beard; I hid not my face from shame and spitting. For the Lord God helps me; therefore I have not been confounded; therefore I have set my face like a flint, and I know that I shall not be put to shame; he who vindicates me is near. Who will contend with me? Let us stand up together. Who is my adversary? Let him come near to me. Behold, the Lord God helps me; who will declare me guilty? Behold, all of them will wear out like a garment; the moth will eat them up.

Psalm 116 [page 759]   or   *Psalm 116:1-8* [page 759]

A Reading (Lesson) from the Letter of James
[2:1-5, 8-10, 14-18]

My brethren, show no partiality as you hold the faith of our Lord Jesus Christ, the Lord of glory. For if a man with gold rings and in fine clothing comes into your assembly, and a poor man in shabby clothing also comes in, and you pay attention to the one who wears the fine clothing and say, "Have a seat here, please," while you say to the poor man, "Stand there," or, "Sit at my feet," have you not made distinctions among yourselves, and become judges with evil thoughts? Listen, my beloved brethren. Has not God chosen those who are poor in the world to be rich in faith and heirs of the kingdom which he has promised to those who love him? If you really fulfill the royal law, according to the scripture, "You shall love your neighbor as yourself," you do well. But if you show partiality, you commit sin, and are convicted by the law as transgressors. For whoever keeps the whole law but fails in one point has become guilty of all of it. What does it profit, my brethren, if a man says he has faith but has not works? Can his faith save him? If a brother or sister is ill-clad and in lack of daily food, and one of you says to them, "Go in peace, be warmed and filled," without giving them the things needed for the body, what does it profit? So faith by itself, if it has no works, is dead. But some one will say, "You have faith and I have works." Show me your faith apart from your works, and I by my works will show you my faith.

✠ *The Holy Gospel of Our Lord Jesus Christ According to Mark* [8:27-38]

Jesus went on with his disciples, to the villages of Caesare'a Philippi; and on the way he asked his disciples, "Who do men say that I am?" And they told him, "John the Baptist; and others say, Eli'jah; and others one of the prophets." And he asked them, "But who do you say that I am?" Peter answered him, "You are the Christ." And he charged them to tell no one about him. And he began to teach them that the Son of man must suffer many things, and be rejected by the elders and the chief priests and the scribes, and be killed, and after three days rise again. And he said this plainly. And Peter took him, and began to rebuke him. But turning and seeing his disciples, he rebuked Peter, and said, "Get behind me, Satan! For you are not on the side of God, but of men." And he called to him the multitude with his disciples, and said to them, "If any man would come after me, let him deny himself and take up his cross and follow me. For whoever would save his life will lose it; and whoever loses his life for my sake and the gospel's will save it. For what does it profit a man, to gain the whole world and forfeit his life? For what can a man give in return for his life? For whoever is ashamed of me and of my words in this adulterous and sinful generation, of him will the Son of man also be ashamed, when he comes in the glory of his Father with the holy angels."

or the following

✝ *The Holy Gospel of Our Lord Jesus Christ*
According to Mark [9:14-29]

When Jesus with Peter and James and John came to the disciples, they saw a great crowd about them, and scribes arguing with them. And immediately all the crowd, when they saw him, were greatly amazed, and ran up to him and greeted him. And he asked them, "What are you discussing with them?" And one of the crowd answered him, "Teacher, I brought my son to you, for he has a dumb spirit; and wherever it seizes him, it dashes him down; and he foams and grinds his teeth and becomes rigid; and I asked your disciples to cast it out, and they were not able." And he answered them, "O faithless generation, how long am I to be with you? How long am I to bear with you? Bring him to me." And they brought the boy to him; and when the spirit saw him, immediately it convulsed the boy, and he fell on the ground and rolled about, foaming at the mouth. And Jesus asked his father, "How long has he had this?" And he said, "From childhood. And it has often cast him into the fire and into the water, to destroy him; but if you can do anything, have pity on us and help us." And Jesus said to him, "If you can! All things are possible to him who believes." Immediately the father of the child cried out and said, "I believe; help my unbelief!" And when Jesus saw that a crowd came running together, he rebuked the unclean spirit, saying to it, "You dumb and deaf spirit, I command you, come out of him, and never enter him again." And after crying out and convulsing him terribly, it came out, and the boy was like a corpse; so that most of them said, "He is dead." But Jesus took him by the hand and lifted him up, and he arose. And when he had entered the house, his disciples asked him privately, "Why could we not cast it out?" And he said to them, "This kind cannot be driven out by anything but prayer."

A Reading (Lesson) from the Book of Wisdom
[1:16—2:1 (6-11)12-22]

The ungodly by their words and deeds summoned death;
considering him a friend, they pined away, and they made
a covenant with him, because they are fit to belong to his
party. For they reasoned unsoundly, saying to themselves,
"Short and sorrowful is our life, and there is no remedy
when a man comes to his end, and no one has been known
to return from Hades.

> "Come, therefore, let us enjoy the good things that exist,
> and make use of the creation to the full as in youth. Let
> us take our fill of costly wine and perfumes, and let no
> flower of spring pass by us. Let us crown ourselves with
> rosebuds before they wither. Let none of us fail to share in
> our revelry, everywhere let us leave signs of enjoyment,
> because this is our portion, and this our lot. Let us
> oppress the righteous poor man; let us not spare the
> widow nor regard the grey hairs of the aged. But let our
> might be our law of right, for what is weak proves itself
> to be useless.

"Let us lie in wait for the righteous man, because he is
inconvenient to us and opposes our actions; he reproaches
us for sins against the law, and accuses us of sins against our
training. He professes to have knowledge of God, and calls
himself a child of the Lord. He became to us a reproof of our
thoughts; the very sight of him is a burden to us, because his
manner of life is unlike that of others, and his ways are
strange. We are considered by him as something base, and
he avoids our ways as unclean; he calls the last end of the
righteous happy, and boasts that God is his father. Let us see
if his words are true, and let us test what will happen at the
end of his life; for if the righteous man is God's son, he will
help him, and will deliver him from the hand of his

adversaries. Let us test him with insult and torture, that we may find out how gentle he is, and make trial of his forbearance. Let us condemn him to a shameful death, for, according to what he says, he will be protected." Thus they reasoned, but they were led astray, for their wickedness blinded them, and they did not know the secret purposes of God, nor hope for the wages of holiness, nor discern the prize for blameless souls.

Psalm 54 [page 659]

A Reading (Lesson) from the Letter of James [3:16—4:6]

Where jealousy and selfish ambition exist, there will be disorder and every vile practice. But the wisdom from above is first pure, then peaceable, gentle, open to reason, full of mercy and good fruits, without uncertainty or insincerity. And the harvest of righteousness is sown in peace by those who make peace. What causes wars, and what causes fightings among you? Is it not your passions that are at war in your members? You desire and do not have; so you kill. And you covet and cannot obtain; so you fight and wage war. You do not have, because you do not ask. You ask and do not receive, because you ask wrongly, to spend it on your passions. Unfaithful creatures! Do you not know that friendship with the world is enmity with God? Therefore whoever wishes to be a friend of the world makes himself an enemy of God. Or do you suppose it is in vain that the scripture says, "He yearns jealously over the spirit which he has made to dwell in us"? But he gives more grace; therefore it says, "God opposes the proud, but gives grace to the humble."

✝ *The Holy Gospel of Our Lord Jesus Christ According to Mark* [9:30-37]

Jesus and his disciples went on and passed through Galilee. And Jesus would not have any one know it; for he was teaching his disciples, saying to them, "The Son of man will be delivered into the hands of men, and they will kill him; and when he is killed, after three days he will rise." But they did not understand the saying, and they were afraid to ask him. And they came to Caper'na-um; and when he was in the house he asked them, "What were you discussing on the way?" But they were silent; for on the way they had discussed with one another who was the greatest. And he sat down and called the twelve; and he said to them, "If any one would be first, he must be last of all and servant of all." And he took a child, and put him in the midst of them; and taking him in his arms, he said to them, "Whoever receives one such child in my name receives me; and whoever receives me, receives not me but him who sent me."

Proper 21   *The Sunday Closest to September 28*

A Reading (Lesson) from the Book of Numbers
[11:4-6, 10-16, 24-29]

Now the rabble that was among the people had a strong craving; and the people of Israel also wept again, and said, "O that we had meat to eat! We remember the fish we ate in Egypt for nothing, the cucumbers, the melons, the leeks, the onions, and the garlic; but now our strength is dried up, and there is nothing at all but this manna to look at." Moses heard the people weeping throughout their families, every man at the door of his tent; and the anger of the Lord blazed hotly, and Moses was displeased. Moses said to the Lord, "Why hast thou dealt ill with thy servant? And why have I not found favor in thy sight, that thou dost lay the burden of all this people upon me? Did I conceive all this people? Did I bring them forth, that thou shouldst say to me, 'Carry them in your bosom, as a nurse carries the sucking child, to the land which thou didst swear to give their fathers?' Where am I to get meat to give to all this people? For they weep before me and say, 'Give us meat, that we may eat.' I am not able to carry all this people alone, the burden is too heavy for me. If thou wilt deal thus with me, kill me at once, if I find favor in thy sight, that I may not see my wretchedness." And the Lord said to Moses, "Gather for me seventy men of the elders of Israel, whom you know to be the elders of the people and officers over them; and bring them to the tent of meeting, and let them take their stand there with you." So Moses went out and told the people the words of the Lord; and he gathered seventy men of the elders of the people, and placed them round about the tent. Then the Lord came down in the cloud and spoke to him, and took some of the spirit that was upon him and put it upon the seventy elders; and when the spirit rested upon them, they prophesied. But they did so no more. Now two men remained in the camp, one named Eldad, and the other named Medad, and the spirit rested upon them; they were among those registered, but they had not gone out to the tent, and so they prophesied in the camp. And a young man ran and told Moses, "Eldad and Medad are prophesying in the camp." And Joshua the son of Nun, the minister of Moses, one of his chosen men, said, "My lord Moses, forbid them." But Moses said to him, "Are you jealous for my sake? Would that all the Lord's people were prophets, that the Lord would put his spirit upon them!"

Psalm 19 [page 606]   or   *Psalm 19:7-14* [page 607]

A Reading (Lesson) from the Letter of James
[4:7-12 (13 — 5:6)]

Submit yourselves to God. Resist the devil and he will flee from you. Draw near to God and he will draw near to you. Cleanse your hands, you sinners, and purify your hearts, you men of double mind. Be wretched and mourn and weep. Let your laughter be turned to mourning and your joy to dejection. Humble yourselves before the Lord and he will exalt you. Do not speak evil against one another, brethren.

He that speaks evil against a brother or judges his brother, speaks evil against the law and judges the law. But if you judge the law, you are not a doer of the law but a judge. There is one lawgiver and judge, he who is able to save and to destroy. But who are you that you judge your neighbor?

Come now, you who say, "Today or tomorrow we will go into such and such a town and spend a year there and trade and get gain"; whereas you do not know about tomorrow. What is your life? For you are a mist that appears for a little time and then vanishes. Instead you ought to say, "If the Lord wills, we shall live and we shall do this or that." As it is, you boast in your arrogance. All such boasting is evil. Whoever knows what is right to do and fails to do it, for him it is sin. Come now, you rich, weep and howl for the miseries that are coming upon you. Your riches have rotted and your garments are motheaten. Your gold and silver have rusted, and their rust will be evidence against you and will eat your flesh like fire. You have laid up treasure for the last days. Behold, the wages of the laborers who mowed your fields, which you kept back by fraud, cry out; and the cries of the harvesters have reached the ears of the Lord of hosts. You have lived on the earth in luxury and in pleasure; you have fattened your hearts in a day of slaughter. You have condemned, you have killed the righteous man; he does not resist you.

✝ *The Holy Gospel of Our Lord Jesus Christ According to Mark* [9:38-43, 45, 47-48]

John said to Jesus, "Teacher, we saw a man casting out demons in your name, and we forbade him, because he was not following us." But Jesus said, "Do not forbid him; for no one who does a mighty work in my name will be able soon after to speak evil of me. For he that is not against us is for us. For truly, I say to you, whoever gives you a cup of water to drink because you bear the name of Christ, will by no means lose his reward. Whoever causes one of these little ones who believe in me to sin, it would be better for him if a great millstone were hung round his neck and he were thrown into the sea. And if your hand causes you to sin, cut it off; it is better for you to enter life maimed than with two hands to go to hell, to the unquenchable fire. And if your foot causes you to sin, cut it off; it is better for you to enter life lame than with two feet to be thrown into hell. And if your eye causes you to sin, pluck it out; it is better for you to enter the kingdom of God with one eye than with two eyes to be thrown into hell, where their worm does not die, and the fire is not quenched."

Proper 22 *The Sunday Closest to October 5*

A Reading (Lesson) from the Book of Genesis [2:18-24]

Then the Lord God said, "It is not good that the man should be alone; I will make him a helper fit for him." So out of the ground the Lord God formed every beast of the field and every bird of the air, and brought them to the man to see what he would call them; and whatever the man called every living creature, that was its name. The man gave names to all cattle, and to the birds of the air, and to every beast of the field; but for the man there was not found a helper fit for him. So the Lord God caused a deep sleep to fall upon the man, and while he slept took one of his ribs and closed up its place with flesh; and the rib which the Lord God had taken from the man he made into a woman and brought her to the man. Then the man said, "This at last is bone of my bones and flesh of my flesh; she shall be called Woman, because she was taken out of Man." Therefore, a man leaves his father and his mother and cleaves to his wife, and they become one flesh.

Psalm 8 [page 592] or *Psalm 128* [page 783]

A Reading (Lesson) from the Letter to the Hebrews
[2:(1-8) 9-18]

We must pay the closer attention to what we have heard, lest we drift away from it. For if the message declared by angels was valid and every transgression or disobedience received a just retribution, how shall we escape if we neglect such a great salvation? It was declared at first by the Lord, and it was attested to us by those who heard him, while God also bore witness by signs and wonders and various miracles and by gifts of the Holy Spirit distributed according to his own will. For it was not to angels that God subjected the world to come, of which we are speaking. It has been testified somewhere, "What is man that thou are mindful of him, or the son of man, that thou carest for him? Thou didst make him for a little while lower than the angels, thou hast crowned him with glory and honor, putting everything in subjection under his feet." Now in putting everything in subjection to him, he left nothing outside his control. As it is, we do not yet see everything in subjection to him.

[*But*] We see Jesus, who for a little while was made lower than the angels, crowned with glory and honor because of the suffering of death, so that by the grace of God he might taste death for every one. For it was fitting that he, for whom and by whom all things exist, in bringing many sons to glory, should make the pioneer of their salvation perfect through suffering. For he who sanctifies and those who are sanctified have all one origin. That is why he is not ashamed to call them brethren, saying, "I will proclaim thy name to my brethren; in the midst of the congregation I will praise thee." And again, "I will put my trust in him." And again, "Here am I, and the children God has given me." Since therefore the children share in flesh and blood, he himself likewise partook of the same nature, that through death he might destroy him who has the power of death, that is, the devil, and deliver all those who through fear of death were subject to lifelong bondage. For surely it is not with angels that he is concerned but with the descendants of Abraham. Therefore he had to be made like his brethren in every respect, so that he might become a merciful and faithful high priest in the service of God, to make expiation for the sins of the people. For because he himself has suffered and been tempted, he is able to help those who are tempted.

✝ *The Holy Gospel of Our Lord Jesus Christ According to Mark* [10:2-9]

The Pharisees came up and in order to test Jesus asked, "Is it lawful for a man to divorce his wife?" He answered them, "What did Moses command you?" They said, "Moses allowed a man to write a certificate of divorce, and to put her away." But Jesus said to them, "For your hardness of heart he wrote you this commandment. But from the beginning of creation, 'God made them male and female.' 'For this reason a man shall leave his father and mother and be joined to his wife, and the two shall become one flesh.' So they are no longer two but one flesh. What therefore God has joined together, let not man put asunder."

Proper 23 *The Sunday Closest to October 12*

A Reading (Lesson) from the Book of Amos [5:6-7, 10-15]

Seek the Lord and live, lest he break out like fire in the house of Joseph, and it devour, with none to quench it for Bethel, O you who turn justice to wormwood, and cast down righteousness to the earth! They hate him who reproves in the gate, and they abhor him who speaks the truth. Therefore because you trample upon the poor and take from him exactions of wheat, you have built houses of hewn stone, but you shall not dwell in them; you have planted pleasant vineyards, but you shall not drink their wine. For I know how many are your transgressions, and how great are your sins — you who afflict the righteous, who take a bribe, and turn aside the needy in the gate. Therefore he who is prudent will keep silent in such a time; for it is an evil time. Seek good, and not evil, that you may live; and so the Lord, the God of hosts, will be with you, as you have said. Hate evil, and love good, and establish justice in the gate; it may be that the Lord, the God of hosts, will be gracious to the remnant of Joseph.

Psalm 90 [page 717]   or   *Psalm 90:1-8, 12* [page 717]

A Reading (Lesson) from the Letter to the Hebrews [3:1-6]

Now my holy brethren, who share in a heavenly call, consider Jesus, the apostle and high priest of our confession. He was faithful to him who appointed him, just as Moses also was faithful in God's house. Yet Jesus has been counted worthy of as much more glory than Moses as the builder of a house has more honor than the house. (For every house is built by some one, but the builder of all things is God.) Now Moses was faithful in all God's house as a servant, to testify to the things that were to be spoken later, but Christ was faithful over God's house as a son. And we are his house if we hold fast our confidence and pride in our hope.

✝ *The Holy Gospel of Our Lord Jesus Christ According to Mark* [10:17-27 (28-31)]

A man ran up to Jesus and knelt before him, and asked him, "Good Teacher, what must I do to inherit eternal life?" And Jesus said to him, "Why do you call me good? No one is good but God alone. You know the commandments: 'Do not kill, Do not commit adultery, Do not steal, Do not bear false witness, Do not defraud, Honor your father and mother.' " And he said to him, "Teacher, all these I have observed from my youth." And Jesus looking upon him loved him, and said to him, "You lack one thing; go, sell what you have, and give to the poor, and you will have treasure in heaven; and come, follow me." At that saying his countenance fell, and he went away sorrowful; for he had great possessions. And Jesus looked around and said to his disciples, "How hard it will be for those who have riches to enter the kingdom of God!" And the disciples were amazed at his words. But Jesus said to them again, "Children, how hard it is to enter the kingdom of God! It is easier for a camel to go through the eye of a needle than for a rich man to enter the kingdom of God." And they were exceedingly astonished, and said to him, "Then who can be saved?" Jesus looked at them and said, "With men it is impossible, but not with God; for all things are possible with God."

Peter began to say to him, "Lo, we have left everything and followed you." Jesus said, "Truly, I say to you, there is no one who has left house or brothers or sisters or mother or father or children or lands, for my sake and for the gospel, who will not receive a hundredfold now in this time, houses and brothers and sisters and mothers and children and lands, with persecutions, and in the age to come eternal life. But many that are first will be last, and the last first."

Proper 24 *The Sunday Closest to October 19*

A Reading (Lesson) from the Book of Isaiah [53:4-12]

Surely he has borne our griefs and carried our sorrows; yet we esteemed him stricken, smitten by God, and afflicted. But he was wounded for our transgressions, he was bruised for our iniquities; upon him was the chastisement that made us whole, and with his stripes we are healed. All we like sheep have gone astray; we have turned every one to his own way; and the Lord has laid on him the iniquity of us all. He was oppressed, and he was afflicted, yet he opened not his mouth; like a lamb that is led to the slaughter, and like a sheep that before its shearers is dumb, so he opened not his mouth. By oppression and judgment he was taken away; and as for his generation, who considered that he was cut off out of the land of the living, stricken for the transgression of my people? And they made his grave with the wicked and with a rich man in his death, although he had done no violence, and there was no deceit in his mouth. Yet it was the will of the Lord to bruise him; he has put him to grief; when he makes himself an offering for sin, he shall see his offspring, he shall prolong his days; the will of the Lord shall prosper in his hand; he shall see the fruit of the travail of his soul and be satisfied; by his knowledge shall the righteous one, my servant, make many to be accounted righteous; and he shall bear their iniquities. Therefore I will divide him a portion with the great, and he shall divide the spoil with the strong; because he poured out his soul to death, and was numbered with the transgressors; yet he bore the sin of many, and made intercession for the transgressors.

Psalm 91 [page 719] or *Psalm 91:9-16* [page 720]

A Reading (Lesson) from the Letter to the Hebrews [4:12-16]

The word of God is living and active, sharper than any two-edged sword, piercing to the division of soul and spirit, of joints and marrow, and discerning the thoughts and intentions of the heart. And before him no creature is hidden, but all are open and laid bare to the eyes of him with whom we have to do. Since, then, we have a great high priest who has passed through the heavens, Jesus, the Son of God, let us hold fast our confession. For we have not a high priest who is unable to sympathize with our weaknesses, but one who in every respect has been tempted as we are, yet without sin. Let us then with confidence draw near to the throne of grace, that we may receive mercy and find grace to help in time of need.

✝ *The Holy Gospel of Our Lord Jesus Christ*
According to Mark [10:35-45]

James and John, the sons of Zeb'edee, came forward to Jesus, and said to him, "Teacher, we want you to do for us whatever we ask of you." And he said to them, "What do you want me to do for you?" And they said to him, "Grant us to sit, one at your right hand and one at your left, in your glory." But Jesus said to them, "You do not know what you are asking. Are you able to drink the cup that I drink, or to be baptized with the baptism with which I am baptized?" And they said to him, "We are able." And Jesus said to them, "The cup that I drink you will drink; and with the baptism with which I am baptized, you will be baptized; but to sit at my right hand or at my left is not mine to grant, but it is for those for whom it has been prepared." And when the ten heard it, they began to be indignant at James and John. And Jesus called them to him and said to them, "You know that those who are supposed to rule over the Gentiles lord it over them, and their great men exercise authority over them. But it shall not be so among you; but whoever would be great among you must be your servant, and whoever would be first among you must be slave of all. For the Son of man also came not to be served but to serve, and to give his life as a ransom for many."

Proper 25   *The Sunday Closest to October 26*

A Reading (Lesson) from the Book of Isaiah [59:(1-4) 9-19]

Behold, the Lord's hand is not shortened, that it cannot save, or his ear dull, that it cannot hear; but your iniquities have made a separation between you and your God, and your sins have hid his face from you, so that he does not hear. For your hands are defiled with blood, and your fingers with iniquity; your lips have spoken lies, your tongue mutters wickedness. No one enters suit justly, no one goes to law honestly; they rely on empty pleas, they speak lies, they conceive mischief and bring forth iniquity.

[*Therefore*] Justice is far from us, and righteousness does not overtake us; we look for light, and behold, darkness, and for brightness, but we walk in gloom. We grope for the wall like the blind, we grope like those who have no eyes; we stumble at noon as in the twilight, among those in full vigor we are like dead men. We all growl like bears, we moan and moan like doves; we look for justice, but there is none; for salvation, but it is far from us. For our transgressions are multiplied before thee, and our sins testify against us; for our transgressions are with us, and we know our iniquities: transgressing, and denying the Lord, and turning away from following our God, speaking oppression and revolt, conceiving and uttering from the heart lying words. Justice is turned back, and righteousness stands afar off; for truth has fallen in the public squares, and uprightness cannot enter. Truth is lacking, and he who departs from evil makes himself a prey. The Lord saw it, and it displeased him that there was no justice. He saw that there was no man, and wondered that there was no one to intervene; then his own arm brought him victory, and his righteousness upheld him. He put on righteousness as a breastplate, and a helmet of salvation upon his head; he put on garments of vengeance for clothing, and wrapped himself in fury as a mantle. According to their deeds, so will he repay, wrath to his adversaries, requital to his enemies; to the coastlands he will render requital. So they shall fear the name of the Lord from the west, and his glory from the rising of the sun; for he will come like a rushing stream, which the wind of the Lord drives.

Psalm 13 [page 597]

A Reading (Lesson) from the Letter to the Hebrews
[5:12—6:1,9-12]

Though by this time you ought to be teachers, you need some one to teach you again the first principles of God's word. You need milk, not solid food; for every one who lives on milk is unskilled in the word of righteousness, for he is a child. But solid food is for the mature, for those who have their faculties trained by practice to distinguish good from evil. Therefore let us leave the elementary doctrine of Christ and go on to maturity, not laying again a foundation of repentance from dead works and of faith toward God. Though we speak thus, yet in your case, beloved, we feel sure of better things that belong to salvation. For God is not so unjust as to overlook your work and the love which you showed for his sake in serving the saints, as you still do. And we desire each one of you to show the same earnestness in realizing the full assurance of hope until the end, so that you may not be sluggish, but imitators of those who through faith and patience inherit the promises.

✝ The Holy Gospel of Our Lord Jesus Christ According to Mark [10:46-52]

Jesus and his disciples came to Jericho; and as he was leaving Jericho with his disciples and a great multitude, Bartimae'us, a blind beggar, the son of Timae'us, was sitting by the roadside. And when he heard that it was Jesus of Nazareth, he began to cry out and say, "Jesus, Son of David, have mercy on me!" And many rebuked him, telling him to be silent; but he cried out all the more, "Son of David, have mercy on me!" And Jesus stopped and said, "Call him." And they called the blind man, saying to him, "Take heart; rise, he is calling you." And throwing off his mantle he sprang up and came to Jesus. And Jesus said to him, "What do you want me to do for you?" And the blind man said to him, "Master, let me receive my sight." And Jesus said to him,

"Go your way; your faith has made you well." And immediately he received his sight and followed him on the way.

Proper 26 *The Sunday Closest to November 2*

A Reading (Lesson) from the Book of Deuteronomy [6:1-9]

Moses said to the people, "Now this is the commandment, the statutes and the ordinances which the Lord your God commanded me to teach you, that you may do them in the land to which you are going over, to possess it; that you may fear the Lord your God, you and your son and your son's son, by keeping all his statutes and his commandments, which I command you, all the days of your life; and that your days may be prolonged. Hear therefore, O Israel, and be careful to do them; that it may go well with you, and that you may multiply greatly, as the Lord, the God of your fathers, has promised you, in a land flowing with milk and honey. Hear, O Israel: The Lord our God is one Lord; and you shall love the Lord your God with all your heart, and with all your soul, and with all your might. And these words which I command you this day shall be upon your heart; and you shall teach them diligently to your children, and shall talk of them when you sit in your house, and when you walk by the way, and when you lie down, and when you rise. And you shall bind them as a sign upon your hand, and they shall be as frontlets between your eyes. And you shall write them on the doorposts of your house and on your gates."

Psalm 119:1-16 [page 763] or *Psalm 119:1-8* [page 763]

A Reading (Lesson) from the Letter to the Hebrews [7:23-28]

The former priests were many in number, because they were prevented by death from continuing in office; but Jesus holds his priesthood permanently, because he continues for ever.

Consequently he is able for all time to save those who draw near to God through him, since he always lives to make intercession for them. For it was fitting that we should have such a high priest, holy, blameless, unstained, separated from sinners, exalted above the heavens. He has no need, like those high priests, to offer sacrifices daily, first for his own sins and then for those of the people; he did this once for all when he offered up himself. Indeed, the law appoints men in their weakness as high priests, but the word of the oath, which came later than the law, appoints a Son who has been made perfect for ever.

✝ *The Holy Gospel of Our Lord Jesus Christ According to Mark* [12:28-34]

One of the scribes came up and heard the Sad'ducees disputing, and seeing that Jesus answered them well, he asked him, "Which commandment is the first of all?" Jesus answered, "The first is, 'Hear, O Israel: The Lord our God, the Lord is one; and you shall love the Lord your God with all your heart, and with all your soul, and with all your mind, and with all your strength.' The second is this, 'You shall love your neighbor as yourself.' There is no other commandment greater than these." And the scribe said to him, "You are right, Teacher; you have truly said that he is one, and there is no other but he; and to love him with all the heart, and with all the understanding, and with all the strength, and to love one's neighbor as oneself, is much more than all whole burnt offerings and sacrifices." And when Jesus saw that he answered wisely, he said to him, "You are not far from the kingdom of God." And after that no one dared to ask him any question.

A Reading (Lesson) from the First Book of the Kings
[17:8-16]

The word of the Lord came to Eli'jah, "Arise, go to
Zar'ephath, which belongs to Sidon, and dwell there.
Behold, I have commanded a widow there to feed you." So
he arose and went to Zar'ephath; and when he came to the
gate of the city, behold, a widow was there gathering sticks;
and he called to her and said, "Bring me a little water in a
vessel, that I may drink." And as she was going to bring it, he
called to her and said, "Bring me a morsel of bread in your
hand." And she said, "As the Lord your God lives, I have
nothing baked, only a handful of meal in a jar, and a little oil
in a cruse; and now, I am gathering a couple of sticks, that I
may go in and prepare it for myself and my son, that we may
eat it, and die." And Eli'jah said to her, "Fear not; go and do
as you have said; but first make me a little cake of it and
bring it to me, and afterward make for yourself and your
son. For thus says the Lord the God of Israel, 'The jar of
meal shall not be spent, and the cruse of oil shall not fail,
until the day that the Lord sends rain upon the earth.'" And
she went and did as Eli'jah said; and she, and he, and her
household ate for many days. The jar of meal was not spent,
neither did the cruse of oil fail, according to the word of the
Lord which he spoke by Eli'jah.

Psalm 146 [page 803]   or   *Psalm 146:4-9* [page 803]

A Reading (Lesson) from the Letter to the Hebrews [9:24-28]

Christ has entered, not into a sanctuary made with hands, a
copy of the true one, but into heaven itself, now to appear in
the presence of God on our behalf. Nor was it to offer
himself repeatedly, as the high priest enters the Holy Place
yearly with blood not his own; for then he would have had
to suffer repeatedly since the foundation of the world. But as

it is, he has appeared once for all at the end of the age to put away sin by the sacrifice of himself. And just as it is appointed for men to die once, and after that comes judgment, so Christ, having been offered once to bear the sins of many, will appear a second time, not to deal with sin but to save those who are eagerly waiting for him.

✝ The Holy Gospel of Our Lord Jesus Christ
According to Mark [12:38-44]

Teaching in the temple Jesus said, "Beware of the scribes, who like to go about in long robes, and to have salutations in the market places and the best seats in the synagogues and the places of honor at feasts, who devour widows' houses and for a pretense make long prayers. They will receive the greater condemnation." And he sat down opposite the treasury, and watched the multitude putting money into the treasury. Many rich people put in large sums. And a poor widow came, and put in two copper coins, which make a penny. And he called his disciples to him, and said to them, "Truly, I say to you, this poor widow has put in more than all those who are contributing to the treasury. For they all contributed out of their abundance; but she out of her poverty has put in everything she had, her whole living."

Proper 28 *The Sunday Closest to November 16*

A Reading (Lesson) from the Book of Daniel [12:1-4a (5-13)]

The Lord spoke to Daniel in a vision and said, "At that time shall arise Michael, the great prince who has charge of your people. And there shall be a time of trouble, such as never has been since there was a nation till that time; but at that time your people shall be delivered, every one whose name shall be found written in the book. And many of those who sleep in the dust of the earth shall awake, some to everlasting life, and some to shame and everlasting contempt. And those who are wise shall shine like the brightness of the firmament; and those who turn many to righteousness, like the stars for ever and ever. But you, Daniel, shut up the words, and seal the book, until the time of the end."

Then I, Daniel, looked, and behold, two others stood, one on this bank of the stream and one on that bank of the stream. And I said to the the man clothed in linen, who was above the waters of the stream, "How long shall it be till the end of these wonders?" The man clothed in linen, who was above the waters of the stream, raised his right hand and his left hand toward heaven; and I heard him swear by him who lives for ever, that it would be for a time, two times, and half a time; and that when the shattering of the power of the holy people comes to an end all these things would be accomplished. I heard, but I did not understand. Then I said, "O my lord, what shall be the issue of these things?" He said, "Go your way, Daniel, for the words are shut up and sealed until the time of the end. Many shall purify themselves, and make themselves white, and be refined; but the wicked shall do wickedly; and none of the wicked shall understand; but those who are wise shall understand. And from the time that the continual burnt offering is taken away, and the abomination that makes desolate is set up, there shall be a thousand two hundred and ninety days. Blessed is he who waits and comes to the thousand three hundred and thirty-five days. But go your way till the end; and you shall rest, and shall stand in your allotted place at the end of the days."

Psalm 16 [page 599] or *Psalm 16:5-11* [page 600]

A Reading (Lesson) from the Letter to the Hebrews
[10:31-39]

It is a fearful thing to fall into the hands of the living God. But recall the former days when, after you were enlightened, you endured a hard struggle with sufferings, sometimes being publicly exposed to abuse and affliction, and sometimes being partners with those so treated. For you had compassion on the prisoners, and you joyfully accepted the plundering of your property, since you knew that you yourselves had a better possession and an abiding one. Therefore do not throw away your confidence, which has a great reward. For you have need of endurance, so that you may do the will of God and receive what is promised. "For yet a little while, and the coming one shall come and shall not tarry; but my righteous one shall live by faith, and if he shrinks back, my soul has no pleasure in him." But we are not of those who shrink back and are destroyed, but of those who have faith and keep their souls.

✝ *The Holy Gospel of Our Lord Jesus Christ*
According to Mark [13:14-23]

Jesus said, "When you see the desolating sacrilege set up where it ought not to be (let the reader understand), then let those who are in Judea flee to the mountains; let him who is on the housetop not go down, nor enter his house, to take anything away; and let him who is in the field not turn back to take his mantle. And alas for those who are with child and for those who give suck in those days! Pray that it may not happen in winter. For in those days there will be such tribulation as has not been from the beginning of the creation which God created until now, and never will be. And if the Lord had not shortened the days, no human being would be saved; but for the sake of the elect, whom he chose, he shortened the days. And then if any one says to you, 'Look, here is the Christ!' or 'Look, there he is!' do not believe it. False Christs and false prophets will arise and show signs and wonders, to lead astray, if possible, the elect. But take heed; I have told you all things beforehand."

Proper 29 *The Sunday Closest to November 23*

A Reading (Lesson) from the Book of Daniel [7:9-14]

Daniel had a vision and wrote down the dream, and said, "As I looked, thrones were placed, and one that was ancient of days took his seat; his raiment was white as snow, and the hair of his head like pure wool; his throne was fiery flames, its wheels were burning fire. A stream of fire issued and came forth from before him; a thousand thousands served him, and ten thousand times ten thousand stood before him; the court sat in judgment, and the books were opened. I looked then because of the sound of the great words which the horn was speaking. And as I looked, the beast was slain and its body destroyed and given over to be burned with fire. As for the rest of the beasts, their dominion was taken away, but their lives were prolonged for a season and a time. I saw in the night visions, and behold, with the clouds of heaven there came one like a son of man, and he came to the Ancient of Days, and was presented before him. And to him was given dominion and glory and kingdom, that all peoples, nations, and languages should serve him; his dominion is an everlasting dominion, which shall not pass away, and his kingdom one that shall not be destroyed."

Psalm 93 [page 722]

A Reading (Lesson) from the Revelation to John [1:1-8]

The revelation of Jesus Christ, which God gave him to show to his servants what must soon take place; and he made it known by sending his angel to his servant John, who bore witness to the word of God and to the testimony of Jesus Christ, even to all that he saw. Blessed is he who reads aloud the words of the prophecy, and blessed are those who hear, and who keep what is written therein; for the time is near. John to the seven churches that are in Asia: Grace to you and peace from him who is, and who was, and who is to come, and from the seven spirits who are before his throne, and from Jesus Christ the faithful witness, the first-born of the dead, and the ruler of kings on earth. To him who loves us and has freed us from our sins by his blood and made us a kingdom, priests to his God and Father, to him be glory and dominion for ever and ever. Amen. Behold, he is coming with the clouds, and every eye will see him, every one who pierced him; and all tribes of the earth will wail on account of him. Even so. Amen. "I am the Alpha and the Omega," says the Lord God, who is, and who was, and who is to come, the Almighty.

✝ *The Holy Gospel of Our Lord Jesus Christ
According to John* [18:33-37]

Pilate entered the praetorium again and called Jesus, and said to him, "Are you the King of the Jews?" Jesus answered, "Do you say this of your own accord, or did others say it to you about me?" Pilate answered, "Am I a Jew? Your own nation and the chief priests have handed you over to me; what have you done?" Jesus answered, "My kingship is not of this world; if my kingship were of this world, my servants would fight, that I might not be handed over to the Jews; but my kingship is not from the world." Pilate said to him, "So you are a king?" Jesus answered, "You say that I am a king. For this I was born, and for this I have come into the world, to bear witness to the truth. Everyone who is of the truth hears my voice."

or this

✝ *The Holy Gospel of Our Lord Jesus Christ
According to Mark* [11:1-11]

When Jesus and those who followed drew near to Jerusalem, to Beth'phage and Bethany, at the Mount of Olives, Jesus sent two of his disciples, and said to them, "Go into the village opposite you, and immediately you enter it you will find a colt tied, on which no one has ever sat; untie it and bring it. If any one says to you, 'Why are you doing this?' say, 'The Lord has need of it and will send it back here immediately.'" And they went away, and found a colt tied at the door out in the open street; and they untied it. And those who stood there said to them, "What are you doing, untying the colt?" And they told them what Jesus had said; and they let them go. And they brought the colt to Jesus, and threw their garments on it; and he sat upon it. And many spread their garments on the road, and others spread leafy branches which they had cut from the fields. And those who went before and those who followed cried out, "Hosanna! Blessed is he who comes in the name of the Lord! Blessed is the kingdom of our father David that is coming! Hosanna in the highest!" And he entered Jerusalem, and went into the temple; and when he had looked round at everything, as it was already late, he went out to Bethany with the twelve.

Holy Days

Saint Andrew   *November 30*

A Reading (Lesson) from the Book of Deuteronomy
[30:11-14]

Moses summoned all Israel and said to them: "This commandment which I command you this day is not too hard for you, neither is it far off. It is not in heaven, that you should say, 'Who will go up for us to heaven, and bring it to us, that we may hear it and do it?' Neither is it beyond the sea, that you should say, 'Who will go over the sea for us, and bring it to us, that we may hear it and do it?' But the word is very near you; it is in your mouth and in your heart, so that you can do it."

Psalm 19 [page 606]   or   *Psalm 19:1-6* [page 606]

A Reading (Lesson) from the Letter of Paul to the Romans
[10:8b-18]

The word is near you, on your lips and in your heart (that is, the word of faith which we preach); because, if you confess with your lips that Jesus is Lord and believe in your heart that God raised him from the dead, you will be saved. For man believes with his heart and so is justified, and he confesses with his lips and so is saved. The scripture says, "No one who believes in him will be put to shame." For there is no distinction between Jew and Greek; the same

Lord is Lord of all and bestows his riches upon all who call upon him. For, "every one who calls upon the name of the Lord will be saved." But how are men to call upon him in whom they have not believed? And how are they to believe in him of whom they have never heard? And how are they to hear without a preacher? And how can men preach unless they are sent? As it is written, "How beautiful are the feet of those who preach good news!" But they have not all obeyed the gospel; for Isaiah says, "Lord, who has believed what he has heard from us?" So faith comes from what is heard, and what is heard comes by the preaching of Christ. But I ask, have they not heard? Indeed they have; for "Their voice has gone out to all the earth, and their words to the ends of the world."

✝ *The Holy Gospel of Our Lord Jesus Christ
According to Matthew* [4:18-22]

As Jesus walked by the Sea of Galilee, he saw two brothers, Simon who is called Peter and Andrew his brother, casting a net into the sea; for they were fishermen. And he said to them, "Follow me, and I will make you fishers of men." Immediately they left their nets and followed him. And going on from there he saw two other brothers, James the son of Zeb'edee and John his brother, in the boat with Zeb'edee their father, mending their nets, and he called them. Immediately they left the boat and their father, and followed him.

Saint Thomas   *December 21*

A Reading (Lesson) from the Book of Habakkuk [2:1-4]

I will take my stand to watch, and station myself on the tower, and look forth to see what he will say to me, and what I will answer concerning my complaint. And the Lord answered me, "Write the vision; make it plain upon tablets, so he may run who reads it. For still the vision awaits its time; it hastens to the end — it will not lie. If it seem slow, wait for it; it will surely come, it will not delay. Behold, he whose soul is not upright in him shall fail, but the righteous shall live by his faith."

Psalm 126 [page 782]

A Reading (Lesson) from the Letter to the Hebrews
[10:35—11:1]

Do not throw away your confidence, which has a great reward. For you have need of endurance, so that you may do the will of God and receive what is promised. "For yet a little while, and the coming one shall come and shall not tarry; but my righteous one shall live by faith, and if he shrinks back, my soul has no pleasure in him." But we are not of those who shrink back and are destroyed, but of those who have faith and keep their souls. Now faith is the assurance of things hoped for, the conviction of things not seen.

✝ *The Holy Gospel of Our Lord Jesus Christ According to John* [20:24-29]

Thomas, one of the twelve, called the Twin, was not with the other disciples when Jesus came. So the other disciples told him, "We have seen the Lord." But he said to them, "Unless I see in his hands the print of the nails, and place my finger in the mark of the nails, and place my hand in his side, I will not believe." Eight days later, his disciples were again in the house, and Thomas was with them. The doors were shut, but Jesus came and stood among them, and said, "Peace be with you." Then he said to Thomas, "Put your finger here, and see my hands; and put out your hand, and place it in my side; do not be faithless, but believing." Thomas answered him, "My Lord and my God!" Jesus said to him, "Have you believed because you have seen me? Blessed are those who have not seen and yet believe."

Saint Stephen   *December 26*

A Reading (Lesson) from the Book of Jeremiah [26:1-9, 12-15]

In the beginning of the reign of Jehoi'akim the son of Josi'ah, king of Judah, this word came from the Lord, "Thus says the Lord: Stand in the court of the Lord's house, and speak to all the cities of Judah which come to worship in the house of the Lord all the words that I command you to speak to them; do not hold back a word. It may be they will listen, and every one turn from his evil way, that I may repent of the evil which I intend to do to them because of their evil doings. You shall say to them, 'Thus says the Lord: If you will not listen to me, to walk in my law which I have set before you, and to heed the words of my servants the prophets whom I send to you urgently, though you have not heeded, then I will make this house like Shiloh, and I will make this city a curse for all the nations of the earth.' " The priests and the prophets and all the people heard Jeremiah speaking these words in the house of the Lord. And when Jeremiah had finished speaking all that the Lord had commanded him to speak to all the people, then the priests and the prophets and all the people laid hold of him, saying, "You shall die! Why have you prophesied in the name of the Lord, saying, 'This house shall be like Shiloh, and this city shall be desolate, without inhabitant'?" And all the people gathered about Jeremiah in the house of the Lord. Then Jeremiah spoke to all the princes and all the people, saying, "The Lord sent me to prophesy against this house and this city all the words you have heard. Now therefore amend your ways and your doings, and obey the voice of the Lord your God, and the Lord will repent of the evil which he has pronounced against you. But as for me, behold, I am in your hands. Do with me as seems good and right to you. Only know for certain that if you put me to death, you will bring innocent blood upon yourselves and upon this city and its inhabitants, for in truth the Lord sent me to you to speak all these words in your ears."

Psalm 31 [page 622]   or   *Psalm 31:1-5* [page 622]

A Reading (Lesson) from the Acts of the Apostles
[6:8—7:2a, 51c-60]

Stephen, full of grace and power, did great wonders and signs among the people. Then some of those who belonged to the synagogue of the Freedmen (as it was called), and of the Cyre'nians, and of the Alexandrians, and of those from Cili'cia and Asia, arose and disputed with Stephen. But they could not withstand the wisdom and the Spirit with which he spoke. Then they secretly instigated men, who said, "We have heard him speak blasphemous words against Moses and God." And they stirred up the people and the elders and the scribes, and they came upon him and seized him and brought him before the council, and set up false witnesses who said, "This man never ceases to speak words against this holy place and the law; for we have heard him say that this Jesus of Nazareth will destroy this place, and will change the customs which Moses delivered to us." And gazing at him, all who sat in the council saw that his face was like the face of an angel. And the high priest said, "Is this so?" And Stephen said, "Brethren and fathers, hear me. As your fathers did, so do you. Which of the prophets did not your fathers persecute? And they killed those who announced beforehand the coming of the Righteous One, whom you have now betrayed and murdered, you who received the law as delivered by angels and did not keep it." Now when they heard these things they were enraged, and they ground their teeth against him. But he, full of the Holy Spirit, gazed into heaven and saw the glory of God, and Jesus standing at the right hand of God; and he said, "Behold, I see the heavens opened, and the Son of man standing at the right hand of God." But they cried out with a loud voice and stopped their ears and rushed together upon him. Then they cast him out of the city and stoned him; and the witnesses laid down their garments at the feet of a young man named Saul. And as they were stoning Stephen, he prayed, "Lord Jesus, receive my spirit." And he knelt down and cried with a loud voice, "Lord, do not hold this sin against them." And when he had said this, he fell asleep.

✝ *The Holy Gospel of Our Lord Jesus Christ*
According to Matthew [23:34-39]

Jesus said, "I will send you prophets and wise men and scribes, some of whom you will kill and crucify, and some you will scourge in your synagogues and persecute from town to town, that upon you may come all the righteous blood shed on earth, from the blood of innocent Abel to the blood of Zechari'ah the son of Barachi'ah, whom you murdered between the sanctuary and the altar. Truly, I say to you, all this will come upon this generation. O Jerusalem, Jerusalem, killing the prophets and stoning those who are sent to you! How often would I have gathered your children together as a hen gathers her brood under her wings, and you would not! Behold, your house is forsaken and desolate. For I tell you, you will not see me again, until you say, 'Blessed is he who comes in the name of the Lord.'"

Saint John   *December 27*

A Reading (Lesson) from the Book of Exodus [33:18-23]

Moses said to God, "I pray thee, show me thy glory." And he said, "I will make all my goodness pass before you, and will proclaim before you my name 'The Lord'; and I will be gracious to whom I will be gracious, and will show mercy on whom I will show mercy. But," he said, "you cannot see my face; for man shall not see me and live." And the Lord said, "Behold, there is a place by me where you shall stand upon the rock; and while my glory passes by I will put you in a cleft of the rock, and I will cover you with my hand until I have passed by; then I will take away my hand, and you shall see my back; but my face shall not be seen."

Psalm 92 [page 720] or *Psalm 92: 1-4, 11-14* [page 720]

A Reading (Lesson) from the First Letter of John [1:1-9]

That which was from the beginning, which we have heard, which we have seen with our eyes, which we have looked upon and touched with our hands, concerning the word of life — the life was made manifest, and we saw it, and testify to it, and proclaim to you the eternal life which was with the Father and was made manifest to us — that which we have seen and heard we proclaim also to you, so that you may have fellowship with us; and our fellowship is with the Father and with his Son Jesus Christ. And we are writing this that our joy may be complete. This is the message we have heard from him and proclaim to you, that God is light and in him is no darkness at all. If we say we have fellowship with him while we walk in darkness, we lie and do not live according to the truth; but if we walk in the light, as he is in the light, we have fellowship with one another, and the blood of Jesus his Son cleanses us from all sin. If we say we have no sin, we deceive ourselves, and the truth is not in us. If we confess our sins, he if faithful and just, and will forgive our sins and cleanse us from all unrighteousness.

✝ *The Holy Gospel of Our Lord Jesus Christ According to John* [21:19b-24]

Jesus said to Peter, "Follow me." Peter turned and saw following them the disciple whom Jesus loved, who had lain close to his breast at the supper and had said, "Lord, who is it that is going to betray you?" When Peter saw him, he said to Jesus, "Lord, what about this man?" Jesus said to him, "If it is my will that he remain until I come, what is that to you? Follow me!" The saying spread abroad among the brethren that this disciple was not to die; yet Jesus did not say to him that he was not to die, but, "If it is my will that he remain until I come, what is that to you?" This is the disciple who is bearing witness to these things, and who has written these things; and we know that his testimony is true.

The Holy Innocents   December 28

A Reading (Lesson) from the Book of Jeremiah [31:15-17]

Thus says the Lord: "A voice is heard in Ramah, lamentation and bitter weeping. Rachel is weeping for her children; she refuses to be comforted for her children, because they are not." Thus says the Lord: "Keep your voice from weeping, and your eyes from tears; for your work shall be rewarded, says the Lord, and they shall come back from the land of the enemy. There is hope for your future, says the Lord, and your children shall come back to their own country."

Psalm 124 [page 781]

A Reading (Lesson) from the Revelation to John [21:1-7]

I saw a new heaven and a new earth; for the first heaven and the first earth had passed away, and the sea was no more. And I saw the holy city, new Jerusalem, coming down out of heaven from God, prepared as a bride adorned for her husband; and I heard a loud voice from the throne saying, "Behold, the dwelling of God is with men. He will dwell with them, and they shall be his people, and God himself will be with them; he will wipe away every tear from their eyes, and death shall be no more, neither shall there be mourning nor crying nor pain any more, for the former things have passed away." And he who sat upon the throne said, "Behold, I make all things new." Also he said, "Write this, for these words are trustworthy and true." And he said to me, "It is done! I am the Alpha and the Omega, the beginning and the end. To the thirsty I will give from the fountain of the water of life without payment. He who conquers shall have this heritage, and I will be his God and he shall be my son."

✝ *The Holy Gospel of Our Lord Jesus Christ According to Matthew* [2:13-18]

When the wise men had departed, behold, an angel of the Lord appeared to Joseph in a dream and said, "Rise, take the child and his mother, and flee to Egypt, and remain there till I tell you; for Herod is about to search for the child, to destroy him." And he rose and took the child and his mother by night, and departed to Egypt, and remained there until the death of Herod. This was to fulfill what the Lord had spoken by the prophet, "Out of Egypt have I called my son." Then Herod, when he saw that he had been tricked by the wise men, was in a furious rage, and he sent and killed all the male children in Bethlehem and in all that region who were two years old or under, according to the time which he had ascertained from the wise men. Then was fulfilled what was spoken by the prophet Jeremiah: "A voice was heard in Ramah, wailing and loud lamentation, Rachel weeping for her children; she refused to be consoled, because they were no more."

Confession of Saint Peter *January 18*

A Reading (Lesson) from the Acts of the Apostles [4:8-13]

Peter, filled with the Holy Spirit, said, "Rulers of the people and elders, if we are being examined today concerning a good deed done to a cripple, by what means this man has been healed, be it known to you all, and to all the people of Israel, that by the name of Jesus Christ of Nazareth, whom you crucified, whom God raised from the dead, by him this man is standing before you well. This is the stone which was rejected by you builders, but which has become the head of the corner. And there is salvation in no one else, for there is no other name under heaven given among men by which we must be saved." Now when they saw the boldness of Peter and John, and perceived that they were uneducated, common men, they wondered; and they recognized that they had been with Jesus.

Psalm 23 [page 612]

A Reading (Lesson) from the First Letter of Peter [5:1-4]

I exhort the elders among you, as a fellow elder and a witness of the sufferings of Christ as well as a partaker in the glory that is to be revealed. Tend the flock of God that is your charge, not by constraint but willingly, not for shameful gain but eagerly, not as domineering over those in your charge but being examples to the flock. And when the chief Shepherd is manifested you will obtain the unfading crown of glory.

✝ *The Holy Gospel of Our Lord Jesus Christ According to Matthew* [16:13-19]

When Jesus came into the district of Caesare'a Philippi, he asked his disciples, "Who do men say that the Son of man is?" And they said, "Some say John the Baptist, others say Eli'jah, and others Jeremiah or one of the prophets." He said to them, "But who do you say that I am?" Simon Peter replied, "You are the Christ, the Son of the living God." And Jesus answered him. "Blessed are you, Simon Bar-Jona! For flesh and blood has not revealed this to you, but my Father who is in heaven. And I tell you, you are Peter, and on this rock I will build my church, and the powers of death shall not prevail against it. I will give you the keys of the kingdom of heaven, and whatever you bind on earth shall be bound in heaven, and whatever you loose on earth shall be loosed in heaven."

A Reading (Lesson) from the Acts of the Apostles [26:9-21]

Paul said to King Agrippa, "I myself was convinced that I ought to do many things in opposing the name of Jesus of Nazareth. And I did so in Jerusalem; I not only shut up many of the saints in prison, by authority from the chief priests, but when they were put to death I cast my vote against them. And I punished them often in all the synagogues and tried to make them blaspheme; and in raging fury against them, I persecuted them even to foreign cities. Thus I journeyed to Damascus with the authority and commission of the chief priests. At midday, O king, I saw on the way a light from heaven, brighter than the sun, shining round me and those who journeyed with me. And when we had all fallen to the ground, I heard a voice saying to me in the Hebrew language, 'Saul, Saul, why do you persecute me? It hurts you to kick against the goads.' And I said, 'Who are you, Lord?' And the Lord said, 'I am Jesus whom you are persecuting. But rise and stand upon your feet; for I have appeared to you for this purpose, to appoint you to serve and bear witness to the things in which you have seen me and to those in which I will appear to you, delivering you from the people and from the Gentiles — to whom I send you to open their eyes, that they may turn from darkness to light and from the power of Satan to God, that they may receive forgiveness of sins and a place among those who are sanctified by faith in me.' Wherefore, O King Agrippa, I was not disobedient to the heavenly vision, but declared first to those at Damascus, then at Jerusalem and throughout all the country of Judea, and also to the Gentiles, that they should repent and turn to God and perform deeds worthy of their repentance. For this reason the Jews seized me in the temple and tried to kill me."

Psalm 67 [page 675]

A Reading (Lesson) from the Letter of Paul to the Galatians
[1:11-24]

I would have you know, brethren, that the gospel which was preached by me is not man's gospel. For I did not receive it from man, nor was I taught it, but it came through a revelation of Jesus Christ. For you have heard of my former life in Judaism, how I persecuted the church of God violently and tried to destroy it; and I advanced in Judaism beyond many of my own age among my people, so extremely zealous was I for the traditions of my fathers. But when he who had set me apart before I was born, and had called me through his grace, was pleased to reveal his Son to me, in order that I might preach him among the Gentiles, I did not confer with flesh and blood, nor did I go up to Jerusalem to those who were apostles before me, but I went away into Arabia; and again I returned to Damascus. Then after three years I went up to Jerusalem to visit Cephas, and remained with him fifteen days. But I saw none of the other apostles except James the Lord's brother. (In what I am writing to you, before God, I do not lie!) Then I went into the regions of Syria and Cilicia. And I was still not known by sight to the churches of Christ in Judea; they only heard it said, "He who once persecuted us is now preaching the faith he once tried to destroy." And they glorified God because of me.

✝ *The Holy Gospel of Our Lord Jesus Christ According to Matthew* [10:16-22]

Jesus said, "Behold, I send you out as sheep in the midst of wolves; so be wise as serpents and innocent as doves. Beware of men; for they will deliver you up to councils, and flog you in their synagogues, and you will be dragged before governors and kings for my sake, to bear testimony before them and the Gentiles. When they deliver you up, do not be anxious how you are to speak or what you are to say; for what you are to say will be given to you in that hour; for it is not you who speak, but the Spirit of your Father speaking through you. Brother will deliver up brother to death, and the father his child, and children will rise against parents and have them put to death; and you will be hated by all for my name's sake. But he who endures to the end will be saved."

The Presentation   *February 2*

A Reading (Lesson) from the Book of Malachi [3:1-4]

Thus says the Lord, "Behold, I send my messenger to prepare the way before me, and the Lord whom you seek will suddenly come to his temple; the messenger of the covenant in whom you delight, behold, he is coming, says the Lord of hosts. But who can endure the day of his coming, and who can stand when he appears? For he is like a refiner's fire and like fullers' soap; he will sit as a refiner and purifier of silver, and he will purify the sons of Levi and refine them like gold and silver, till they present right offerings to the Lord. Then the offering of Judah and Jerusalem will be pleasing to the Lord as in the days of old and as in former years."

Psalm 84 [page 707]   or   *Psalm 84:1-6* [page 707]

A Reading (Lesson) from the Letter to the Hebrews [2:14-18]

Since God's children share in flesh and blood, Jesus himself likewise partook of the same nature, that through death he might destroy him who has the power of death, that is, the devil, and deliver all those who through fear of death were subject to lifelong bondage. For surely it is not with angels that he is concerned but with the descendants of Abraham. Therefore he had to be made like his brethren in every respect, so that he might become a merciful and faithful high priest in the service of God, to make expiation for the sins of the people. For because he himself has suffered and been tempted, he is able to help those who are tempted.

✝ *The Holy Gospel of Our Lord Jesus Christ*
According to Luke [2:22-40]

When the time came for their purification according to the law of Moses, the parents of Jesus brought him up to Jerusalem to present him to the Lord (as it is written in the law of the Lord, "Every male that opens the womb shall be called holy to the Lord") and to offer a sacrifice according to what is said in the law of the Lord, "a pair of turtledoves, or two young pigeons." Now there was a man in Jerusalem, whose name was Simeon, and this man was righteous and devout, looking for the consolation of Israel, and the Holy Spirit was upon him. And it had been revealed to him by the Holy Spirit that he should not see death before he had seen the Lord's Christ. And inspired by the Spirit he came into the temple; and when the parents brought in the child Jesus, to do for him according to the custom of the law, he took him up in his arms and blessed God and said, "Lord, now lettest thou thy servant depart in peace, according to thy word; for mine eyes have seen thy salvation which thou hast prepared in the presence of all peoples, a light for revelation to the Gentiles, and for glory to thy people Israel." And his father and his mother marveled at what was said about him; and Simeon blessed them and said to Mary his mother, "Behold, this child is set for the fall and rising of many in Israel, and for a sign that is spoken against (and a sword will pierce through your own soul also), that thoughts out of many hearts may be revealed." And there was a prophetess, Anna, the daughter of Pha'nu-el, of the tribe of Asher; she was of great age, having lived with her husband seven years from her viginity, and as a widow till she was eighty-four. She did not depart from the temple, worshiping with fasting and prayer night and day. And coming up at that very hour she gave thanks to God, and spoke of him to all who were looking for the redemption of Jerusalem. And when they had performed everything according to the law of the Lord, they returned into Galilee, to their own city, Nazareth. And the child grew and became strong, filled with wisdom; and the favor of God was upon him.

Saint Matthias   *February 24*

A Reading (Lesson) from the Acts of the Apostles [1:15-26]

Peter stood up among the brethren (the company of persons was in all about a hundred and twenty), and said, "Brethren, the scripture had to be fulfilled, which the Holy Spirit spoke beforehand by the mouth of David, concerning Judas who was guide to those who arrested Jesus. For he was numbered among us, and was allotted his share in this ministry. (Now this man bought a field with the reward of his wickedness; and falling headlong he burst open in the middle and all his bowels gushed out. And it became known to all the inhabitants of Jerusalem, so that the field was called in their language Akel'dama, that is, Field of Blood.) For it is written in the book of Psalms, 'Let his habitation become desolate, and let there be no one to live in it'; and 'His office let another take.' So one of the men who have accompanied us during all the time that the Lord Jesus went in and out among us, beginning from the baptism of John until the day when he was taken up from us — one of these men must become with us a witness to his resurrection." And they put forward two, Joseph called Barsab'bas, who was surnamed Justus, and Matthi'as. And they prayed and said, "Lord, who knowest the hearts of all men, show which one of these two thou hast chosen to take the place in this ministry and apostleship from which Judas turned aside, to go to his own place." And they cast lots for them, and the lot fell on Matthi'as; and he was enrolled with the eleven apostles.

Psalm 15 [page 599]

A Reading (Lesson) from the Letter of Paul to the
Philippians [3:13b-21]

One thing I do, forgetting what lies behind and straining forward to what lies ahead, I press on toward the goal for the prize of the upward call of God in Christ Jesus. Let those of us who are mature be thus minded; and if in anything you are otherwise minded, God will reveal that also to you. Only let us hold true to what we have attained. Brethren, join in imitating me, and mark those who so live as you have an example in us. For many, of whom I have often told you and now tell you even with tears, live as enemies of the cross of Christ. Their end is destruction, their god is the belly, and they glory in their shame, with minds set on earthly things. But our commonwealth is in heaven, and from it we await a Savior, the Lord Jesus Christ, who will change our lowly body to be like his glorious body, by the power which enables him even to subject all things to himself.

✝ *The Holy Gospel of Our Lord Jesus Christ*
According to John [15:1, 6-16]

Jesus said, "I am the true vine, and my Father is the vinedresser. If a man does not abide in me, he is cast forth as a branch and withers; and the branches are gathered, thrown into the fire and burned. If you abide in me, and my words abide in you, ask whatever you will, and it shall be done for you. By this my Father is glorified, that you bear much fruit, and so prove to be my disciples. As the Father has loved me, so have I loved you; abide in my love. If you keep my commandments, you will abide in my love, just as I have kept my Father's commandments and abide in his love. These things I have spoken to you, that my joy may be in you, and that your joy may be full. This is my commandment, that you love one another as I have loved you. Greater love has no man than this, that a man lay down his life for his friends. You are my friends if you do what I command you. No longer do I call you servants, for the servant does not know what his master is doing; but I have called you friends, for all that I have heard from my Father I have made known to you. You did not choose me, but I chose you and appointed you that you should go and bear fruit and that your fruit should abide; so that whatever you ask the Father in my name, he may give it to you."

Saint Joseph *March 19*

A Reading (Lesson) from the Second Book of Samuel
[7:4, 8-16]

The word of the Lord came to Nathan, "Thus you shall say to my servant David: 'Thus says the Lord of hosts, I took you from the pasture, from following the sheep, that you should be prince over my people Israel; and I have been with you wherever you went, and have cut off all your enemies from before you; and I will make for you a great name, like the name of the great ones of the earth. And I will appoint a place for my people Israel, and will plant them, that they may dwell in their own place, and be disturbed no more; and violent men shall afflict them no more, as formerly, from the time that I appointed judges over my people Israel; and I will give you rest from all your enemies. Moreover the Lord declares to you that the Lord will make you a house. When your days are fulfilled and you lie down with your fathers, I will raise up your offspring after you, who shall come forth from your body, and I will establish his kingdom. He shall build a house for my name, and I will establish the throne of his kingdom for ever. I will be his father, and he shall be my son. When he commits iniquity, I will chasten him with the rod of men, with the stripes of the sons of men; but I will not take my steadfast love from him, as I took it from Saul, whom I put away from before you. And your house and your kingdom shall be made sure for ever before me; your throne shall be established for ever."

Psalm 89:1-29 [page 713]   or
Psalm 89:1-4, 26-29 [page 713]

A Reading (Lesson) from the Letter of Paul to the Romans
[4:13-18]

The promise to Abraham and his descendants, that they should inherit the world, did not come through the law but through the righteousness of faith. If it is the adherents of the law who are to be the heirs, faith is null and the promise is void. For the law brings wrath, but where there is no law there is no transgression. That is why it depends on faith, in order that the promise may rest on grace and be guaranteed to all his descendants — not only to the adherents of the law but also to those who share the faith of Abraham, for he is the father of us all, as it is written, "I have made you the father of many nations" — in the presence of the God in whom he believed, who gives life to the dead and calls into existence the things that do not exist. In hope he believed against hope, that he should become the father of many nations; as he had been told, "So shall your descendants be."

✝ *The Holy Gospel of Our Lord Jesus Christ*
According to Luke [2:41-52]

Jesus' parents went to Jerusalem every year at the feast of the Passover. And when he was twelve years old, they went up according to custom; and when the feast was ended, as they were returning, the boy Jesus stayed behind in Jerusalem. His parents did not know it, but supposing him to be in the company they went a day's journey, and they sought him among their kinsfolk and acquaintances; and when they did not find him, they returned to Jerusalem, seeking him. After three days they found him in the temple, sitting among the teachers, listening to them and asking them questions; and all who heard him were amazed at his understanding and his answers.And when they saw him they were astonished; and his mother said to him, "Son, why have you treated us so? Behold, your father and I have been looking for you anxiously." And he said to them, "How is it that you sought me? Did you not know that I must be in my Father's house?" And they did not understand the saying which he spoke to them. And he went down with them and came to Nazareth, and was obedient to them; and his mother kept all these things in her heart. And Jesus increased in wisdom and in stature, and in favor with God and man.

The Annunciation   *March 25*

A Reading (Lesson) from the Book of Isaiah [7:10-14]

The Lord spoke to Ahaz, "Ask a sign of the Lord your God; let it be deep as Sheol or high as heaven." But Ahaz said, "I will not ask, and I will not put the Lord to the test." And he said, "Hear then, O house of David! Is it too little for you to weary men, that you weary my God also? Therefore the Lord himself will give you a sign. Behold, a young woman shall conceive and bear a son, and shall call his name Imman'u-el."

Psalm 40:1-11 [page 640]   or   *Psalm 40:5-10* [page 640]   or
The Magnificat, Canticle 3 or 15 [page 50 or 91]

A Reading (Lesson) from the Letter to the Hebrews [10:5-10]

When Christ came into the world, he said, "Sacrifices and offerings thou hast not desired, but a body hast thou prepared for me; in burnt offerings and sin offerings thou hast taken no pleasure. Then I said, 'Lo, I have come to do thy will, O God,' as it is written of me in the roll of the book." When he said above, "Thou hast neither desired nor taken pleasure in sacrifices and offerings and burnt offerings and sin offerings" (these are offered according to the law), then he added, "Lo, I have come to do thy will." He abolishes the first in order to establish the second. And by that will we have been sanctified through the offering of the body of Jesus Christ once for all.

✝ *The Holy Gospel of Our Lord Jesus Christ*
According to Luke [1:26-38]

In the sixth month the angel Gabriel was sent from God to a city of Galilee named Nazareth, to a virgin betrothed to a man whose name was Joseph, of the house of David; and the virgin's name was Mary. And he came to her and said, "Hail, O favored one, the Lord is with you!" But she was greatly troubled at the saying, and considered in her mind what sort of greeting this might be. And the angel said to her, "Do not be afraid, Mary, for you have found favor with God. And behold, you will conceive in your womb and bear a son, and you shall call his name Jesus. He will be great, and will be called the Son of the Most High; and the Lord God will give to him the throne of his father David, and he will reign over the house of Jacob for ever; and of his kingdom there will be no end." And Mary said to the angel, "How shall this be, since I have no husband?" And the angel said to her, "The Holy Spirit will come upon you, and the power of the Most High will overshadow you; therefore the child to be born will be called holy, the Son of God. And behold, your kinswoman Elizabeth in her old age has also conceived a son; and this is the sixth month with her who was called barren. For with God nothing will be impossible." And Mary said, "Behold, I am the handmaid of the Lord; let it be to me according to your word." And the angel departed from her.

Saint Mark   *April 25*

A Reading (Lesson) from the Book of Isaiah [52:7-10]

How beautiful upon the mountains are the feet of him who brings good tidings, who publishes peace, who brings good tidings of good, who publishes salvation, who says to Zion, "Your God reigns." Hark, your watchmen lift up their voice, together they sing for joy; for eye to eye they see the return of the Lord to Zion. Break forth together into singing, you waste places of Jerusalem; for the Lord has comforted his people, he has redeemed Jerusalem. The Lord has bared his holy arm before the eyes of all the nations; and all the ends of the earth shall see the salvation of our God.

Psalm 2 [page 586]   or   *Psalm 2:7-10* [page 586]

A Reading (Lesson) from the Letter of Paul to the Ephesians [4:7-8, 11-16]

Grace was given to each of us according to the measure of Christ's gift. Therefore it is said, "When he ascended on high he led a host of captives, and he gave gifts to men." And his gifts were that some should be apostles, some prophets, some evangelists, some pastors and teachers, to equip the saints for the work of ministry, for building up the body of Christ, until we all attain to the unity of the faith and of the knowledge of the Son of God, to mature manhood, to the measure of the stature of the fulness of Christ; so that we may no longer be children, tossed to and fro and carried about with every wind of doctrine, by the cunning of men, by their craftiness in deceitful wiles. Rather, speaking the truth in love, we are to grow up in every way into him who is the head, into Christ, from whom the whole body, joined and knit together by every joint with which it is supplied, when each part is working properly, makes bodily growth and upbuilds itself in love.

✝ *The Holy Gospel of Our Lord Jesus Christ*
According to Mark [1:1-15]

The beginning of the gospel of Jesus Christ, the Son of God. As it is written in Isaiah the prophet, "Behold, I send my messenger before thy face, who shall prepare thy way; the voice of one crying in the wilderness: Prepare the way of the Lord, make his paths straight." John the baptizer appeared in the wilderness, preaching a baptism of repentance for the forgiveness of sins. And there went out to him all the country of Judea, and all the people of Jerusalem; and they were baptized by him in the river Jordan, confessing their sins. Now John was clothed with camel's hair, and had a leather girdle around his waist, and ate locusts and wild honey. And he preached, saying, "After me comes he who is mightier than I, the thong of whose sandals I am not worthy to stoop down and untie. I have baptized you with water; but he will baptize you with the Holy Spirit." In those days Jesus came from Nazareth of Galilee and was baptized by John in the Jordan. And when he came up out of the water, immediately he saw the heavens opened and the Spirit descending upon him like a dove; and a voice came from heaven, "Thou art my beloved Son; with thee I am well pleased." The Spirit immediately drove him out into the wilderness. And he was in the wilderness forty days, tempted by Satan; and he was with the wild beasts; and the angels ministered to him. Now after John was arrested, Jesus came into Galilee, preaching the gospel of God, and saying, "The time is fulfilled, and the kingdom of God is at hand; repent, and believe in the gospel."

or this

✝ *The Holy Gospel of Our Lord Jesus Christ*
   According to Mark [16:15-20]

Jesus said to the apostles, "Go into all the world and preach the gospel to the whole creation. He who believes and is baptized will be saved; but he who does not believe will be condemned. And these signs will accompany those who believe: in my name they will cast out demons; they will speak in new tongues; they will pick up serpents, and if they drink any deadly thing, it will not hurt them; they will lay their hands on the sick, and they will recover." So then the Lord Jesus, after he had spoken to them, was taken up into heaven, and sat down at the right hand of God. And they went forth and preached everywhere, while the Lord worked with them and confirmed the message by the signs that attended it.

Saint Philip and Saint James   *May 1*

A Reading (Lesson) from the Book of Isaiah [30:18-21]

The Lord waits to be gracious to you; therefore he exalts himself to show mercy to you. For the Lord is a God of justice; blessed are all those who wait for him. Yea, O people in Zion who dwell at Jerusalem; you shall weep no more. He will surely be gracious to you at the sound of your cry; when he hears it, he will answer you. And though the Lord give you the bread of adversity and the water of affliction, yet your Teacher will not hide himself any more, but your eyes shall see your Teacher. And your ears shall hear a word behind you, saying, "This is the way, walk in it," when you turn to the right or when you turn to the left.

Psalm 119:33 - 40 [page 766]

A Reading (Lesson) from the Second Letter of Paul to the Corinthians [4:1-6]

Having this ministry by the mercy of God, we do not lose heart. We have renounced disgraceful, underhanded ways; we refuse to practice cunning or to tamper with God's word, but by the open statement of the truth we would commend ourselves to every man's conscience in the sight of God. And even if our gospel is veiled, it is veiled only to those who are perishing. In their case the god of this world has blinded the minds of the unbelievers, to keep them from seeing the light of the gospel of the glory of Christ, who is the likeness of

God. For what we preach is not ourselves, but Jesus Christ as Lord, with ourselves as your servants for Jesus' sake. For it is the God who said, "Let light shine out of darkness," who has shone in our hearts to give the light of the knowledge of the glory of God in the face of Christ.

✝ *The Holy Gospel of Our Lord Jesus Christ According to John* [14:6-14]

Jesus said to Thomas, "I am the way, and the truth, and the life; no one comes to the Father, but by me. If you had known me, you would have known my Father also; henceforth you know him and have seen him." Philip said to him, "Lord, show us the Father, and we shall be satisfied." Jesus said to him, "Have I been with you so long, and yet you do not know me, Philip? He who has seen me has seen the Father; how can you say, 'Show us the Father'? Do you not believe that I am in the Father and the Father in me? The words that I say to you I do not speak on my own authority; but the Father who dwells in me does his works. Believe me that I am in the Father and the Father in me; or else believe me for the sake of the works themselves. Truly, truly, I say to you, he who believes in me will also do the works that I do; and greater works than these will he do, because I go to the Father. Whatever you ask in my name, I will do it, that the Father may be glorified in the Son; if you ask anything in my name, I will do it."

The Visitation   *May 31*

A Reading (Lesson) from the Book of Zephaniah [3:14-18a]

Sing aloud, O daughter of Zion; shout, O Israel! Rejoice and exult with all your heart, O daughter of Jerusalem! The Lord has taken away the judgments against you, he has cast out your enemies. The King of Israel, the Lord, is in your midst; you shall fear evil no more. On that day it shall be said to

Jerusalem, "Do not fear, O Zion; let not your hands grow weak. The Lord, your God, is in your midst, a warrior who gives victory; he will rejoice over you with gladness, he will renew you in his love; he will exult over you with loud singing as on a day of festival."

Psalm 113 [page 756]   or

The First Song of Isaiah, Canticle 9 [page 86]

A Reading (Lesson) from the Letter of Paul to the Colossians [3:12-17]

Put on, as God's chosen ones, holy and beloved, compassion, kindness, lowliness, meekness, and patience, forbearing one another and, if one has a complaint against another, forgiving each other; as the Lord has forgiven you, so you also must forgive. And above all these put on love, which binds everything together in perfect harmony. And let the peace of Christ rule in your hearts, to which indeed you were called in the one body. And be thankful. Let the word of Christ dwell in you richly, teach and admonish one another in all wisdom, and sing psalms and hymns and spiritual songs with thankfulness in your hearts to God. And whatever you do, in word or deed, do everything in the name of the Lord Jesus, giving thanks to God the Father through him.

✝ *The Holy Gospel of Our Lord Jesus Christ According to Luke* [1:39-49]

Mary arose and went with haste into the hill country, to a city of Judah, and she entered the house of Zechari'ah and greeted Elizabeth. And when Elizabeth heard the greeting of Mary, the babe leaped in her womb; and Elizabeth was filled with the Holy Spirit and she exclaimed with a loud cry, "Blessed are you among women, and blessed is the fruit of your womb! And why is this granted me, that the mother of my Lord should come to me? For behold, when the voice of your greeting came to my ears, the babe in my womb leaped for joy. And blessed is she who believed that there would be a fulfillment of what was spoken to her from the Lord." And Mary said, "My soul magnifies the Lord, and my spirit rejoices in God my Savior, for he has regarded the low estate of his handmaiden. For behold, henceforth all generations will call me blessed; for he who is mighty has done great things for me, and holy is his name."

Saint Barnabas *June 11*

A Reading (Lesson) from the Book of Isaiah [42:5-12]

Thus says God, the Lord, who created the heavens and stretched them out, who spread forth the earth and what comes from it, who gives breath to the people upon it and spirit to those who walk in it: "I am the Lord, I have called you in righteousness, I have taken you by the hand and kept you; I have given you as a covenant to the people, a light to the nations, to open the eyes that are blind, to bring out the prisoners from the dungeon, from the prison those who sit in darkness. I am the Lord, that is my name; my glory I give to no other, nor my praise to graven images. Behold, the former things have come to pass, and new things I now declare; before they spring forth I tell you of them." Sing to the Lord a new song, his praise from the end of the earth! Let the sea roar and all that fills it, the coastlands and their inhabitants. Let the desert and its cities lift up their voice, the villages that Kedar inhabits; let the inhabitants of Sela sing for joy, let them shout from the top of the mountains. Let them give glory to the Lord, and declare his praise in the coastlands.

Psalm 112 [page 755]

A Reading (Lesson) from the Acts of the Apostles
[11:19-30; 13:1-3]

Those who were scattered because of the persecution that arose over Stephen traveled as far as Phoeni'cia and Cyprus and Antioch, speaking the word to none except Jews. But there were some of them, men of Cyprus and Cyre'ne, who on coming to Antioch spoke to the Greeks also, preaching the Lord Jesus. And the hand of the Lord was with them, and a great number that believed turned to the Lord. News of this came to the ears of the church in Jerusalem, and they sent Barnabas to Antioch. When he came and saw the grace of God, he was glad; and he exhorted them all to remain faithful to the Lord with steadfast purpose; for he was a good man, full of the Holy Spirit and of faith. And a large company was added to the Lord. So Barnabas went to Tarsus to look for Saul; and when he had found him, he brought him to Antioch. For a whole year they met with the church, and taught a large company of people; and in Antioch the disciples were for the first time called Christians. Now in these days prophets came down from Jerusalem to Antioch. And one of them named Ag'abus stood up and foretold by the Spirit that there would be a great famine over all the world; and this took place in the days of Claudius. And the disciples determined, every one according to his ability, to send relief to the brethren who lived in Judea; and they did so, sending it to the elders by the hand of Barnabas and Saul. Now in the church at Antioch there were prophets and teachers, Barnabas, Simeon who was called Niger, Lucius of Cy'rene, Man'a-en a member of the court of Herod the tetrarch, and Saul. While they were worshiping the Lord and fasting, the Holy Spirit said, "Set apart for me Barnabas and Saul for the work to which I have called them." Then after fasting and praying they laid their hands on them and sent them off.

✝ *The Holy Gospel of Our Lord Jesus Christ*
According to Matthew [10:7-16]

Jesus said to the twelve, "Preach as you go, saying, 'The kingdom of heaven is at hand.' Heal the sick, raise the dead, cleanse lepers, cast out demons. You received without paying, give without pay. Take no gold, nor silver, nor copper in your belts, no bag for your journey, nor two tunics, nor sandals, nor a staff; for the laborer deserves his food. And whatever town or village you enter, find out who is worthy in it, and stay with him until you depart. As you enter the house, salute it. And if the house is worthy, let your peace come upon it; but if it is not worthy, let your peace return to you. And if any one will not receive you or listen to your words, shake off the dust from your feet as you leave that house or town. Truly, I say to you, it shall be more tolerable on the day of judgment for the land of Sodom and Gomor'rah than for that town. Behold, I send you out as sheep in the midst of wolves; so be wise as serpents and innocent as doves."

Nativity of Saint John the Baptist   *June 24*

A Reading (Lesson) from the Book of Isaiah [40:1-11]

Comfort, comfort my people, says your God. Speak tenderly to Jerusalem, and cry to her that her warfare is ended, that her iniquity is pardoned, that she has received from the Lord's hand double for all her sins. A voice cries: "In the wilderness prepare the way of the Lord, make straight in the desert a highway for our God. Every valley shall be lifted up, and every mountain and hill be made low; the uneven ground shall become level, and the rough places a plain. And the glory of the Lord shall be revealed, and all flesh shall see it together, for the mouth of the Lord has spoken." A voice says, "Cry!" and I said, "What shall I cry?" All flesh is grass, and all its beauty is like the flower of the field. The grass withers, the flower fades, when the breath of the Lord blows upon it; surely the people is grass. The grass withers, the flower fades; but the word of our God will stand for ever. Get you up to a high mountain, O Zion, herald of good tidings; lift up your voice with strength, O Jerusalem, herald of good tidings, lift it up, fear not; say to the cities of Judah, "Behold your God!" Behold, the Lord God comes with might, and his arm rules for him; behold, his reward is with him, and his recompense before him. He will feed his flock like a shepherd, he will gather the lambs in his arms, he will carry them in his bosom, and gently lead those that are with young.

Psalm 85 [page 708] or *Psalm 85:7-13* [page 709]

A Reading (Lesson) from the Acts of the Apostles
[13:14b-26]

On the sabbath day Paul and his company went into the synagogue and sat down. After the reading of the law and the prophets, the rulers of the synagogue sent to them, saying, "Brethren, if you have any word of exhortation for the people, say it." So Paul stood up, and motioning with his hands said: "Men of Israel, and you that fear God, listen. The God of this people Israel chose our fathers and made the people great during their stay in the land of Egypt, and with uplifted arm he led them out of it. And for about forty years he bore with them in the wilderness. And when he had destroyed seven nations in the land of Canaan, he gave them their land as an inheritance, for about four hundred and fifty years. And after that he gave them judges until Samuel the prophet. Then they asked for a king; and God gave them Saul the son of Kish, a man of the tribe of Benjamin, for forty years. And when he had removed him, he raised up David to be their king; of whom he testified and said, 'I have found in David the son of Jesse a man after my heart, who will do all my will.' Of this man's posterity God has brought to Israel a Savior, Jesus, as he promised. Before his coming John had preached a baptism of repentance to all the people of Israel. And as John was finishing his course, he said, 'What do you suppose that I am? I am not he. No, but after me one is coming, the sandals of whose feet I am not worthy to untie.' Brethren, sons of the family of Abraham, and those among you that fear God, to us has been sent the message of this salvation."

✝ *The Holy Gospel of Our Lord Jesus Christ According to Luke* [1:57-80]

The time came for Elizabeth to be delivered, and she gave birth to a son. And her neighbors and kinsfolk heard that the Lord had shown great mercy to her, and they rejoiced with her. And on the eighth day they came to circumcise the child; and they would have named him Zechari'ah after his father, but his mother said, "Not so; he shall be called John." And they said to her, "None of your kindred is called by this name." And they made signs to his father, inquiring what he would have him called. And he asked for a writing tablet, and wrote, "His name is John." And they all marveled. And immediately his mouth was opened and his tongue loosed, and he spoke, blessing God. And fear came on all their neighbors. And all these things were talked about through all the hill country of Judea; and all who heard them laid them up in their hearts, saying, "What then will this child be?" For the hand of the Lord was with him. And his father Zechari'ah was filled with the Holy Spirit, and prophesied, saying, "Blessed be the Lord God of Israel, for he has visited and redeemed his people, and has raised up a horn of salvation for us in the house of his servant David, as he spoke by the mouth of his holy prophets from of old, that we should be saved from our enemies, and from the hand of all who hate us; to perform the mercy promised to our fathers, and to remember his holy covenant, the oath which he swore to our father Abraham, to grant us that we, being delivered from the hand of our enemies, might serve him without fear, in holiness and righteousness before him all the days of our life. And you, child, will be called the prophet of the Most High; for you will go before the Lord to prepare his ways, to give knowledge of salvation to his people in the forgiveness of their sins, through the tender mercy of our God, when the day shall dawn upon us from on high to give light to those who sit in darkness and in the shadow of death, to guide our feet into the way of peace." And the child grew and became strong in spirit, and he was in the wilderness till the day of his manifestation to Israel.

Saint Peter and Saint Paul *June 29*

A Reading (Lesson) from the Book of Ezekiel [34:11-16]

Thus says the Lord God: "Behold, I, I myself will search for my sheep, and will seek them out. As a shepherd seeks out his flock when some of his sheep have been scattered abroad, so will I seek out my sheep; and I will rescue them from all places where they have been scattered on a day of clouds and thick darkness. And I will bring them out from the peoples, and gather them from the countries, and will bring them into their own land; and I will feed them on the mountains of Israel, by the fountains, and in all the inhabited places of the country. I will feed them with good pasture, and upon the mountain heights of Israel shall be their pasture; there they shall lie down in good grazing land, and on fat pasture they shall feed on the mountains of Israel. I myself will be the shepherd of my sheep, and I will make them lie down, says the Lord God. I will seek the lost, and I will bring back the strayed, and I will bind up the crippled, and I will strengthen the weak, and the fat and the strong I will watch over; I will feed them in justice."

A Reading (Lesson) from the Second Letter of Paul to Timothy [4:1-8]

I charge you in the presence of God and of Christ Jesus who is to judge the living and the dead, and by his appearing and his kingdom: preach the word, be urgent in season and out of season, convince, rebuke, and exhort, be unfailing in patience and in teaching. For the time is coming when people will not endure sound teaching, but having itching ears they will accumulate for themselves teachers to suit their own likings, and will turn away from listening to the truth and wander into myths. As for you, always be steady, endure suffering, do the work of an evangelist, fulfill your ministry. For I am already on the point of being sacrificed; the time of my departure has come. I have fought the good fight, I have finished the race, I have kept the faith. Henceforth there is laid up for me the crown of righteousness, which the Lord, the righteous judge, will award to me on that Day, and not only to me but also to all who have loved his appearing.

✝ *The Holy Gospel of Our Lord Jesus Christ According to John* [21:15-19]

When they had finished breakfast, Jesus said to Simon Peter, "Simon, son of John, do you love me more than these?" He said to him, "Yes, Lord; you know that I love you." He said to him, "Feed my lambs." A second time he said to him, "Simon, son of John, do you love me?" He said to him, "Yes, Lord; you know that I love you." He said to him, "Tend my sheep." He said to him the third time, "Simon, son of John, do you love me?" Peter was grieved because he said to him the third time, "Do you love me?" And he said to him, "Lord, you know everything; you know that I love you." Jesus said to him, "Feed my sheep. Truly, truly, I say to you, when you were young, you girded yourself and walked where you would; but when you are old, you will stretch out your hands, and another will gird you and carry you where you do not wish to go." (This he said to show by what death he was to glorify God.) And after this he said to him, "Follow me."

Independence Day   *July 4*

The Lessons and Psalm "For the Nation," may be used in place of the following. [See texts and citations on pages 248-250 below]

A Reading (Lesson) from the Book of Deuteronomy
[10:17-21]

The Lord your God is God of gods and Lord of lords, the great, the mighty, and the terrible God, who is not partial and takes no bribe. He executes justice for the fatherless and the widow, and loves the sojourner, giving him food and clothing. Love the sojourner therefore; for you were sojourners in the land of Egypt. You shall fear the Lord your God; you shall serve him and cleave to him, and by his name you shall swear. He is your praise; he is your God, who has done for you these great and terrible things which your eyes have seen.

Psalm 145 [page 801]   or   *Psalm 145:1-9* [page 801]

A Reading (Lesson) from the Letter to the Hebrews [11:8-16]

By faith Abraham obeyed when he was called to go out to a place which he was to receive as an inheritance; and he went out, not knowing where he was to go. By faith he sojourned in the land of promise, as in a foreign land, living in tents with Isaac and Jacob, heirs with him of the same promise. For he looked forward to the city which has foundations, whose builder and maker is God. By faith Sarah herself received power to conceive, even when she was past the age, since she considered him faithful who had promised.

Therefore from one man, and him as good as dead, were born descendants as many as the stars of heaven and as the innumerable grains of sand by the seashore. These all died in faith, not having received what was promised, but having seen it and greeted it from afar, and having acknowledged that they were strangers and exiles on the earth. For people who speak thus make it clear that they are seeking a homeland. If they had been thinking of that land from which they had gone out, they would have had opportunity to return. But as it is, they desire a better country, that is, a heavenly one. Therefore God is not ashamed to be called their God, for he has prepared for them a city.

✝ *The Holy Gospel of Our Lord Jesus Christ According to Matthew* [5:43-48]

Jesus said, "You have heard that it was said, 'You shall love your neighbor and hate your enemy.' But I say to you, Love your enemies and pray for those who persecute you, so that you may be sons of your Father who is in heaven; for he makes his sun rise on the evil and on the good, and sends rain on the just and on the unjust. For if you love those who love you, what reward have you? Do not even the tax collectors do the same? And if you salute only your brethren, what more are you doing than others? Do not even the Gentiles do the same? You, therefore, must be perfect, as your heavenly Father is perfect."

For the Nation *July 4*

Alternative for Independence Day above.

A Reading (Lesson) from the Book of Isaiah [26:1-8]

In that day this song will be sung in the land of Judah: "We have a strong city; he sets up salvation as walls and bulwarks. Open the gates, that the righteous nation which keeps faith may enter in. Thou dost keep him in perfect peace, whose mind is stayed on thee, because he trusts in thee. Trust in the Lord for ever, for the Lord God is an everlasting rock. For he has brought low the inhabitants of the height, the lofty city. He lays it low, lays it low to the ground, casts it to the dust. The foot tramples it, the feet of the poor, the steps of the needy." The way of the righteous is level; thou dost make smooth the path of the righteous. In the path of thy judgments, O Lord, we wait for thee; thy memorial name is the desire of our soul.

Psalm 47 [page 650]

A Reading (Lesson) from the Letter of Paul to the Romans [13:1-10]

Let every person be subject to the governing authorities. For there is no authority except from God, and those that exist have been instituted by God. Therefore he who resists the authorities resists what God has appointed, and those who resist will incur judgment. For rulers are not a terror to good conduct, but to bad. Would you have no fear of him who is in authority? Then do what is good, and you will receive his approval, for he is God's servant for your good. But if you do wrong, be afraid, for he does not bear the sword in vain; he is the servant of God to execute his wrath on the wrongdoer. Therefore one must be subject, not only to avoid God's wrath but also for the sake of conscience. For the same reason you also pay taxes, for the authorities are ministers of God, attending to this very thing. Pay all of them their dues, taxes to whom taxes are due, revenue to whom revenue is due, respect to whom respect is due, honor to whom honor is due. Owe no one anything, except to love one another; for he who loves his neighbor has fulfilled the law. The commandments, "You shall not commit adultery, You shall not kill, You shall not steal, You shall not covet," and any other commandment, are summed in this sentence, "You shall love your neighbor as yourself." Love does no wrong to a neighbor; therefore love is the fulfilling of the law.

✝ **The Holy Gospel of Our Lord Jesus Christ**
According to Mark [12:13-17]

Some of the Pharisees and some of the Herodians were sent to Jesus to entrap him in his talk. And they came and said to him, "Teacher, we know that you are true, and care for no man; for you do not regard the position of men, but truly teach the way of God. Is it lawful to pay taxes to Caesar, or not? Should we pay them, or should we not?" But knowing their hypocrisy, he said to them, "Why put me to the test? Bring me a coin, and let me look at it." And they brought one. And he said to them, "Whose likeness and inscription is this?" They said to him, "Caesar's." Jesus said to them, "Render to Caesar the things that are Caesar's, and to God the things that are God's." And they were amazed at him.

Saint Mary Magdalene   *July 22*

A Reading (Lesson) from the Book of Judith [9:1, 11-14]

Judith fell upon her face, and put ashes on her head, and uncovered the sackcloth she was wearing; and at the very time when that evening's incense was being offered in the house of God in Jerusalem, Judith cried out to the Lord with a loud voice, and said, "O God my God, hear me. Thy power depends not upon numbers, nor thy might upon men of strength; for thou art God of the lowly, helper of the oppressed, upholder of the weak, protector of the forlorn, savior of those without hope. Hear, O hear me, God of my father, God of the inheritance of Israel, Lord of heaven and earth, Creator of the waters, King of all thy creation, hear my prayer! Make my deceitful words to be their wound and stripe, for they have planned cruel things against thy covenant, and against thy consecrated house, and against the top of Zion, and against the house possessed by thy children. And cause thy whole nation and every tribe to know and understand that thou art God, the God of all power and might, and that there is no other who protects the people of Israel but thou alone!"

Psalm 42:1-7 [page 643]

A Reading (Lesson) from the Second Letter of Paul to the Corinthians [5:14-18]

The love of Christ controls us, because we are convinced that one has died for all; therefore all have died. And he died for all, that those who live might live no longer for themselves but for him who for their sake died and was raised. From now on, therefore, we regard no one from a human point of view; even though we once regarded Christ from a human point of view, we regard him thus no longer. Therefore, if any one is in Christ, he is a new creation; the old has passed away, behold, the new has come. All this is from God, who through Christ reconciled us to himself and gave us the ministry of reconciliation.

✝ *The Holy Gospel of Our Lord Jesus Christ According to John* [20:11-18]

Mary stood weeping outside the tomb, and as she wept she stooped to look into the tomb; and she saw two angels in white, sitting where the body of Jesus had lain, one at the head and one at the feet. They said to her, "Woman, why are you weeping?" She said to them, "Because they have taken away my Lord, and I do not know where they have laid him." Saying this, she turned around and saw Jesus standing, but she did not know that it was Jesus. Jesus said to her, "Woman, why are you weeping? Whom do you seek?" Supposing him to be the gardener, she said to him, "Sir, if you have carried him away, tell me where you have laid him, and I will take him away." Jesus said to her, "Mary."

She turned and said to him in Hebrew, "Rab-bo'ni!" (which means Teacher). Jesus said to her, "Do not hold me, for I have not yet ascended to the Father; but go to my brethren and say to them, I am ascending to my Father and your Father, to my God and your God." Mary Mag'dalene went and said to the disciples, "I have seen the Lord"; and she told them that he had said these things to her.

Saint James   *July 25*

A Reading (Lesson) from the Book of Jeremiah   [45:1-5]

The word that Jeremiah the prophet spoke to Baruch the son of Neri'ah, when he wrote these words in a book at the dictation of Jeremiah, in the fourth year of Jehoi'akim the son of Josi'ah, king of Judah: "Thus says the Lord, the God of Israel, to you, O Baruch: You said, 'Woe is me! For the Lord has added sorrow to my pain; I am weary with my groaning, and I find no rest.' Thus shall you say to him, Thus says the Lord: Behold, what I have built I am breaking down, and what I have planted I am plucking up — that is, the whole land. And do you seek great things for yourself? Seek them not; for, behold, I am bringing evil upon all flesh, says the Lord; but I will give you your life as a prize of war in all places to which you may go."

Psalm 7:1-10   [page 590]

A Reading (Lesson) from the Acts of the Apostles
[11:27 — 12:3]

In these days prophets came down from Jerusalem to Antioch. And one of them named Ag'abus stood up and foretold by the Spirit that there would be a great famine over all the world; and this took place in the days of Claudius. And the disciples determined, every one according to his ability, to send relief to the brethren who lived in Judea; and they did so, sending it to the elders by the hand of Barnabas and Saul. About that time Herod the king laid violent hands upon some who belonged to the church. He killed James the brother of John with the sword; and when he saw that it pleased the Jews, he proceeded to arrest Peter also. This was during the days of Unleavened Bread.

✝ *The Holy Gospel of Our Lord Jesus Christ
According to Matthew* [20:20-28]

The mother of the sons of Zeb'edee came up to Jesus with her sons, and kneeling before him she asked him for something. And he said to her, "What do you want?" She said to him, "Command that these two sons of mine may sit, one at your right hand and one at your left, in your kingdom." But Jesus answered, "You do not know what you are asking. Are you able to drink the cup that I am to drink?" They said to him, "We are able." He said to them, "You will drink my cup, but to sit at my right hand and at my left is not mine to grant, but it is for those for whom it has been prepared by my Father." And when the ten heard it, they were indignant at the two brothers. But Jesus called them to him and said, "You know that the rulers of the Gentiles lord it over them, and their great men exercise authority over them. It shall not be so among you; but whoever would be great among you must be your servant, and whoever would be first among you must be your slave; even as the Son of man came not to be served but to serve, and to give his life as a ransom for many."

The Transfiguration   *August 6*

A Reading (Lesson) from the Book of Exodus [34:29-35]

When Moses came down from Mount Sinai, with the two tables of the testimony in his hand as he came down from the mountain, Moses did not know that the skin of his face shone because he had been talking with God. And when Aaron and all the people of Israel saw Moses, behold, the skin of his face shone, and they were afraid to come near him. But Moses called to them; and Aaron and all the leaders of the congregation returned to him, and Moses talked with them. And afterward all the people of Israel came near, and he gave them in commandment all that the Lord had spoken with him in Mount Sinai. And when Moses had finished speaking with them, he put a veil on his face; but whenever Moses went in before the Lord to speak with him, he took the veil off, until he came out; and when he came out, and told the people of Israel what he was commanded, the people of Israel saw the face of Moses, that the skin of Moses' face shone; and Moses would put the veil upon his face again, until he went in to speak with him.

Psalm 99 [page 728]   or   *Psalm 99:5-9* [page 729]

A Reading (Lesson) from the Second Letter of Peter
[1:13-21]

I think it right, as long as I am in this body, to arouse you by way of reminder, since I know that the putting off of my body will be soon, as our Lord Jesus Christ showed me. And I will see to it that after my departure you may be able at any time to recall these things. For we did not follow cleverly devised myths when we made known to you the power and coming of our Lord Jesus Christ, but we were eyewitnesses of his majesty. For when he received honor and glory from God the Father and the voice was borne to him by the Majestic Glory, "This is my beloved Son, with whom I am well pleased," we heard this voice borne from heaven, for we were with him on the holy mountain. And we have the prophetic word made more sure. You will do well to pay attention to this as to a lamp shining in a dark place, until the day dawns and the morning star rises in your hearts. First of all you must understand this, that no prophecy of scripture is a matter of one's own interpretation, because no prophecy ever came by the impulse of man, but men moved by the Holy Spirit spoke from God.

✝ *The Holy Gospel of Our Lord Jesus Christ*
According to Luke [9:28-36]

Now about eight days after Jesus had foretold his death and resurrection, he took with him Peter and John and James, and went up on the mountain to pray. And as he was praying, the appearance of his countenance was altered, and his raiment became dazzling white. And behold, two men talked with him, Moses and Eli'jah, who appeared in glory and spoke of his departure, which he was to accomplish at Jerusalem. Now Peter and those who were with him were heavy with sleep, and when they wakened they saw his glory and the two men who stood with him. And as the men were parting from him, Peter said to Jesus, "Master, it is well that we are here; let us make three booths, one for you and one for Moses and one for Eli'jah" — not knowing what he said. As he said this, a cloud came and overshadowed them; and they were afraid as they entered the cloud. And a voice came out of the cloud, saying, "This is my Son, my Chosen; listen to him!" And when the voice had spoken, Jesus was found alone. And they kept silence and told no one in those days anything of what they had seen.

Saint Mary the Virgin   *August 15*

A Reading (Lesson) from the Book of Isaiah [61:10-11]

I will greatly rejoice in the Lord, my soul shall exult in my God; for he has clothed me with the garments of salvation, he has covered me with the robe of righteousness, as a bridegroom decks himself with a garland, and as a bride adorns herself with her jewels. For as the earth brings forth its shoots, and as a garden causes what is sown in it to spring up, so the Lord God will cause righteousness and praise to spring forth before all the nations.

Psalm 34 [page 627] or *Psalm 34:1-9* [page 627]

A Reading (Lesson) from the Letter of Paul to the Galatians [4:4-7]

When the time had fully come, God sent forth his Son, born of woman, born under the law, to redeem those who were under the law, so that we might receive adoption as sons. And because you are sons, God has sent the Spirit of his Son into our hearts, crying, "Abba! Father!" So through God you are no longer a slave but a son, and if a son then an heir.

✝ *The Holy Gospel of Our Lord Jesus Christ According to Luke* [1:46-55]

Mary said, "My soul magnifies the Lord, and my spirit rejoices in God my Savior, for he has regarded the low estate of his handmaiden. For behold, henceforth all generations will call me blessed; for he who is mighty has done great things for me, and holy is his name. And his mercy is on those who fear him from generation to generation. He has shown strength with his arm, he has scattered the proud in the imagination of their hearts, he has put down the mighty from their thrones, and exalted those of low degree; he has filled the hungry with good things, and the rich he has sent empty away. He has helped his servant Israel, in remembrance of his mercy, as he spoke to our fathers, to Abraham and to his posterity for ever."

Saint Bartholomew *August 24*

A Reading (Lesson) from the Book of Deuteronomy [18:15-18]

Moses said to the people, "The Lord your God will raise up for you a prophet like me from among you, from your brethren — him you shall heed — just as you desired of the Lord your God at Horeb on the day of the assembly, when you said, 'Let me not hear again the voice of the Lord my God, or see this great fire any more, lest I die.' And the Lord said to me, 'They have rightly said all that they have spoken. I will raise up for them a prophet like you from among their brethren; and I will put my words in his mouth, and he shall speak to them all that I command him.'"

Psalm 91 [page 719] or *Psalm 91:1-4* [page 719]

A Reading (Lesson) from the First Letter of Paul to the Corinthians [4:9-15]

I think that God has exhibited us apostles as last of all, like men sentenced to death; because we have become a spectacle to the world, to angels and to men. We are fools for Christ's sake, but you are wise in Christ. We are weak, but you are strong. You are held in honor, but we in disrepute. To the present hour we hunger and thirst, we are ill-clad and buffeted and homeless, and we labor, working with our own hands. When reviled, we bless; when persecuted, we endure; when slandered, we try to conciliate; we have become, and are now, as the refuse of the world, the offscouring of all things. I do not write this to make you ashamed, but to admonish you as my beloved children. For though you have countless guides in Christ, you do not have many fathers. For I became your father in Christ Jesus through the gospel.

✝ *The Holy Gospel of Our Lord Jesus Christ According to Luke* [22:24-30]

A dispute arose among the apostles, which of them was to be regarded as the greatest.And Jesus said to them, "The kings of the Gentiles exercise lordship over them; and those in authority over them are called benefactors. But not so with you; rather let the greatest among you become as the youngest, and the leader as one who serves. For which is the greater, one who sits at table, or one who serves? Is it not the one who sits at table? But I am among you as one who serves. You are those who have continued with me in my trials; and I assign to you, as my Father assigned to me, a kingdom, that you may eat and drink at my table in my kingdom, and sit on thrones judging the twelve tribes of Israel."

Holy Cross Day *September 14*

A Reading (Lesson) from the Book of Isaiah [45:21-25]

Thus says the Lord: "Declare and present your case; let them take counsel together! Who told this long ago? Who declared it of old? Was it not I, the Lord? And there is no other god besides me, a righteous God and a Savior; there is none besides me. Turn to me and be saved, all the ends of the earth! For I am God, and there is no other. By myself I have sworn, from my mouth has gone forth in righteousness a word that shall not return: 'To me every knee shall bow, every tongue shall swear.' Only in the Lord, it shall be said of me, are righteousness and strength; to him shall come and be ashamed, all who were incensed against him. In the Lord all the offspring of Israel shall triumph and glory."

Psalm 98 [page 727] or *Psalm 98:1-4* [page 727]

A Reading (Lesson) from the Letter of Paul to the Philippians [2:5-11]

Have this mind among yourselves, which is yours in Christ Jesus, who, though he was in the form of God, did not count equality with God a thing to be grasped, but emptied himself, taking the form of a servant, being born in the likeness of men. And being found in human form he humbled himself and became obedient unto death, even death on a cross. Therefore God has highly exalted him and bestowed on him the name which is above every name, that at the name of Jesus every knee should bow, in heaven and

on earth and under the earth, and every tongue confess that
Jesus Christ is Lord, to the glory of God the Father.

or this

A Reading (Lesson) from the Letter of Paul to the Galatians
[6:14-18]

Far be it from me to glory except in the cross of our Lord
Jesus Christ, by which the world has been crucified to me,
and I to the world. For neither circumcision counts for
anything, nor uncircumcision, but a new creation. Peace and
mercy be upon all who walk by this rule, upon the Israel of
God. Henceforth let no man trouble me; for I bear on my
body the marks of Jesus. The grace of our Lord Jesus Christ
be with your spirit, brethren. Amen.

✝ *The Holy Gospel of Our Lord Jesus Christ
According to John* [12:31-36a]

Jesus said, "Now is the judgment of this world, now shall
the ruler of this world be cast out; and I, when I am lifted up
from the earth, will draw all men to myself." He said this to
show by what death he was to die. The crowd answered
him, "We have heard from the law that the Christ remains
for ever. How can you say that the Son of man must be lifted
up? Who is this Son of man?" Jesus said to them, "The light
is with you for a little longer. Walk while you have the light,
lest the darkness overtake you; he who walks in the darkness
does not know where he goes. While you have the light,
believe in the light, that you may become sons of light."

Saint Matthew   *September 21*

A Reading (Lesson) from the Book of Proverbs [3:1-6]

My son, do not forget my teaching, but let your heart keep
my commandments; for length of days and years of life and
abundant welfare will they give you. Let not loyalty and

faithfulness forsake you; bind them about your neck, write them on the tablet of your heart. So you will find favor and good repute in the sight of God and man. Trust in the Lord with all your heart, and do not rely on your own insight. In all your ways acknowledge him, and he will make straight your paths.

Psalm 119:33-40 [page 766]

A Reading (Lesson) from the Second Letter of Paul to Timothy [3:14-17]

As for you, continue in what you have learned and have firmly believed, knowing from whom you learned it and how from childhood you have been acquainted with the sacred writings which are able to instruct you for salvation through faith in Christ Jesus. All scripture is inspired by God and profitable for teaching, for reproof, for correction, and for training in righteousness, that the man of God may be complete, equipped for every good work.

✝ *The Holy Gospel of Our Lord Jesus Christ According to Matthew* [9:9-13]

Jesus saw a man called Matthew sitting at the tax office; and he said to him, "Follow me." And he rose and followed him. And as he sat at table in the house, behold, many tax collectors and sinners came and sat down with Jesus and his disciples. And when the Pharisees saw this, they said to his disciples, "Why does your teacher eat with tax collectors and sinners?" But when he heard it, he said, "Those who are well have no need of a physician, but those who are sick. Go and learn what this means, 'I desire mercy, and not sacrifice.' For I came not to call the righteous, but sinners."

Saint Michael and All Angels   *September 29*

A Reading (Lesson) from the Book of Genesis [28:10-17]

Jacob left Beer-sheba, and went toward Haran. And he came
to a certain place, and stayed there that night, because the
sun had set. Taking one of the stones of the place, he put it
under his head and lay down in that place to sleep. And he
dreamed that there was a ladder set up on the earth, and the
top of it reached to heaven; and behold, the angels of God
were ascending and descending on it! And behold, the Lord
stood above it and said, "I am the Lord, the God of
Abraham your father and the God of Isaac; the land on
which you lie I will give to you and to your descendants; and
your descendants shall be like the dust of the earth, and you
shall spread abroad to the west and to the east and to the
north and to the south; and by you and your descendants
shall all the families of the earth bless themselves. Behold,
I am with you and will keep you wherever you go, and
will bring you back to this land; for I will not leave you until
I have done that of which I have spoken to you." Then Jacob
awoke from his sleep and said, "Surely the Lord is in this
place; and I did not know it." And he was afraid, and said,
"How awesome is this place! This is none other than the
house of God, and this is the gate of heaven."

Psalm 103 [page 733]   or   *Psalm 103:19-22* [page 734]

A Reading (Lesson) from the Revelation to John [12:7-12]

Now war arose in heaven, Michael and his angels fighting
against the dragon; and the dragon and his angels fought,
but they were defeated and there was no longer any place for
them in heaven. And the great dragon was thrown down,
that ancient serpent, who is called the Devil and Satan, the
deceiver of the whole world — he was thrown down to the
earth, and his angels were thrown down with him. And
I heard a loud voice in heaven, saying, "Now the salvation

and the power and the kingdom of our God and the
authority of his Christ have come, for the accuser of our
brethren has been thrown down, who accuses them day and
night before our God. And they have conquered him by the
blood of the Lamb and by the word of their testimony; for
they loved not their lives even unto death. Rejoice then, O
heaven and you that dwell therein! But woe to you, O earth
and sea, for the devil has come down to you in great wrath,
because he knows that his time is short!"

✝ The Holy Gospel of Our Lord Jesus Christ
   According to John [1:47-51]

Jesus saw Nathan'a-el coming to him, and said of him,
"Behold, an Israelite indeed, in whom is no guile!" Nathan'a-el
said to him, "How do you know me?" Jesus answered
him, "Before Philip called you, when you were under the fig
tree, I saw you." Nathan'a-el answered him, "Rabbi, you are
the son of God! You are the King of Israel!" Jesus answered
him, "Because I said to you, I saw you under the fig tree, do
you believe? You shall see greater things than these." And he
said to him, "Truly, truly, I say to you, you will see heaven
opened, and the angels of God ascending and descending
upon the Son of man."

Saint Luke   *October 18*

A Reading (Lesson) from the Book of Ecclesiasticus
[38:1-4, 6-10, 12-14]

Honor the physician with the honor due him, according to
your need of him, for the Lord created him; for healing
comes from the Most High, and he will receive a gift from
the king. The skill of the physician lifts up his head, and in
the presence of great men he is admired. The Lord created
medicines from the earth, and a sensible man will not
despise them. And he gave skill to men that he might be
glorified in his marvelous works. By them he heals and takes

away pain; the pharmacist makes of them a compound. His works will never be finished; and from him health is upon the face of the earth. My son, when you are sick do not be negligent, but pray to the Lord, and he will heal you. Give up your faults and direct your hands aright, and cleanse your heart from all sin. And give the physician his place, for the Lord created him; let him not leave you, for there is need of him. There is a time when success lies in the hands of physicians, for they too will pray to the Lord that he should grant them success in diagnosis and in healing, for the sake of preserving life.

Psalm 147 [Page 804]] or *Psalm 147:1-7* [page 804]

A Reading (Lesson) from the Second Letter of Paul to Timothy [4:5-13]

As for you, always be steady, endure suffering, do the work of an evangelist, fulfill your ministry. For I am already on the point of being sacrificed; the time of my departure has come. I have fought the good fight, I have finished the race, I have kept the faith. Henceforth there is laid up for me the crown of righteousness, which the Lord, the righteous judge, will award to me on that Day, and not only to me but also to all who have loved his appearing. Do your best to come to me soon. For Demas, in love with this present world, has deserted me and gone to Thessalon'ica; Crescens has gone to Galatia, Titus to Dalmatia. Luke alone is with me. Get Mark and bring him with you; for he is very useful in serving me. Tychi'cus I have sent to Ephesus. When you come, bring the cloak that I left with Carpus at Tro'as, also the books, and above all the parchments.

✝ *The Holy Gospel of Our Lord Jesus Christ According to Luke* [4:14-21]

Jesus returned in the power of the Spirit into Galilee, and a report concerning him went out through all the surrounding country. And he taught in their synagogues, being glorified by all. And he came to Nazareth, where he had been brought up; and he went to the synagogue, as his custom was, on the sabbath day. And he stood up to read; and there was given to him the book of the prophet Isaiah. He opened the book and found the place where it was written, "The Spirit of the Lord is upon me, because he has anointed me to preach good news to the poor. He has sent me to proclaim release to the captives and recovering of sight to the blind, to set at liberty those who are oppressed, to proclaim the acceptable year of the Lord." And he closed the book, and gave it back to the attendant, and sat down; and the eyes of all in the synagogue were fixed on him. And he began to say to them, "Today this scripture has been fulfilled in your hearing."

Saint James of Jerusalem   *October 23*

A Reading (Lesson) from the Acts of the Apostles [15:12-22a]

All the assembly kept silence; and they listened to Barnabas and Paul as they related what signs and wonders God had done through them among the Gentiles. After they finished speaking, James replied, "Brethren, listen to me. Simeon has related how God first visited the Gentiles, to take out of them a people for his name. And with this the words of the prophets agree, as it is written, 'After this I will return, and I will rebuild the dwelling of David, which has fallen; I will rebuild its ruins, and I will set it up, that the rest of men may seek the Lord, and all the Gentiles who are called by my name, says the Lord, who has made these things known from of old.' Therefore my judgment is that we should not trouble those of the Gentiles who turn to God, but should write to them to abstain from the pollutions of idols and from unchastity and from what is strangled and from blood. For from early generations Moses has had in every city those who preach him, for he is read every sabbath in the synagogues." Then it seemed good to the apostles and the elders, with the whole church, to choose men from among them and send them to Antioch with Paul and Barnabas.

Psalm 1 [page 585]

A Reading (Lesson) from the First Letter of Paul to the Corinthians [15:1-11]

I would remind you, brethren, in what terms I preached to you the gospel, which you received, in which you stand, by which you are saved, if you hold it fast — unless you believed in vain. For I delivered to you as of first importance what I also received, that Christ died for our sins in accordance with the scriptures, that he was buried, that he was raised on the third day in accordance with the scriptures, and that he appeared to Cephas, then to the twelve. Then he appeared to more than five hundred brethren at one time, most of whom are still alive, though some have fallen asleep. Then he appeared to James, then to all the apostles. Last of all, as to one untimely born, he appeared also to me. For I am the least of the apostles, unfit to be called an apostle, because I persecuted the church of God. But by the grace of God I am what I am, and his grace toward me was not in vain. On the contrary, I worked harder than any of them, though it was not I, but the grace of God which is with me. Whether then it was I or they, so we preach and so you believed.

✝ *The Holy Gospel of Our Lord Jesus Christ According to Matthew* [13:54-58]

Coming to his own country, Jesus taught them in their synagogue, so that they were astonished, and said, "Where did this man get this wisdom and these mighty works? Is not this the carpenter's son? Is not his mother called Mary? And are not his brothers James and Joseph and Simon and Judas? And are not all his sisters with us? Where then did this man get all this?" And they took offense at him. But Jesus said to them, "A prophet is not without honor except in his own country and in his own house." And he did not do many mighty works there, because of their unbelief.

Saint Simon and Saint Jude *October 28*

A Reading (Lesson) from the Book of Deuteronomy [32:1-4]

Moses spoke the words of this song, "Give ear, O heavens, and I will speak; and let the earth hear the words of my mouth. May my teaching drop as the rain, my speech distill as the dew, as the gentle rain upon the tender grass, and as the showers upon the herb. For I will proclaim the name of the Lord. Ascribe greatness to our God! The Rock, his work is perfect; for all his ways are justice. A God of faithfulness and without iniquity, just and right is he."

Psalm 119:89-96 [page 770]

A Reading (Lesson) from the Letter of Paul to the Ephesians [2:13-22]

Now in Christ Jesus you Gentiles, who once were far off have been brought near in the blood of Christ. For he is our peace, who has made us both one, and has broken down the dividing wall of hostility, by abolishing in his flesh the law of commandments and ordinances, that he might create in himself one new man in place of the two, so making peace, and might reconcile us both to God in one body through the cross, thereby bringing the hostility to an end. And he came and preached peace to you who were far off and peace to those who were near; for through him we both have access in one Spirit to the Father. So then you are no longer strangers and sojourners, but you are fellow citizens with the saints and members of the household of God, built upon the foundation of the apostles and prophets, Christ Jesus himself being the cornerstone, in whom the whole structure is joined together and grows into a holy temple in the Lord; in whom you also are built into it for a dwelling place of God in the Spirit.

✝ The Holy Gospel of Our Lord Jesus Christ
   According to John [15:17-27]

Jesus said to his disciples, "This I command you, to love one another. If the world hates you, know that it has hated me before it hated you. If you were of the world, the world would love its own; but because you are not of the world, but I chose you out of the world, therefore the world hates you. Remember the word that I said to you, 'A servant is not greater than his master.' If they persecuted me, they will persecute you; if they kept my word, they will keep yours also. But all this they will do to you on my account, because they do not know him who sent me. If I had not come and spoken to them, they would not have sin; but now they have no excuse for their sin. He who hates me hates my Father also. If I had not done among them the works which no one else did, they would not have sin; but now they have seen and hated both me and my Father. It is to fulfill the word that is written in their law, 'They hated me without a cause.' But when the Counselor comes, whom I shall send to you from the Father, even the Spirit of truth, who proceeds from the Father, he will bear witness to me; and you also are witnesses, because you have been with me from the beginning."

All Saints' Day I *November 1*

A Reading (Lesson) from the Book of Ecclesiasticus
[44:1-10, 13-14]

Let us now praise famous men, and our fathers in their generations. The Lord apportioned to them great glory, his majesty from the beginning. There were those who ruled in their kingdoms, and were men renowned for their power, giving counsel by their understanding, and proclaiming prophecies; leaders of the people in their deliberations and in understanding of learning for the people, wise in their words of instruction; those who composed musical tunes, and set forth verses in writing; rich men furnished with resources, living peaceably in their habitations — all these were honored in their generations, and were the glory of their times. There are some of them who have left a name, so that men declare their praise. And there are some who have no memorial, who have perished as though they had not lived; they have become as though they had not been born, and so have their children after them. But these were men of mercy, whose righteous deeds have not been forgotten. Their posterity will continue for ever, and their glory will not be blotted out. Their bodies were buried in peace, and their name lives to all generations.

Psalm 149 [page 807]

A Reading (Lesson) from the Revelation to John [7:2-4, 9-17]

I saw another angel ascend from the rising of the sun, with the seal of the living God, and he called with a loud voice to the four angels who had been given power to harm earth and sea, saying, "Do not harm the earth or the sea or the trees, till we have sealed the servants of our God upon their foreheads." And I heard the number of the sealed, a hundred and forty-four thousand sealed, out of every tribe of the sons of Israel. After this I looked, and behold, a great multitude which no man could number, from every nation, from all tribes and peoples and tongues, standing before the throne and before the Lamb, clothed in white robes, with palm branches in their hands, and crying out with a loud voice, "Salvation belongs to our God who sits upon the throne, and to the Lamb!" And all the angels stood round the throne and round the elders and the four living creatures, and they fell on their faces before the throne and worshiped God, saying, "Amen! Blessing and glory and wisdom and thanksgiving and honor and power and might be to our God for ever and ever! Amen." Then one of the elders addressed me, saying, "Who are these, clothed in white robes, and whence have they come?" I said to him, "Sir, you know." And he said to me, "These are they who have come out of the great tribulation; they have washed their robes and made them white in the blood of the Lamb. Therefore are they before the throne of God, and serve him day and night within his temple; and he who sits upon the throne will shelter them with his presence. They shall hunger no more, neither thirst any more; the sun shall not strike them, nor any scorching heat. For the Lamb in the midst of the throne will be their shepherd, and he will guide them to springs of living water; and God will wipe away every tear from their eyes."

✝ *The Holy Gospel of Our Lord Jesus Christ*
According to Matthew [5:1-12]

Seeing the crowds, Jesus went up on the mountain, and when he sat down his disciples came to him. And he opened his mouth and taught them, saying: "Blessed are the poor in spirit, for theirs is the kingdom of heaven. Blessed are those who mourn, for they shall be comforted. Blessed are the meek, for they shall inherit the earth. Blessed are those who hunger and thirst for righteousness, for they shall be satisfied. Blessed are the merciful, for they shall obtain mercy. Blessed are the pure in heart, for they shall see God. Blessed are the peacemakers, for they shall be called sons of God. Blessed are those who are persecuted for righteousness' sake, for theirs is the kingdom of heaven. Blessed are you when men revile you and persecute you and utter all kinds of evil against you falsely on my account. Rejoice and be glad, for your reward is great in heaven, for so men persecuted the prophets who were before you."

All Saints' Day II   *November 1 (or the Sunday following)*

A Reading (Lesson) from the Book of Ecclesiasticus
[2:(1-6) 7-11]

> My son, if you come forward to serve the Lord, prepare
> yourself for temptation. Set your heart right and be
> steadfast, and do not be hasty in time of calamity. Cleave
> to him and do not depart, that you may be honored at
> the end of your life. Accept whatever is brought upon
> you, and in changes that humble you be patient. For gold
> is tested in the fire, and acceptable men in the furnace of
> humiliation. Trust in him, and he will help you; make
> your ways straight, and hope in him.

You who fear the Lord, wait for his mercy; and turn not
aside, lest you fall. You who fear the Lord, trust in him, and
your reward will not fail; you who fear the Lord, hope for
good things, for everlasting joy and mercy. Consider the
ancient generations and see: who ever trusted in the Lord
and was put to shame? Or who ever persevered in the fear of
the Lord and was forsaken? Or who ever called upon him
and was overlooked? For the Lord is compassionate and
merciful; he forgives sins and saves in time of affliction.

Psalm 149 [page 807]

A Reading (Lesson) from the Letter of Paul to the Ephesians
[1:(11-14) 15-23]

> In Christ, according to the purpose of him who
> accomplishes all things according to the counsel of his
> will, we who first hoped in Christ have been destined and
> appointed to live for the praise of his glory. In him you
> also, who have heard the word of truth, the gospel of
> your salvation, and have believed in him, were sealed with
> the promised Holy Spirit, which is the guarantee of our
> inheritance until we acquire possession of it, to the praise
> of his glory.

For this reason, because I have heard of your faith in the Lord Jesus and your love toward all the saints, I do not cease to give thanks for you, remembering you in my prayers, that the God of our Lord Jesus Christ, the Father of glory, may give you a spirit of wisdom and of revelation in the knowledge of him, having the eyes of your hearts enlightened, that you may know what is the hope to which he has called you, what are the riches of his glorious inheritance in the saints, and what is the immeasurable greatness of his power in us who believe, according to the working of his great might which he accomplished in Christ when he raised him from the dead and made him sit at his right hand in the heavenly places, far above all rule and authority and power and dominion, and above every name that is named, not only in this age but also in that which is to come; and he has put all things under his feet and has made him the head over all things for the church, which is his body, the fullness of him who fills all in all.

✝ *The Holy Gospel of Our Lord Jesus Christ*
According to Luke [6:20-26(27-36)]

Jesus lifted up his eyes on his disciples, and said: "Blessed are you poor, for yours is the kingdom of God. Blessed are you that hunger now, for you shall be satisfied. Blessed are you that weep now, for you shall laugh. Blessed are you when men hate you, and when they exclude you and revile you, and cast out your name as evil, on account of the Son of man! Rejoice in that day, and leap for joy, for behold, your reward is great in heaven; for so their fathers did to the prophets. But woe to you that are rich, for you have received your consolation. Woe to you that are full now, for you shall hunger. Woe to you that laugh now, for you shall mourn and weep. Woe to you, when all men speak well of you, for so their fathers did to the false prophets."

"But I say to you that hear, Love your enemies, do good to those who hate you, bless those who curse you, pray for those who abuse you. To him who strikes you on the cheek, offer the other also; and from him who takes away your coat do not withhold even your shirt. Give to every one who begs from you; and of him who takes away your goods do not ask them again. And as you wish that men would do to you, do so to them. If you love those who love you, what credit is that to you? For even sinners love those who love them. And if you do good to those who do good to you, what credit is that to you? For even sinners do the same. And if you lend to those from whom you hope to receive, what credit is that to you? Even sinners lend to sinners, to receive as much again. But love your enemies, and do good, and lend, expecting nothing in return; and your reward will be great, and you will be sons of the Most High; for he is kind to the ungrateful and the selfish. Be merciful, even as your Father is merciful."

Thanksgiving Day

A Reading (Lesson) from the Book of Deuteronomy
[8:1-3, 6-10 (17-20)]

Moses said to all Israel, "All the commandments which I command you this day you shall be careful to do, that you may live and multiply, and go in and possess the land which the Lord swore to give to your fathers. And you shall remember all the way which the Lord your God has led you these forty years in the wilderness, that he might humble you, testing you to know what was in your heart, whether you would keep his commandments, or not. And he humbled you and let you hunger and fed you with manna, which you did not know, nor did your fathers know; that he might make you know that man does not live by bread alone, but that man lives by everything that proceeds out of the mouth of the Lord. So you shall keep the commandments of the Lord your God, by walking in his ways and by fearing him. For the Lord your God is bringing you into a good land, a land of brooks of water, of fountains and springs, flowing forth in valleys and hills, a land of wheat and barley, of vines and fig trees and pomegranates, a land of olive trees and honey, a land in which you will eat bread without scarcity, in which you will lack nothing, a land whose stones are iron, and out of whose hills you can dig copper. And you shall eat and be full, and you shall bless the Lord your God for the good land he has given you.

> "Beware lest you say in your heart, 'My power and the might of my hand have gotten me this wealth.' You shall remember the Lord your God, for it is he who gives you power to get wealth; that he may confirm his covenant which he swore to your fathers, as at this day. And if you forget the Lord your God and go after other gods and serve them and worship them, I solemnly warn you this day that you shall surely perish. Like the nations that the Lord makes to perish before you, so shall you perish, because you would not obey the voice of the Lord your God."

Psalm 65 [page 672] or *Psalm 65:9-14* [page 673]

A Reading (Lesson) from the Letter of James [1:17-18, 21-27]

Every good endowment and every perfect gift is from above, coming down from the Father of lights with whom there is no variation or shadow due to change. Of his own will he brought us forth by the word of truth that we should be a kind of first fruits of his creatures. Therefore put away all filthiness and rank growth of wickedness and receive with meekness the implanted word, which is able to save your souls. But be doers of the word, and not hearers only, deceiving yourselves. For if any one is a hearer of the word and not a doer, he is like a man who observes his natural face in a mirror; for he observes himself and goes away and at once forgets what he was like. But he who looks into the perfect law, the law of liberty, and perseveres, being no hearer that forgets but a doer that acts, he shall be blessed in his doing. If any one thinks he is religious, and does not bridle his tongue but deceives his heart, this man's religion is vain. Religion that is pure and undefiled before God and the Father is this: to visit orphans and widows in their affliction, and to keep oneself unstained from the world.

✝ *The Holy Gospel of Our Lord Jesus Christ*
  According to Matthew [6:25-33]

Jesus said, "Do not be anxious about your life, what you shall eat or what you shall drink, nor about your body, what you shall put on. Is not life more than food, and the body more than clothing? Look at the birds of the air: they neither sow nor reap nor gather into barns, and yet your heavenly Father feeds them. Are you not of more value than they? And which of you by being anxious can add one cubit to his span of life? And why are you anxious about clothing? Consider the lilies of the field, how they grow; they neither toil nor spin; yet I tell you, even Solomon in all his glory was not arrayed like one of these. But if God so clothes the grass of the field, which today is alive and tomorrow is thrown into the oven, will he not much more clothe you, O men of little faith? Therefore do not be anxious, saying, 'What shall we eat?' or 'What shall we drink?' or 'What shall we wear?' For the Gentiles seek all these things; and your heavenly Father knows that you need them all. But seek first his kingdom and his righteousness, and all these things shall be yours as well."